can we talk ?

the power and influence
of talk shows

can we talk ?

the power and influence of talk shows

Gini Graham Scott, Ph. D., J. D.

INSIGHT BOOKS

Plenum Press • New York and London

Library of Congress Cataloging-in-Publication Data

Scott, Gini Graham.
    Can we talk? : the power and influence of talk shows / Gini Graham
Scott.
        p.   cm.
    Includes bibliographical references and index.
    ISBN 0-306-45401-7
    1. Talk shows.   2. Radio broadcasting--Social aspects--United
States.   3. Television broadcasting--Social aspects--United States.
I. Title.
PN1990.9.T34S36   1996
302.23'44'0973--dc20   96-28343
                                                                   CIP

ISBN 0-306-45401-7

© 1996 Gini Graham Scott
Insight Books is a Division of Plenum Publishing Corporation
233 Spring Street, New York, N.Y. 10013-1578

An Insight Book

10 9 8 7 6 5 4 3 2 1

Printed in the United States of America

contents

introduction

T V and radio talk shows have become a powerful new influence on the way we think and behave. They are like the town hall or community forum that binds us together in an increasingly digitized and atomized global village. We may not know our neighbor next door; we may not want to; we may be afraid of the stranger or possible criminal on the street. But radio and TV talk shows have become welcome visitors that help us know what's going on and make sense of an increasingly dangerous, alienating world.

At the same time, as these shows have grown up along with the radio and TV medium, they have chronicled America's increasing dysfunction in a more and more chaotic world. Thus, while they may help us understand what is happening around us and give us some feeling of solace and protection, they have stirred up feelings of anger and fear as well. That's because talk shows have that incredible potential that comes with the power to attract millions—to do harm or good. And increasingly they are being accused of stirring up anger and fear, particularly on the political radio call-in shows, and undermining civility and personal relationships, particularly in the world of daytime talk TV.

In the case of TV, the warning shot was literally fired when one guest on *The Jenny Jones Show*, Jonathan Schmitz, killed another, his neighbor 32-year-old Scott Amadeur, after Jones arranged for a surprise confrontation. Schmitz had been invited to come on the show to meet a secret admirer, who he imagined with

1

pleasure would be a woman from his neighborhood. But when he learned his admirer was instead a male neighbor, he went to the neighbor's house a few days later with a 12-gauge shotgun, killed him, and then turned himself in, later pleading not guilty to charges of first-degree murder.[1]

The big question for TV was: did *Jenny Jones,* by provoking an emotional confrontation, irresponsibly open up psychological wounds it wasn't prepared to heal, thereby leading to this incident? In the fallout after the show, numerous psychologists commenting on talk shows and in print thought so. Also, the incident led many media critics to question whether these relationship shows in general were causing psychological harm by the topics they covered and the confrontations of guests they brought together. It is an issue that is still hotly debated as the relationship shows continue.

Meanwhile, in the case of radio, the big concern has erupted over explicit sex talk and right-leaning political shows at a time when there is a climate of growing fear over sexual activity, crime, the breakdown of the family, social decay, and a growing anti-government movement. Given this general atmosphere of fear and malaise, there has been an increasing concern about the popularity of so-called "shock jocks" (so named because of their confrontative let-it-all-hang-out attitude), such as Howard Stern, who talks openly and aggressively about sex and other intimate acts. While both types of radio may have resulted as a way of confronting modern day anxieties—escapist release on the one hand, the open expression of anger on the other—many people are concerned about what these shows themselves might unleash. For instance, while conservative politicians, religious leaders, and ordinary citizens are especially disturbed by the open sexuality of radio talk personalities like Stern, supposedly contributing to the breakdown of the family and its traditional values, the liberals feel threatened by the growing antigovernment attitude of the political shows that are lashing out at the IRS, FBI, and other government agencies with their antitax government-out-of-control message. In fact, many liberals suggest that these growing conservative diatribes against the power of government and the decline of traditional values have contributed to a rash of terrorist acts, from assaults on abortion clinics, to firings on the White House and the Oklahoma City bombing. Even President Clinton has accused many of the conservative talk show hosts, like Rush Limbaugh and G. Gordon Liddy, of inspiring these desperate acts with their antigovernment rhetoric.

But do these shows really have such power? Or are they just reflecting the increasing despair and dysfunction in the United States and global society? And might these shows use their power to help us deal with and heal some of these problems? Today, apart from the growing din of voices attacking radio and TV talk, many within the industry are speaking out in support of this potential for good.

Meanwhile, as this debate over talk shows rages on, it helps to put these shows in perspective. For both radio and TV have grown up at a time when America and the whole world have been going through an unprecedented period of turmoil and technological upheaval. Radio itself came of age after World War I during the 1920s and 1930s, when America was transformed from an isolationist power focused on material growth to a member of a world community which experienced major cultural changes and a worldwide depression. Then, television followed in the 1950s, after another disruptive war followed by a period of relative calm, innocence, and the denial of growing social fissures in the 1950s. In the 1960s, the reach of television expanded rapidly, and its ability to show on-the-spot news helped to document the rising alienation and antigovernment movements of the times.

Now in the 1990s, all of these social strains have only gotten worse—and these deep pains are dramatically reflected in the content of current radio and TV programming and in the fears about radio and TV. And perhaps much of this concern about the messenger as well as the message is because we do not like looking in the mirror and seeing what it reflects. As a result, much of the hue and cry is over taking away that mirror, breaking it, covering it up, or enclosing it, so we can only see certain things we want to, rather than trying to fix what's in the mirror.

Ironically, radio and TV talk shows have gained their great

power—and their ability to inspire great fear—only recently. Until about the early 1990s, talk shows were mainly confined to late night radio and TV or relegated to smaller public interest stations. Typically, too, they dealt with serious topics through interviews and panel discussions. They were more of an adjunct of news or public service programming, at a time when the big money in radio was in popular music programming, while on TV the big money was in popular game, comedy, and drama shows.

But in the last few years, the audience for real life radio and TV has mushroomed to tens of millions of listeners and viewers. Suddenly, people want to hear what others—both celebrities and everyday people—have to say. And as the number of these shows have grown, along with new outlets, such as cable TV and the national syndication of both radio and TV shows, so has the power of the most popular hosts. Some have even become superstars, like Rush Limbaugh and Howard Stern, who have spawned books and merchandising tie-ins, though their stardom has in turn inspired an antistar movement—like the efforts of FAIR, the independent media watch group whose initials stand for Fairness and Accuracy in Reporting, who among other things have tracked and reported on the many false statements by Rush Limbaugh, published in 1995 as the book *The Way Things Aren't: Rush Limbaugh's Reign of Error*.[2]

Meanwhile, the number of people seeking their own fame and money by appearing on these shows has grown. And increasingly people have been willing to talk about almost anything, including putting their own pain and emotional anguish on the air, for all to see. In fact, the interest in all sorts of dysfunction—from tragedy and scandal to disturbed relationships—has never seemed greater. Perhaps one reason is that as much as we like to see someone triumph against adversity or see the underdog achieve victory, we also want to see that anger and pain—because it helps us feel better about our own difficulties and deficiencies. Thus, in a sense, these shows are an antidote for the individual and society in an age of disorder, despair, and angst.

That antidote reflects the positive side of these shows, in that they are contributing to a national dialogue that is helping people become more informed about current events and more understanding about the personal relationships aired on these shows.

But there is a growing negative side, in the way many shows, in their competition to attract audiences, have helped to spotlight and increase the social disruption and personal anguish many feel today. For example, some shows have gone too far in advocating violent and/or antigovernment actions (which have led some individuals to engage in violence such as killing abortion doctors or blowing up buildings). Other shows have gone too far in subjecting callers and guests to insults, public humiliation, revelations of private information, or pranks that have gone awry, leading to criminal charges and lawsuits. For example, apart from the *Jenny Jones* incident already noted, there was a storm of controversy when Connie Chung, since dropped by CBS, invited Newt Gingrich's mom to tell her "off the record, just between us" what Newt thought of First Lady Hillary Rodham Clinton. Gingrich's mom did, and her remarks were soon aired nationally, raising debate on what should or should not be kept confidential. On a day-to-day basis, people now seem to come on popular tell-all shows revealing their deepest and darkest secrets—from incest to affairs to past crimes. Sometimes they spill the secrets of others in the process—or freely talk about what's wrong with those currently in their life, like the men on many of these daytime shows complaining their wife or girlfriend is too fat or sloppy.

Meanwhile, on radio, the rising level of anger and the potential for violence and disrupting society has many concerned. For example, some see a direct connection between radio hosts urging people to arm themselves against the government following the government attacks on David Koresch and his followers in Waco, Texas, and on Randy Weaver in his cabin in Ruby Ridge, Idaho, and the subsequent bombing of the federal building in Oklahoma on April 19, 1995, the two-year anniversary of the Waco blast. And many others, from liberal columnists and radio commentators to President Clinton, are disturbed by G. Gordon Liddy's statements on his radio program about the best way to kill federal agents if they are coming after you (aim for the head or the groin area, which are unprotected).

But on the other side of the fence, many others see these radio hosts speaking out as free speech saviors. That's why the board of the National Association of Radio Talk Show Hosts (NARTSH) decided to give Liddy its annual Freedom of Speech Award at its 7th annual convention in 1995. The board supported his courage in airing his outspoken program (at the time number two in the nation, right after Rush Limbaugh), an act that provoked still more controversy from those who see Liddy as a felon advocating criminal violence rather than as a free speech advocate.

The same kind of good–evil controversy has swirled about Howard Stern and some other "let-it-all-hang-out" shock jocks. For example, while the Federal Communications Commission (FCC) hit some of Stern's stations with $1.7 million in fines for airing explicit sexual statements, his first autobiographical volume, *Private Parts*,[3] turned out to be the fastest-selling book ever the week of its release in October, 1993, by Simon and Schuster, with reportedly 6000 people lined up at the opening of one New York bookstore[4] and about 8000–10,000 people a couple of months later at a bookstore in Pasadena.[5] As of this writing, Mr. Stern has a second bestseller, *Miss America*,[6] and his radio show is filmed and aired on the E! cable television network.

And so the debate goes on. Are talk shows on radio and TV contributing to the national dialogue; or are they corrupting it? Are they reflecting the major concerns in society; or are they contributing to further diminishing American society?

Certainly, some talk show hosts have become the new superstars, with many migrating from radio to TV or doing both as their star power has grown. At the same time, more and more celebrities and big-name politicians—from Mario Cuomo and Jerry Brown on the left to Oliver North on the right—have turned their own star power into nationally and internationally syndicated radio or TV shows.

But amid all the glitz and hoopla, what do these developments say about what's happening in our own society? What do our talk shows tell us about ourselves? What dangers do we face from them individually and as a society? And to what extent are these shows helping us become aware of or overcome the dangers we face?

Can We Talk? is designed to look at these issues by exploring the state of talk shows today and their effect on our society. My own view is that these shows are all of these things. They are a mirror reflecting our problems, a window making us aware of what is wrong, and sometimes they can either add to these problems or help us resolve them. Those hosting and producing these shows have the power to do any and all of these things. And we as a society have power too in choosing what to listen to or watch.

Here I hope to provide a broad overview of how today's talk shows have become powerful and then focus on the dynamics of these shows that make them so compelling and appealing. What is their message? What types of shows are there? What makes certain shows especially popular? Who is the audience for different kinds of shows? Why? How do people launch shows? What is it like to host or be a guest? And importantly, what can we as individuals and a society do to use the power of these shows to help solve many of today's problems?

The next chapter looks at social backdrop that has contributed to the rise of these shows. Then, Part I deals with radio talk shows; II with talk shows on television. While this book is written for the average listener or viewer—essentially most of America—professionals in communications, sociology, history, and popular culture may find this of special interest, namely, in better understanding the power of on-air talk today.

notes

1. Marc Peyser, "Making a Killing on Talk TV," *Newsweek*, March 20, 1995, p. 30.
2. Steven Rendall, Jim Naureckas, and Jeff Cohen, *The Way Things Aren't: Rush Limbaugh's Reign of Error*, New York: The New Press, 1995.
3. Howard Stern, *Private Parts*, New York: Simon & Schuster, 1993.
4. Reuter's Press Release, October 15, 1993.
5. James Anderson, "Stern Draws 10,000 to Book Signing," *Orange County Register*, December 17, 1993.
6. Howard Stern, *Miss America*, New York: Regan Books, 1995.

chapter one

creating a climate of anger and pain

a powerful draw of radio and TV shows is that they are a way for listeners to release and express their feelings of anger and pain. Also, in today's global village, these shows are the equivalent of the old face-to-face community forums where people could meet to discuss current issues, share gossip, or talk philosophy, arts, and letters.

But most are simply listeners or viewers, like eavesdroppers on what others are talking about. Recent audience research, such as a 1993 study by the Times Mirror Center for the People and the Press, shows that only about 11% of the American population has ever tried to call a talk show, and only 6% ever made it on the air.[1] However, this more vocal minority of callers—mostly adult males according to other surveys—tends to be composed of those who are feeling more anger, anxiety, and pain. They feel a more intense desire to escape or make changes from the painful reality of the day, and so are prompted to call.

In the early days of both radio and TV—the late 1920s for radio, the mid-1950s for TV—the programs were characterized by a lightheartedness and playfulness. This tone was related in part to stricter network and sponsor standards, as well as a more upbeat climate of public opinion in which most Americans still supported the popular image of the "American dream"—the ideal of seeking material success in a nation committed to progress and democracy. But now shows with that more lighthearted, playful feeling are primarily the game and late night comedy shows on TV, and the early morning DJs who favor light talk with music.

But mostly there seems to be a deep sense of anger and pain. The anger is especially expressed on radio on the liberal and conservative political and issues-oriented shows in which people express the view that something has gone terribly wrong in society. Meanwhile, the pain is especially visible on TV on the personal relationships and self-help shows, in which people share what's wrong with themselves or others.

In turn, these audiences reflect a common psychological dynamic in the way men and women deal differently with anger and pain. When men experience this, they tend to direct it outward and find external sources to blame for it, whereas women tend to direct their anger and pain inward and blame or try to change themselves. As a result, the listeners and callers on the political "blame society or the government" shows on radio tend much more to be men, projecting their anger outward. By contrast, the audience and participants in the relationship and self-help shows on TV tend much more to be women, directing their pain inward and seeking understanding and help to change themselves or their relationships.

Yet, whether these shows appeal to men or women, or to those who seek to blame society or themselves for what is wrong, this powerful undercurrent of anger and pain helps to create a community of listeners and viewers for these shows.

Why? A number of commentators, like Charles J. Sykes, author of *A Nation of Victims*,[2] have explored some of the social and psychological dynamics that have helped create this eager audience. It has grown at the same time that the technology of radio and television has created the forum for releasing these feelings.

the creation of an alienated, anxious audience

Essentially, this angry, alienated, and anxious pain-filled audience was created by two major forces. On the one hand, people increasingly felt a loss of power in their lives as society became more complex since the early 1900s. They also came to see themselves as victims who deserved pity or had a right to blame others for their plight. On the other hand, because people increasingly felt that their views were not being represented by the mainstream media, they wanted to directly express themselves. If the increasingly powerful media journalists, commentators, and news anchors would not speak for them, the people wanted to speak out themselves.

In *A Nation of Victims: The Decay of the American Character*, Charles J. Sykes, a professor from Wisconsin, makes a powerful case for the rise of this angry and anxious group of Americans. They have contributed the core audience for these talk shows that allow them to express these feelings. Though Sykes doesn't focus on the connection between this growing alienation and anxiety in American society and the rising popularity of talk shows, the connection is readily apparent as one listens to these shows.

As Sykes describes it, this rising chorus of people who feel victimized has been gaining steam since the 1950s, as people have more and more come to believe that the American dream has failed and to feel that they themselves are inadequate, diseased, or addicted. In Sykes's view, this disillusionment has occurred as the language of psychology has been increasingly used to explain and excuse personal behavior and the individual's failure to succeed.[2]

As Sykes notes, growing numbers of upset, disappointed people have become members of groups for people with a variety of inadequacies and behavioral lacks, now redefined as diseases. These groups include people who consider themselves "addicts" or in "recovery" from some problem, such as Gamblers Anonymous, Unwed Parents Anonymous, Debtors Anonymous, and Batterers Anonymous.[2] In a parallel development, growing numbers have joined numerous antiestablishment political and social groups—ranging from left-leaning liberal and radical groups to right-leaning conservative and libertarian groups. On the left, the groups want the government to do more for the underprivileged while staying out of life-style choices; on the right, they want the government to do less for everyone, except where they feel the government should act to help restore the traditional middle-class family virtues of hard work, personal responsibility, and sexual restraint. But in either case, group members are angry about something, feeling that the government or society is flawed and needs to be fixed in some way.

Who are these victims? Why do they feel this way? As Sykes describes it, since the 1950s, more and more people are insisting that "I am a victim," adopting the mantra: "I am not responsible; it's not my fault." Instead of taking responsibility for their own difficulties, they blame and project their sense of guilt onto others. They value feelings rather than reasons, and have become overly sensitized to detecting racism, sexism, oppression, or other sources of put-downs from others.[2]

Many of these individuals claiming to be victims are not only listening and viewing but also calling the talk shows. When they get their chance to go on the air, they describe how society has taken advantage of a whole class of victims like themselves or how they have personally been scarred by abuse, incest, toxic parents, or other causes of personal pain. As Sykes notes:

> [Besides] the genuine victims of misfortune or injustice … the list of certifiable victims continues to grow; victim status is now claimed not only by members of minority groups but increasingly by members of the middle class…and the otherwise psychically scarred—all of whom are engaged in an elaborate game of victim one-upmanship. Celebrities vie with one another in confessing graphic stories of abuse they suffered as children, while television talk shows feature a parade of victims ranging from overweight incest victims to handicapped sex addicts.[3]

In short, the growing personal pain and social anger people feel has provided a wealth of subject matter for these talk shows.

But why have people become so especially sensitive as victims? Outwardly, we are the most powerful nation on earth. Communism has been discredited; Japan has not overtaken us economically as feared. So why the deepening sense of victimization leading many to turn to the talk shows as an outlet for all this anger and pain?

Sykes creates a powerful argument that the breakdown of traditional sources of authority and the loss of traditional values have led to our feelings of distrust and alienation and the "therapizing" of society that have fueled this growing sense of victim-hood. In turn, this attitude of distrust and unease in our relation-ships makes it difficult to talk reasonably with each other. Instead, our society experiences a growing divisiveness across racial, class, gender, and other group lines, as America becomes more trib-alized and people identify themselves with different groups of victims. Concurrently, we are driven by emotions to shout, make demands, and insult one another.[2]

These reactions are reflected in the increasingly emotional and strident tone on many talk shows. People react this way, because they are giving vent to what we feel collectively as a nation—a loss of power, even self-hatred, because we increasingly identify ourselves by our weaknesses and deficiencies as victims. Then, in response, we often blame our ills externally on such things as oppression, society, racism, and sexism, or internally on psychological maladjustment to give ourselves an explanation for the anguish we feel. Also, sharing this blame helps us feel a sense of belonging to a community of others who feel the same way.

Ironically, though, this dynamic is a recipe for social decline and disaster, as we become more and more mired in wanting to blame others or ourselves and feel better about our anger and pain. The radio and TV talk shows help us cope by giving us an outlet to express these feelings. So we feel better. Yet the underly-ing problems still remain. So we continue to see ourselves as angry, anxious victims.

how we became an angry, anxious audience

The process of being transformed into victims began, as Sykes explains, in the 1950s. In essence, it resulted from the growing overconcern with the self and the desire to project blame outward that grew out of the 1960s reaction to the conformity of the 1950s.

This conformity was described by a number of sociologists and social commentators of the day, such as William H. Whyte, author of *The Organization Man*, and C. Wright Mills, author of *White Collar: The American Middle Class*, who decried this growing homogenization of culture resulting from the rise of a new corporate order that celebrated sameness, conformity, predictability, and order. Some even described this darkly as a controlling, tyrannical bureaucratic world. Ironically, though, this dark view of the world came from a culture created by the very corporations that commentators now attacked, since corporate business had helped to create the economic wealth that shaped this new society. But despite this seeming success, there was a growing undercurrent of distress, particularly among the young and among the intellectuals.

For example, this alienation from superficial materialism was captured by James Dean in the film *Rebel Without a Cause* and in the growing subculture of "rocks" and "hoods" in the high schools—teens who wanted to let loose and have fun. Meanwhile, social critics like David Riesman, who wrote *The Lonely Crowd*, published in 1961 about the 1950s' corporate culture, pointed to a gradual erosion of the strength of the American character in the new bureaucratic world. As Riesman explained it, in a traditional society, people looked to their families or tradition for personal guidance. Then, with the social changes caused by the Industrial Revolution, society became more entrepreneurial, and in response the individual became more inner directed, by internalizing social norms and mores, including being committed to hard work and becoming adaptable to changing conditions. In effect, the individual developed a strong stable sense of self and was now guided by an internal "gyroscope" rooted in a strong sense of "character." But then in the 1950s, the new affluent mass culture led to the emergence of a new, more other-oriented, type of person concerned with paying attention to others to get cues on what to do and how to think, instead of being guided by a firm set of internal values or by tradition.[4]

Then, because people were so much more attuned to others, they began to be receptive to the advice of experts, and particularly professional therapists and psychologists, who offered to help them make personal choices. The result was the rise of a new therapeutic culture based on relying on experts in response to the angst of the times. Or as Sykes puts it: "The rise of the therapeutic professions seemed to promise access to and understanding of the central preoccupation of the age, the self."[5]

The booming economy of the 1950s and early 1960s also contributed to this growing interest in the self. That occurred because in an affluent culture, people had less concern with day-to-day survival or achieving prosperity, since that was already a given. Instead, they could turn inward and work on reshaping and molding the self.

Then, too, the breakdown of traditional sources of values, such as the family and traditional religious and educational institutions, contributed to this shift in orientation from community to self. That's because with the decline in support for traditional ideals and institutions, the self became the measure of all values, leading the individual to question the traditional standards of morality, responsibility, and cause–effect consequences once taken for granted.[2]

And so the reaction to the 1950s' sugarcoated conformity combined with the new focus on the self as the true arbiter of right and wrong helped prepare the way for the alienation, anxiety, and breakdown of today, triggered by the questioning and rebellion that started in the 1960s.

This interest in self was expressed by phrases such as "do your own thing." The ideal was to express one's unfettered creative and emotional impulses to achieve true personal freedom and independence. Self-absorption and instant gratification were encouraged and celebrated. In short, selfishness, characterized as "discovering and expressing one's individuality" and being "truly free," was fine.

Unfortunately, one result of this focus on the self and the psychologizing of life was that people began to turn just about everything into a mental or emotional disorder. So increasingly they began to feel they were suffering from some sort of psychological problem[2]—and these difficulties provided much of the gist for the self-help TV and radio talk shows. And in time these problems acquired catchy names as well. For example, women with libido problems became "women who loved too much";

people with obsessive-compulsive disorders became people "who can't let go of an old love."

Then, making feelings of victimization worse and more common, people developed increasing expectations of social and psychological possibilities. As a result, they felt dissatisfied when these ideals weren't met, and even more disappointed because they not only expected and hoped for but felt they "deserved" fulfillment. For that's what the growing variety of self-help books and experts proliferating in the 1970s promised. Worse, if they didn't achieve their expanded ideal, they came to envy those who did, blame others for their own lack of success, and otherwise feel cheated and victimized.[2] And with a slowed-down economy, more and more people found their unrealistic or exaggerated hopes not fulfilled.

Additionally, the expression of this anger and pain was fueled by the push to provide support and compassion for a growing number of victims as the definition of who was a victim expanded beyond the seriously disadvantaged, like the serious accident victim. Traditionally, people would feel pity and offer charity to help the victim get back on his feet or better manage. But now there was a trend to romanticize and glorify the victim, often through the news and other programming on radio and TV. For example, as author Joseph Amato notes in *Victims and Values*, "Sorrow, misery, and suffering provided fertile material for self-dramatization.... [It was] a way to assert one's own sincerity and profundity.... To suffer...made one sensitive, serious, interesting, something other than a superficial, materialistic, and vulgar member of the middle class."[6]

This romanticized view of suffering at one time appealed to the Romantics who rebelled against the middle-class bourgeois tradition, seeing an idealized ennobling virtue in suffering. But now, Sykes suggests, this vision spread throughout society, creating a community of sufferers, in which people could feel a sense of belonging and support from others for their pain and oppression.[2]

It's the kind of response many radio callers and TV guests get on the talk shows. They get to share their anger, fear, or shame with others, and many get a degree of adulation for what they've gone through that turns them into a hero for what they have endured, even if caused by their own mistakes, rather than their achievement. It's an attitude that's led many modern victims to the radio–TV talk circuit and to taking their victimization to the bank.

A classic case is the glorification of the Stolpas, the Colorado couple with a baby, who had driven onto an isolated road in a blinding snowstorm, just concerned with getting to their destination, not thinking about the consequences. Their truck got stuck in the snow miles from anything. But somehow they managed to survive and get rescued after two weeks, because James Stolpa trudged through the snow in time to get help while his wife waited in a cave with their baby. This is not to deny their great suffering or not to recognize that Stolpa overcame great odds to get rescued. But instead of popular interest focusing on the heroism of the rescuers who managed to save them, the glory went to the victims.

One downside of glorifying the victim, according to Sykes, is that in supporting them because they have suffered so much, we harshly judge and criticize those who question their victimhood.[2] For example, we can see this response in the critical attack on the more conservative radio and TV talk show hosts and participants who have resisted this support-the-victim trend, asserting instead that victims should be responsible for their own acts that created their victimization, not given emotional support. Their view is opposed to the sympathy participants get on many programs like *Oprah* and the radio self-help shows, which is one reason these conservative shows have been attacked so strongly by those who feel victims should be supported, not judged.

But then, the conservatives have their own anger over being victimized, too, though for different reasons. For them, their victimization comes not so much from psychological damage but from an out-of-control government. So they, too, having high expectations of what society should be, feel disappointed and use the shows as a forum for expressing their anger and pain.

the loss of a national voice

Radio and TV talk shows have also become a popular outlet because many people feel they don't otherwise have anyone speaking up for them, reflecting their ideas. They feel that the mass media have created an elite class of media stars and pundits, like Barbara Walters and Ted Koppel, who have grown out of touch with the ideas of the average person. They mostly speak to other stars and celebrities. By contrast, the talk shows help the ordinary person feel a renewed sense of community and connection with others in a similar position in society.

This sense of losing touch is highlighted in a study of the new media powerbrokers, *The Media Elite* by S. Robert Lichter, Stanley Rothman, and Linda S. Lichter, respectively a professor in political science at George Washington University, a professor of government at Smith College, and a codirector of the Center of Media and Public Affairs in Washington, DC.[7] As they point out, America grew up ideologically as a "quintessential bourgeois capitalist nation," committed to "individualism, freedom, equality, private property, and democracy"—a view once widely accepted by both liberals and conservatives. This attitude led to the development of a "journalism for the masses," which was primarily owned by private businesses, unlike the media in Europe, which had strong government links. So from the beginning, the U.S. press was strongly influenced by the profit motive, though some newspapers were affiliated with political parties and there was a socially conscious Catholic press, which supported the interests of the blue collar worker and the poor.[7]

This widely supported profit motive helped to give most of the media a more pragmatic nonideological bent, during the 19th and early 20th century, since people generally believed in the promise of liberal capitalism and its ethic of free enterprise and progress. So the media reflected this pragmatic outlook with its objective news reporting approach, rather than the more interpretive commentary style in Europe.

The media were also initially characterized by a populist strain, in which the press at times eagerly exposed and denounced political leaders, though without questioning the basic structure of the sociopolitical system. Another big difference from today is that before World War II, there was no national press and reporters were typically from the working class and from the local community. As a result, they shared an affinity with the mass culture they represented.

Despite the cultural changes of the 1920s and depression of the 1930s, this general faith in democratic capitalism remained, as did this locally based mass culture orientation of the media. Most Americans were still not especially conscious of New York or even Washington, and, according to Lichter *et al.*, "Most also accepted the basic cultural and social parameters of their society as good and right and thought that those who wished to change them radically were either odd or evil."[8]

In turn, this ethos was supported by the program content in the new radio medium and in Hollywood, since the owners and producers of the media of the day—newspapers, radio stations, and motion pictures—were all relatively conservative and almost exclusively male. Though there were a few small groups of radicals in New York and other urban centers publishing journals, organizing workers, and starting to enter government after Roosevelt's New Deal was passed, they were a small minority.

However, after World War II, the media began to change dramatically as a result of the new technology and the growing affluence of the population. One big change was the emergence of a new elite media class increasingly out of the touch with the basic conservatism of the country. Some of these influences that transformed the media are quite obvious. Because of improvements in communications, for example, a new large national audience became possible for the first time. At the same time, other changes, such as the development of the jet plane, spreading automobile ownership, and creation of a national highway system, led to a decline in regional differences and isolation.

In response, beginning in the 1930s and expanding rapidly after the war, national media emerged. Radio began to link the living rooms around America, and newspaper chains and new national mass magazines like *Time* and *Life* helped to create a new national consciousness. Increasingly, too, as the media became national, most of it became centered in New York, and secondarily, for political news, in Washington.[7]

Then, in the late 1950s and early 1960s, the power of the national media was further strengthened by the emergence of television, which became extremely powerful very quickly. By 1958, there were almost as many television sets as homes in America, and within a few years, the distribution of television programming became controlled by the three major networks—ABC, CBS, and NBC—centered in New York. Meanwhile, national TV networks, like the BBC in Britain, developed in other countries. Another centralizing force was the economics of production and distribution. Because producing programs was so expensive, the local stations quickly turned to the networks for most of their programming, both news and entertainment.[7]

The result, as we know well today, is that a national audience was more solidly linked together than ever before by the visual power of television. By the mid-1960s, TVs were owned by most Americans; adults and children were watching TV about six to seven hours a day; and TV executives were focused on doing whatever they could to attract large audiences to build the bottom line.[7]

Soon this development contributed to creating a professionalized, homogenized class of media stars, who increasingly represented the culture of a few urban centers in America, most notably New York and Los Angeles. This culture tended to discount the views of those living in other regions, particularly those still living in small-town America. The result was that a large class of Americans were now increasingly out of the loop, disenfranchised by the rise of a new media elite that powered the new mass media and represented the style and culture of urban metropolitan America.[7]

Yet much was lost in the process. For as the values of the cities became enshrined in the popular media, this helped to undermine the traditional ties Americans once felt to their family, locality, and church. Moreover, the new values of the media discredited old values as being old fashioned. As a result, many Americans—most notably members of the working class or those living in small towns—increasingly felt a sense of losing their moorings and sense of place. And for many this meant feeling conflicting loyalties and values, a kind of split consciousness, in which their local culture and values were at odds with those they saw supported by the national media and the increasingly powerful media figures, who they often saw as heroes and role models, and sometimes felt very close to, even though they never met them. That's because these media stars—including news anchors, politicians, Hollywood and TV stars—had become in effect what scholar Richard Merelman calls "pseudo-intimate acquaintances."[9]

One can see that today in some of the deeply emotional feelings surrounding the glamorous figures whose everyday comings and goings, loves and losses, are the source of everyday conversation and the staple of popular magazines and tabloids like *People* and *The National Enquirer*. We sympathize with Oprah Winfrey's struggles to lose weight and wonder if she will finally marry her current suitor. We suffer along with Liz Taylor through her various surgeries and debate whether she should have married a younger man, Larry Fortensky. And for many people, the trial of O.J. Simpson was not just a mystery or search for the truth; they agonized along with O.J. or with the Goldmans and Browns and victims Ron and Nicole, seeing them as a kind of surrogate family.

But this idolization of media superstars can itself contribute to the values gap and sense of confusion many people feel when the norms and values of these media icons are so different from those of the mass culture to whom and for whom they presumably speak. That's because this increasingly well-educated, professional, urban-based media elite has, more than the general American public, tended to hold a mix of liberal social values, in part inspired by the flowering of the civil rights and counterculture movements of the 1960s, when this new media elite began to emerge.[7] In turn, it is this audience outside these urban centers, this "middle America," that has so eagerly responded to the radio and TV mass culture that is more closely aligned with their own views.

Then, through the 1970s and 1980s, this trend continued, and was documented by several surveys in the early 1980s showing that journalists in Washington and other big cities tended to have characteristics strongly distinguishing them from the average working-class American, such as supporting a more progressive social agenda promoting such things as women's rights, homosexual rights, sexual freedom, affirmative action, and environmental protection.[10] Likewise, an extensive 1985 survey by the *Los Angeles Times* of about 3000 newspaper reporters and editors throughout the country, who were compared with a national random sample of 3300 adults, found the journalists consistently more liberal than the general public in their attitude. For example, they were much more likely to favor government regulation of business, oppose prayer in public schools, and oppose increased defense spending.[11]

Thus, the result of this transformation in the media—both in the new technologies and in the new personnel in leadership positions—was a growing culture gap with a large percentage of the population, essentially with "middle America." And it is this audience that so eagerly responded to the radio and TV talk shows as a forum to express the traditional ideals and values downplayed or disparaged by the mainstream media.

the growing desire to take back the media

The feeling of anger at being left out, the dismay at the direction the United States has been going, and the desire to regain a voice are reflected in the growing tide of conservatism sweeping the country. It's a trend reflected in everything from political changes to a growing chorus of popular books on what's wrong with America and what to do about it. The Republican Revolution that turned control of the House over to the Republicans for the first time in about 40 years and made Newt Gingrich the new Speaker of the House is but one example. More recently, Gingrich's book *Renew America*, has expressed this desire to return the nation to its traditional capitalist democratic roots, along with a prescription of how to do it. Still another example is the popularity of books by Rush Limbaugh, such as *See, I Told You So* and *The Way Things Ought to Be*, which express commonsense maxims about the conservative course correction now needed.

Some examples of this approach are well expressed in the observations of conservative newspaper columnist and radio commentator Cal Thomas, in his 1993 book, *The Things That Matter Most*, with a foreword by Limbaugh. Positioning himself in opposition to the mainstream media elite, he speaks directly to the mainstream middle American who feels left out, observing that:

> You are the people who the "experts" ignore, whose faith and values are regularly criticized and satirized. You are often forced to suffer indignities in relative silence because your access to the major media organs is blocked. You are called names when you refuse to accept the elite's view of the world by people who label you "intolerant" if you question their ideas and practices....
>
> You know the old solutions work and that by their having been ignored the old problems have returned, bringing some new ones with them.[12]

Then, after encapsulating the anger of this group with observations such as "Taxpayers are tired of being asked to cough up more money for a bigger government that doesn't work and rarely addresses their concerns,"[13] he identifies various liberal sacred cows he argues it is time to retire, such as "liberation from the traditional family," "progressive education," and "the promise that bigger government will do it for you."[14]

In sum, because of a variety of developments in society and media over the last few decades, increasingly ordinary people want to find their own voice through the media. They feel a growing sense of anger, pain, and a loss of their voice as a result of the centralization, standardization, and professionalization of the media. And they are reacting to the bureaucratization of big government shutting the average person out. On the one hand, many conservative writers like Thomas have given vent to these ideals. But on the other side of the political fence, many liberals also feel squelched by the expanding power of a repressive bureaucratic society that curtails free expression and sometimes resembles a police state trying to control social and life-style choices.

But whatever the source of people's anger, pain, and frustration, these feelings have led to this growing interest in talk radio and TV. So whether people simply want to listen or watch or want to become callers and guests too, the growing trend has been for people to reach out and try to connect. It's a way of re-creating some of the traditional feelings of community that have been increasingly lost in modern bureaucratic society.

In fact, the rise of Internet newsgroups and on-line bulletin boards is another example of this desire to connect on a more personal level in society today. But then, the growing on-line community is another story for another book.

notes

1. "The Vocal Minority in American Politics," Washington, DC: Times Mirror Center for the People and the Press, 1993, cited in Peter Laufer, *Inside Talk Radio: America's Voice or Just Hot Air?*, New York: Birch Lane Press, 1995.
2. Charles J. Sykes, *A Nation of Victims: The Decay of the American Character*, New York: St. Martin's Press, 1992.
3. Sykes, p. 12.
4. David Riesman, *The Lonely Crowd*, New Haven: Yale University Press, 1961.
5. Sykes, p. 37.
6. Joseph Amato, *Victims and Values*, New York: Praeger Publishers, 1990, p. 105.
7. Robert Lichter, Stanley Rothman, and Linda S. Lichter, *The Media Elite: America's New Powerbrokers*, New York: Hastings House, 1990.
8. Lichter, Rothman, and Lichter, p. 6.
9. Richard Merelman, *Making Something of Ourselves*, Berkeley: University of California Press, 1984.
10. Some of these surveys were done or reported on by: Charlotte

Hayes and Jonathan Rowe, "Reporters: The New Washington Elite," *Washington Monthly*, July–August 1995; Michael Robinson and Margaret Sheehan, *Over the Wire and On TV*, New York: Russell Sage Foundation, 1993; Joseph Kraft, "The Imperial Media," *Commentary*, May 1981.

11. *Los Angeles Times*, August 12, 1985.

12. Cal Thomas, *The Things That Matter Most*, New York: HarperCollins, 1993, pp. xiii–xiv.

13. Thomas, p. xv.

14. Thomas, pp. 3–6.

part one

talk radio

chapter two

a nation of talkers
the rise of talk radio

as talk radio grew up with the beginnings of radio, creating a new type of community forum, the voice of America talking became a national one, linked together by the first radio networks—at least until the rise of TV in the 1950s. Then, for a time, radio turned local and the most popular shows were the pop musical programs for the next few decades. But since the 1980s, America has become networked again, with new syndicated shows of the late 1980s and 1990s.

So what was it like in the early more innocent days of talk radio? This chapter focuses on what is sometimes called the "golden age" of radio through the 1930s and 40s, and touches briefly on the 1950s. Then, the following chapter looks at the roots of today's highly charged world of politics, sex, and psychology in radio that arrived with the revolution in American society in the 1960s.

the roots of the talk show in the community forums

Where did it all begin? In *All Talk: The Talkshow in Media Culture*, Professor Wayne Munson suggests that the roots of the talk show can be traced back to the first gathering of an audience to discuss the issues of the day in the English coffeehouses of the

18th century.[1] Before the development of these coffeehouses, people were largely passive spectators in public forums, such as church pulpits, palace and court proclamations, or parliamentary decisions. But they had little or no influence on information or on the larger culture generally, because in an authoritarian world, the religious, political, social, and cultural influences generally came down from the top. Thus, a sharp cultural split divided the aristocratic culture of the royal courts, governments, and church and the local community culture of the peasants.

Then, in the late 17th and 18th century, with the rise of cities, the Renaissance, mercantile culture, and the middle classes, new middle class centers of culture began to emerge in the cities of England and Western Europe. And the coffeehouse emerged in these centers. These were like salons where the new urban dwellers of the Enlightenment could talk about philosophy, the arts, and other ideas of the day.[2]

During the 18th century, this middle class talk tradition spread even more, helped along by the spread of printing and the first popular magazines, which supported this new talk tradition. These magazines featured commentary by many of the writers who participated in these coffeehouse salons, and so was born the first "audience participation in the media," as Munson describes it. Even the names of many of these new magazines, like the *Tatler*, *Spectator*, *Town Talk*, *Tea Table*, and *Chit Chat*, highlighted the appeal of ordinary conversation.

So what did people talk about? Generally, much the same type of conversation as today. On the more serious side, both the coffeehouse conversation and magazine articles were devoted to politics, social issues, and the arts. But on a lighter note, people had a growing interest in everyday gossip, much of it devoted to satirizing or ridiculing pretense, and promoting "simplicity of manner" and ordinary common sense. So two centuries ago the media were much like today—eager to talk about and deflate those who put on airs.[1] In turn, these early coffeehouses and magazines enabled the individual for the first time to become a participant, not just a spectator, in the informal public pursuit of knowledge and self-expression outside of official government and church auspices.

And soon this institution spread to the American colonies, where other forums for informal conversation developed, too.

early talk in america

Besides the coffeehouse, other popular forums for talk quickly developed in 19th century America. The more intellectual ones in the urban centers were the philosophical society, in which participants talked about issues they read about in the early newspapers; the literary circle, in which they discussed current books; and the lyceum, in which local groups invited noted authors to speak to them. Also, in the small towns and rural areas, many people gathered in the saloons, sat around the grocery store cracker barrel, or just spoke over the back fence.[1]

Most of these forums remained quite localized, face-to-face ways of sharing ideas and reinforcing community ties. By contrast, the lyceum, which began in 1826, turned into a lecture circuit, with parallels to the rise of talk radio today. Started by Josiah Holbrook in Massachusetts, these lyceums were at first local groups of community members who sponsored lectures and discussions, organized libraries, and occasionally put on scientific experiments to share useful information, mostly among young workingmen, since few women were then involved in work or public affairs.[1]

But while the lyceum started small, much like talk radio, it soon changed from having local control and participation to being a lecture circuit for current celebrities.[1] It was like the mostly local radio shows of the 1950s through 1970s giving way to the modern syndicated talk shows with nationally known hosts like Rush Limbaugh and Howard Stern. Meanwhile, this transformation process was helped along by the growth of the media of the day— newspapers, magazines, and the telegraph, and by the national linkup created by the railroads. Soon well-paid stars like Ralph

Waldo Emerson became the featured draw. Much like today, the speakers were frequently authors with books to plug, and by the mid-1800s, several large booker-promoter agencies, like the American Literary Bureau, had sprung up to represent them.

In contrast to the largely male lyceum audience, the women's magazines that emerged in the late 19th century primarily appealed to women and their subject matter was focused around the romance and self-help topics featured on the radio and TV relationship programs today, which also appeal largely to women. Like these programs, magazines such as *The Ladies' Home Journal* found ways to encourage audience participation, by having contests, doing reader surveys with prizes for respondents, and inviting readers to write in for advice. And some of these magazines, like many talk shows today, increasingly used experts to give advice on living—particularly on health, home, and child rearing—at a time when the home, and only the home, was seen as woman's proper sphere.[1]

Meanwhile, alongside these developments, toward the end of the 19th century and early 20th century, a variety of commercial centers for recreation developed in the cities, such as the saloons, dance halls, amusement parks, and cabarets. But unlike the early forums—lyceums for men and magazines for women—which were generally segregated by sex, increasingly, these new forms of recreation were open to both sexes.[1] In fact, the women who joined the men in flocking to the dance halls, amusement parks, and early movie houses called the nickelodeon were the first wave of women to reject the ideal of the domesticated gentle nurturing woman confined to the home.

In turn, these changes generally, and the development of the cabaret and nightclub in particular, according to Munson, helped to create a new environment that encouraged more spontaneous audience participation, which prepared the way for the game and talk shows of the next decades. This occurred because a rising group of "leisure entrepreneurs" helped promote these new attractions to a younger group, which now included working women, as the "modern" thing to do. In the process, they encouraged younger women to get out of the house and express their "autonomy, self-discovery, and self-invention"—a complete switch from the 19th century ideal of the "passive, repressed, domestic" woman—which contributed to the birth of the liberated flapper women of the 1920s.[2]

Significantly, these nightclubs and cabarets invited volunteers from the audience to join in. These participants were considered "sports" for doing so, and according to Munson, this participation, along with the lighthearted entertainment offered at these night spots—such as the 1910s' ragtime dance craze—helped to break down the boundaries between the entertainer and respectable members of the audience. In turn, this breaking of barriers helped prepare the way for everyday members of society to eagerly participate in the early game and talk shows, initially on radio. Or as Munson explains:

> The cabaret opened the door to greater expressiveness through the intimacy, spontaneity, and informality of its performance.... The cabaret became "a new public environment for the exploration of alternatives to the private character of the nineteenth century," bringing "intimacy and expressiveness into everyday life."[3]

Additionally, the cabaret opened the door to the rise of a new kind of entertainer, the personable star, who encouraged audience involvement.

In turn, the development of these more spontaneous and participatory entertainment forms helped prepare the way for people to interact more spontaneously and openly as the voice of radio spread nationally in the late 1920s.

the beginnings and the golden age of radio

According to some radio historians, the first talk show was broadcast in 1921 over WBZ in Springfield, Massachusetts. The topic? Farming for a rural audience.[4]

Soon, though, as more and more Americans got plugged in with radios, radio increasingly tapped a small-town and urban audience, and the topics became very diverse. For example, among the 21 programs categorized as "talk" programs on the networks in 1928 and 1929, according to radio historian Munson, were public affairs, religious, daytime homemakers, and miscellaneous talk shows.

Unlike the interactive format popular today, the shows were mostly monologues, with "experts talking *at* the audience rather than dialogue or audience participation shows."[5] Typical of these shows was Alexander Woolcott's program on WOR in New York City called *The Town Crier*. Woolcott started each program by announcing "Hear ye, hear ye, this is Woolcott speaking," and then reported on his recent experiences, such as the people he met, plays he attended, books he read, and some jokes he heard.[4]

Starting around 1933, these programs rapidly expanded. Not only were there more types of programs, but also more opportunities for audience participation. Like today, the shows appeared very much tied to the concerns of the day.

For example, one popular show, *The Voice of Experience*, which ran from 1933 to 1940, invited listeners to contribute to a fund for the "less fortunate" set up by its host, Dr. Marian Sayle Taylor, a social worker. While this approach was much in tune with the hard economic times of the day, it was also an early harbinger of today's sensationalized talk shows, which similarly feature stories of people in trouble.[1]

Other talk programs likewise echoed the types of topics popular today, i.e., news and current issues, religion, hobbies, the arts, and celebrity gossip. Even the early homemaker shows focused on topics still of interest to many women, such as cooking, the home, and gardening.

More and more programs involved audience participation, too, particularly programs featuring interviews and human interest subjects. For instance, one popular interviewer of the 1930s and 1940s was Art Baker, the host of shows with folksy names like *Pull Over Neighbor*, *Paging John Doe*, and *Meet Joe Public*. Another long-running program, from 1933 to 1968, was the *Breakfast Club*, which featured informal morning chatter.

The new "man on the street" interviews proved to be another popular format, and despite the name, they included interviews with women. But unlike some of the more serious current issues interview programs of today, these tended to be lighthearted shows, highlighting amusing comments and foibles. One of the first was *Vox Populi*, the voice of the people. It started in Houston in 1932, went national on NBC, and thereafter moved to CBS and ABC, broadcasting through 1947. Its imitators included the *Inquiring Reporter* on the Mutual Network and *Our Neighbors* on NBC. Typically, these shows featured spontaneous interviews with "political, personal, trick, or 'nonsense' questions calculated to surprise the interviewee into an amusing response," according to Munson.[6] So they were a little like Jay Leno cruising the L.A. streets with a mike and camera to invite funny audience comments. Some shows also added prizes for correct guesses to trick questions, thus combining the excitement of game shows with the interview format.

A key reason for the popularity of these shows was their "spontaneous intimacy," which helped people feel a sense of closeness with the hosts and guests. Additionally, the "unrehearsed intimacy" provided the potential for sensation. "Then as now," to quote Munson, "the talkshow in its spontaneity, courted the risque."[7]

Yet, in contrast to today's more direct humor and blatant sexual innuendo, the questions asked reflected a sort of innocence. For example, when *Vox Populi* first went on network radio in 1935, some of the questions asked by its two midtown Manhattan reporters, Parks Johnson and Jerry Belcher, were: "To which side does a pig's tail curl?" and "Do you use both sides of your mouth when you smile?"[7]

Early radio also featured a growing audience for two other genres that sometimes included talk and interview segments. One was the game show, whose popularity was immediate. The first syndicated show, *The Answer Man*, which debuted in 1937, invited listeners to submit questions on any topic, and the program was soon drawing 1 million letters a year.[8] Another popular game was *Information Please*, which averaged 30,000 letters a week from listeners who vied to win prizes by asking questions that a panel of experts couldn't answer. And then there was *Truth or Conse-*

quences, launched in 1940, which later became a popular TV show, and a top-selling board game. In the show participants selected from the audience tried to answer questions correctly, and if they couldn't they would pay the consequences by participating in a funny race or stunt.

Still another early popular audience participation format was the amateur variety shows, such as *Arthur Godfrey's Talent Scouts* and *Major Bowes' Amateur Hour*, which began in the mid-1930s. Later many continued on TV. A key reason for their popularity, much like the game shows, was the spontaneous real-life quality of the audience involvement. Listeners, and later TV viewers, did not know what to expect. So they might be surprised and pleased when a really talented amateur did appear. Or even if they encountered a talentless amateur who thought he was good, they might enjoy the humor of seeing him struggle along, until he was ignominiously "gonged" or invited to end his performance.[1] The show's appeal was a little like that of the modern *America's Funniest Home Videos*.

These shows attracted millions of responses from eager volunteers. *Ted Mack's Original Amateur Hour*, which debuted in 1935 during the height of the depression, soon was getting 10,000 letters a week from hopefuls—a half million a year—by its second year on the air, though the odds of appearing were daunting. Typically, only 20 participants a week were selected from the approximately 500–700 chosen to be auditioned each week.

There was also a growing category of comedy audience participation shows, which included a mix of nonprofessional performers, informal interviews with ordinary folk, humorous game show competitions, and roving candid mikes. Many made the transition to early TV. Among the most popular were *Art Linkletter's House Party*, Art Linkletter's *People Are Funny*, *Beat the Clock*, and Allen Funt's *Candid Mike*, the precursor to *Candid Camera*.[1] What these shows had in common were the unscripted, spur of the moment humor of nonprofessional performers and guests, who responded in an unexpected, unslick, and often clumsy way. It was radio's equivalent of people willing to appear on TV shows and make fools of themselves today.

Meanwhile, some educational radio talk shows began to gain an audience, although like the more serious public affairs programs of today, they didn't gain the mass popularity of other formats. Woolcott's *Town Crier*, launched in 1929, was an early example, but generally these shows began in the mid-1930s. One long-lasting show was CBS's *The People's Platform*, from 1938 to 1952, which featured a mix of participants: a big-name guest, an expert on the subject of the day, and an average woman or man, plus the well-known educator Lyman Bryson as moderator. Two other long-lasting shows were *America's Town Meeting* on NBC and *American Forum of the Air* on the Mutual Network, which featured debates on current issues and aired from about 1935 through the late 1940s.[1]

According to Munson, this growth of these audience participation shows in the 1930s was sparked by a growing interest in public opinion generally. People wanted to know what other people thought. Radio was one way to find out, as were other new opinion sampling methods that started up in the 1930s. For instance, in 1935, George Gallup launched the American Institute for Public Opinion, the beginning of public polling. And in the 1930s, market researchers began trying to figure out what the average American wanted, so advertisers could direct advertising to that market—in effect the birth of "consumerism."[8]

This glorious age of participatory radio was short-lived, however. For after its brief flowering through the 1930s and into the 1940s, the "golden age" ended in the late 1940s. One reason is that World War II restricted the spontaneity of many of these shows. For example, before the war, the audience questions and comments were spontaneous on the public affairs and street interview shows. But once America was at war, government officials became concerned about what got said on the air and feared the informality of these shows could potentially endanger the public order. As a result, the programs were now subject to censorship regulations, so everything had to be written out in advance.[9] But unfortunately that change undermined these shows, since their popularity strongly depended on their informal spontaneity. So they declined in interest.

Then, with the war's end, radio's "golden age" ended for another reason, namely, the growing popularity of television. I remember those days myself. As a young child, I used to sit with my mother and grandmother in the living room or alone in my room, listening to those wonderful radio dramas, comedies, and audience participation shows. I could imagine everyone was right there in the room with me. Then, in the late 1940s and early 1950s, these shows began disappearing, as one after another of their hosts announced they were going to TV. Oddly, I felt disappointed and resisted this change because I liked creating pictures of these radio characters in my head, and I thought that was far more interesting than watching the simple pictures from TV studios that characterized early TV. But within a year or two I had largely turned from the radio to TV; like most of the nation, I had become an avid TV viewer.

the beginnings of the call-in shows and talk radio in the 1950s

Some of these radio shows did struggle on for awhile, but the tide was clearly turning to TV. As a result, network radio gradually declined and finally died by the 1950s—until the revival of national syndication in the 1980s and 1990s. Instead, radio turned local as local owners increasingly began to run their own stations and choose their own programming. And now instead of talk, dramatic, or comedy programming, radio turned more and more to music programming, such as the new rock and roll, local news, service information, and local ads. Here and there, some national programs were still syndicated (such as the specialized news and programming supplied by the old networks) through barter. Also, some national advertising was placed on local stations. But the big trend was toward localizing radio and turning to music, with popular local personalities acting as DJs.[1]

In turn, some of these DJs paved the way for the next major development in talk radio, i.e., the call-in show, which developed out of these music shows, particularly those with a top-40 format. This format developed as the music programs became increasingly driven by advertising. At first, this localizing trend gave DJs a great deal of freedom in choosing what they wanted to play. But soon, the program directors at the stations began to take control and tell the DJs what to play, basing their choices on the findings of a growing market research industry, which described what was popular to particular market segments. This way the station owners and managers could better sell advertising to those listeners.[1] So now, increasingly, formal playlists began to limit what was played, and DJs had to follow these guidelines, spacing the breaks between music with lively patter and commercials. In fact, I remember those days as a teenager, when I carefully charted the hits of the day as the DJs announced the weekly countdowns on the top-40 stations.

True, some of the initial seeds for the growth of the call-in shows were laid in the 1930s and 1940s. In the 1930s, some DJs invited listeners to call in their comments, and afterwards they would describe what their listeners had said on the air. Then, in 1945, Barry Gray, a popular late-night DJ on WMCA in New York (still on the air on WOR in 1996) , had the first—or at least one of the first—on-air phone conversation with a caller, when he spoke with the popular band leader Woody Herman. Subsequently, he invited celebrities to come to the radio studio and invited members of the audience to call in and ask them questions, and later he had ordinary individuals like cab drivers in as guests, too.[1]

Yet, despite these early seeds, the big growth of call-in shows was strongly influenced by top-40 radio in the 1950s, which opened up request lines to get listeners to call in. Doing so helped them develop personal bonds with listeners as well as play what was popular, and in many cases, these requests turned into brief conversations with listeners.[1]

Again, I have strong memories of such exchanges as a teenager. One time around 1955 I was sleeping over at a girlfriend's house with several other friends because it had snowed heavily that night and none of our parents were able to pick us up. So we called the local radio station with a request for a song dedicated to all of the members of our group, which turned into a discussion about how badly it was snowing and how we felt about being "snowbound." Then, after a couple of minutes of banter, the DJ played our song.

While such talk remained only an occasional break from music on these top hits stations, sometimes DJs allowed more and more time for talk, and by the late 1950s, a growing number of call-in shows were devoted to local news or community topics. At the same time, a growing number of stations began to feature community discussion programs with local officials as guests who fielded questions from callers.[1]

Then in the 1960s this trend to talk accelerated, along with the new concern with social issues and personal identity that marked the turbulent 1960s. It's a change that has continued to the present as we'll see in the following chapter.

notes

1. Wayne Munson, *All Talk: The Talkshow in Media Culture*, Philadelphia: Temple University Press, 1993.
2. Munson, p. 25.
3. Lewis Erenberg, *Steppin' Out: New York Nightlife and the Transformation of American Culture, 1890–1930*, Westport, Connecticut: Greenwood Press, 1981, pp. 246–249, cited in Munson, p. 26.
4. Peter Laufer, *Inside Talk Radio: America's Voice or Just Hot Air?*, New York: Birch Lane Books, 1995.
5. Munson, pp. 26–27.
6. Munson, p. 31.
7. Munson, p. 32.
8. Munson, p. 34.
9. Erik Barnouw, *The Golden Web: A History of Broadcasting in the United States*, Vol. 2, *1933–1953*, New York: Oxford University Press, 1968, p. 156, cited in Munson, p. 31.

Chapter Three

talk radio since the 1960s
politics, psychology, success, and shock jocks

the beginnings of politics and talk radio of the 1960s

In the 1960s, this trend toward talk continued. In the early 1960s, a few stations even converted over to exclusive talk from a music format, such as KABC in L.A. which went to talk exclusively in 1961. By the mid-1960s, according to a 1966 *Broadcasting* report, about 80% of all stations now carried some talk programs.[1] Many of these talk shows featured political issues, in keeping with the growing political concerns of the times.

Unlike most of the locally owned stations that were still emphasizing music, many of these talk stations were owned by the networks, were strong in the news, and/or were based in or near the major urban areas, like New York, L.A., Chicago, and San Francisco. One reason for these differences is that talk programs were much more expensive, especially if they had call-ins, than the music shows, where a DJ just had to put on a record. Also, the urban setting was better for drawing an audience, since urbanites already were more apt to participate in audience participation forums, like nightclubs and cabarets. Plus these urban areas had a bigger pool of available experts, guests, and callers interested in the day's issues.[2] Some even had a growing activist political movement, with members eager to air their views.

Meanwhile, as call-in talk radio grew during the 1960s, so did all-news radio, primarily on big-city stations, like WINS in New York, KYW in Philadelphia, and WNUS in Chicago. Generally, this new type of news or talk programming attracted a different type of audience, i.e., generally older, more affluent, and largely male,[3] a picture still true of much talk radio today.

the rise of underground talk radio

Underground talk radio on FM also developed in the 1960s. Before then, the FM dial was largely a radio backwater, since few radios were manufactured that could receive it. As a result, FM was mostly used on a limited number of stations for classical music, since it had better fidelity, and for some specialty programs with a specialized audience, such as jazz, foreign-language, and religious programs.[4] And here and there some big AM stations had sister FM stations that commonly played the same programs for listeners with better-quality FM reception.

Then in the 1960s, rock and roll music began moving from the top AM stations to FM, and some of this music had a strong appeal to the new hippie subculture that was growing, primarily in certain urban markets, most notably San Francisco, New York, and L.A. This audience was especially drawn to hearing this new rock sound in the highest fidelity possible, and they felt a community connection with FM, because, as noted by Wes 'Scoop' Nisker, one of the first counterculture radio personalities, they liked hearing this high-fidelity music "programmed for us by members of our own tribe."[5]

By the mid-1960s, many new FM stations around the country, like KSAN in San Francisco, where Nisker worked, KPFA in Berkeley, and KPFK in Los Angeles, became a rallying point and chronicle for the new experiments of the age. A variety of talk shows became part of the mix, including call-ins on music shows and interviews with guests active in current political and social movements.

Characteristically, these shows were full of attitude—taking a strong advocacy position against the government, war, police, and anyone representing the establishment generally. Thus, much like today's conservative counterpart, they provided a forum where those who felt angry or wanted change—the liberals back then—could voice what they felt was wrong with society. Additionally, they reported on the latest events, like meetings and protests, so they contributed to encouraging political action and protest, too—a role well captured in the title of Nisker's 1994 book about those times: *If You Don't Like the News … Go Out and Make Some of Your Own*. It was a time when:

> We promoted antigovernment protests, we savagely criticized the president and congress, we preached against capitalism and the Judeo-Christian religions, we openly encouraged the use of marijuana and LSD, and, of course, we played the music to accompany all of these activities. We were truly tribal radio, filling the heads of American youth with a call to sex, drugs, rock-and-roll, and revolution.[6]

the growing shift to talk

Meanwhile, more and more mainstream AM stations joined the shift from music to talk through the 1960s, using a variety of formats, from call-in shows and talk interview programs with studio guests, to a mix of talk and news. Whatever the format, the news was especially important as a catalyst to attract listeners into a dialogue on the activities of the day.

Because talk radio was expensive—about three times the cost of running a music show as a result of the extra staffing needed, unless staff members were volunteers or low-paid employees on shoestring FM stations—the stations that converted were generally the larger stations in the larger cities with 250,000 or more people. These cities also lent themselves to the more dramatic issues that would attract listeners and provoke callers to respond.[2]

In turn, this talk format contributed to the development of a new type of personality, the talk show host, some of whom attracted a strong following. They were characterized by knowing a little bit about a lot of things, being able to talk easily and engagingly about the current subject, whatever it was, and having an appealing style that encouraged audience rapport and involvement. It was a style that appealed to many advertisers, who soon began using these hosts to promote their products. Meanwhile, the stations could capitalize on this development by being able to charge up to twice as much for these host-read ads, which proved more effective, because of the host's authority in talking about the product.[2]

As for content, these shows reflected the major issues of the day, which seem like a list of top topics today. For example, the top issues featured by the first 18 talk stations, according to radio historian Munson, were "money, taxes, religion, teenagers, politics, race troubles." Meanwhile, some of the more controversial late-night shows had more offbeat and antiestablishment topics, such as using LSD and burning draft cards.[7]

Ironically, though much of this discussion reflected the antiestablishment tenor of the times, the stations promoted this format because it was very profitable. Much like today, the stations were concerned with ratings, and this topical orientation was good for the bottom line. Though the callers and guests might challenge the social order and object to materialism, the station could still target its listeners and more effectively sell them something,[2] much like the profit-motivated stations of today.

One of the most popular of these talk formats was the political gripe program, which attracted callers to respond to the latest news and issues. It was so popular because it gave people who might otherwise feel powerless a chance to speak out about whatever was bothering them. And gripe many did! Just like today.

from advice to exploration

Soon another format became popular, namely, advice shows of all types. They became a hit, since more and more people were now seeking to understand, redefine themselves, and discover their personal identity. These questions now came up as people questioned the traditions of society and the power of an impersonal authority. As a result, instead of looking to traditional sources of defining oneself and one's place in society, they looked to the growing number of psychologists, psychiatrists, and other self-help specialists who offered their guidance on these "shrink" and relationship shows.[2]

Such shows, according to radio historian Munson, reflected a kind of revival of a "new Romanticism," because the "self, personality, and ego" were now seen as the modern wellsprings of knowledge. Those who searched for them were much like the 19th century Romantics, who valued the inner emotions and similarly reacted against a society that was becoming more and more subject to rules and restrictions.[3]

Meanwhile, on the alternative FM stations, this exploration of self and society was more free-form and experimental, since these stations didn't have the same commercial incentive to make a profit. Instead, the staffers who flocked to these stations had a desire for meaning. They wanted to be part of the revolution, to change society.[4]

finding that formula for success in an antisuccess era

By contrast, on AM, the driving commercial force behind talk led to an increasingly refined, polished programming format that has become even more refined and polished today. More and more in the late 1960s, the station managers and programmers used a variety of techniques to better control what was being broadcast, such as call screening procedures, delay systems, and computers.[2] Their goal was to maximize what worked.

Then, as certain formulas or host personalities proved especially effective, the next step was syndication—a development that picked up steam in the 1960s, and helped create a renewed network broadcasting. In the late 1940s and 1950s such broadcasting had disappeared with the localizing of pop music radio. But now networking returned with a vengeance. For example, some popular shows of the day that soon went into syndication included *The Joe Pyne Show*, which began as a local program in L.A.

in 1965; *The Jean Shepherd Show*, which got its start in New York; and shows by Dr. Joyce Brothers and William F. Buckley. In time, many of these hosts were able to migrate successfully to TV, such as Buckley, currently on *Crossfire* on CNN.

The 1960s was also a time when the insult talk show, so popular today, originated—another reflection of the "anything goes" attitude of the 1960s. One of the masters of this approach was Joe Pyne, whose show on KLAC in Los Angeles was eventually syndicated to about 165 stations around the country. His popular format involved inviting an unusual guest to appear; then he would zero in on the attack and his listeners loved his aggressive, offensive approach.[9] When he subsequently moved his show to TV in 1966–1969, he invited members of the audience to add their own insults—a precursor to the Howard Sterns, Morton Downeys, and other shock jocks of today.

Meanwhile, many other hosts featured the news and political controversies of the day, though not so combatively. Instead, they provided a relatively safe, supportive environment where people could release their anger and feelings of frustration or disaffection. It was, as Munson describes it, a "calls of the riled" format, with "let it all hang out" hosts. Other big names of the day included Long John Nebel, Barry Farber, Ronn Owens, and Owen Spann.[10]

In turn, the rise of the call-in show during the 1960s helped channel all of this disruption, conversing, politicking, and exploring alternatives into a product or commodity ideally suited to the age.[2] And the feeling of spontaneity, unpredictability, and uncontrollability that characterized these shows helped make them intriguing to the listener. Still, on the major stations, broadcasters did take some steps to control these shows by learning what worked to keep the ratings up, while avoiding overly outrageous shows that provoked lawsuits. They used strategies like delay systems to edit out profane or libelous comments or call screening to weed out uninteresting, off-topic, or off-the-wall callers. And they began using audience demographics to better target programming and advertising to desired listeners[2]—strategies still used today.

the change in radio programming in the 1970s

In the 1970s, as the protests and upheavals of the 1960s died down, the content and format of talk radio shifted, in keeping with the times. By now about 110 stations had a talk format.[11]

One major change was a more prepared show and less spontaneity, since with less controversy, there were fewer angry callers. As a result, talk show hosts had to come prepared with more of their own material to keep the show going if few people called. So commonly the hosts now came with current news items, letters, or other documents related to topics listeners might find of interest. Then, to kick off the program, they would start talking to "churn" up some listeners' enthusiasm to pick up the phone and call—an approach that came to be called the "churn."[12]

But suppose no one calls or calls are few? Or suppose the host just wants to talk? In either case, the host must be able to keep an interesting monologue or on-air performance going, sometimes for one, two, or more hours—an approach later used very successfully by Rush Limbaugh in the 1990s, who combined short monologues—diatribes, according to critics—with humorous and newsy bits, like clips from the news, music selections, and parody. Some hosts also began to keep a list of experts they could call for opinions and commentary, or to help spark up a slow show.

Also, in the 1970s, many stations began to develop ways to appeal to female listeners, since the audience was at all hours largely made up of younger males. For example, they began featuring programs on interpersonal relationships, figuring such subjects would have a strong appeal to women. It was the beginning of the relationship programming that would soon migrate to television and open the doors to shows like *Oprah*, *Donahue*, and *Sally Jessy Raphael*.

One of the first of these shows was *Feminine Forum* hosted by Bill Ballance, launched on KGBS in Los Angeles in 1970. It featured what soon became a common format on these programs, i.e., "light, humorous conversations about the relationships between men and women."[13] The basic approach was to invite women who sounded young (say in their 20s and 30s) to call in anonymously and share their deepest secrets and concerns about their husbands, lovers, and boyfriends. And often the conversation turned to sex.

The format proved so successful that lots of imitators soon followed. As a result, by 1973, about 50 or so stations around the country were running such programs[2], and some hosts became local celebrities, such as Don Chamberlain, host of the popular show *California Girls*. The program was right in step with the free-swinging sexual relationships of the times, and it helped women, and many male listeners, better understand the changing—and increasingly "in"—dynamic between men and women based on a more equal partnership, where women were more assertive and independent, while men were more supportive and nurturing. The shows were a forum where both men and women could learn how to better relate to each other under these new rules; and they provided a safe place where women could not only talk about sex, but men could easily listen in. In addition, these shows helped to supplement the many workshops, seminars, lectures, and other programs on relationships that became a common feature of this exploration in the 1970s.

Soon, though, much like today's crackdown on sex in the media, this sexually oriented programming inspired some key government figures to publicly denounce "smut" on the air, such as then FCC Chairman Dean Burch and Senator John Pastore.[2] But their fulminations never went anywhere, as numerous station managers came to the support of these programs as part of the new freedoms of the decade, as well as being informative for women who were now more open to sex talk generally.

Another big trend of the 1970s was the spread of self-help psychology programs mirroring the growing national movement of psychological and spiritual searching. This was a time when big growth centers like Esalen in Big Sur, California, grew rapidly, and all sorts of workshops of personal discovery were offered by people who claimed they had found the answers. California, and the San Francisco Bay area in particular, helped to lead the way in what later became the national New Age movement. In the 1970s, it was oriented around personal growth and self-discovery; in the 1980s, the focus turned more to success and prosperity.

Radio, in turn, grew hand in hand with this movement, as many of these self-help workshop and seminar leaders not only appeared as guests on these shows, but also launched their own programs. Generally, these were locally based at first; then some of the more popular ones went national through syndication.

These advice shows—all still on the air today, though commonly on the smaller local stations—developed in three major directions. One type of program was the show hosted by a psychologist, such as Dr. Toni Grant, whose syndicated call-in show went national on ABC. Callers would describe their problem, and she would advise them on what to do. Increasingly, this type of general psychological advice show replaced the call-in sex advice shows, though they had a similar appeal in enabling callers to feel safe in revealing their most intimate problems, while listeners could remain safely anonymous, too.[2] And perhaps they were more successful because they offered a broader range of advice, including on sexual subjects.

Another advice show format was the talk-interview program with a guest representing one of the new personal growth perspectives. One of the most popular of these shows was *New Dimensions*, hosted by Michael Toms, which got its start on KQED in San Francisco in 1973. It soon went into national syndication, and is on about 150 stations today. The show featured (and still does) the vanguard of what came to be called the "New Age" humanist and transpersonal psychology movement, with guests such as psychologist Carl Rogers, parapsychologist Jeffrey Mishlove, and Esalen founder Michael Murphy. The show also successfully began a practice common to many of these programs, namely packaging and selling the tapes of guests, as well as promoting and selling their books and workshops through newsletters and announcements.

Additionally, some programs began to feature the psychic approach to giving advice. On these, a psychic would invite listeners to call-in to get a reading on the air, as well as offer advice about relationships and everyday problems from a psychic perspective. For example, a host would talk about what was happening to the "energy of the planet" and explain how one should best draw on these energies for personal success. It was, as they say, "very California," though these shows soon sprung up elsewhere around the country. And today these shows are still attracting callers, talking about much the same things as they did then.

Still another new 1970s format was the mix of music with New Age guests and topics led by a host who was part of the New Age, such as radio personality Scott Nisker, who was on his own journey of spiritual discovery from the late 1960s through the 1970s and introduced these ideas on his show. As he writes in his book,

> I began exploring all sorts of transformational techniques: body therapies, gestalt workshops, consciousness-raising seminars, personality assessments, herbal healings, and even health-enhancing home appliances.... By the mid '70s a veritable gaggle of gurus had descended on California from the Far East.... As special features producer at KSAN, I had the perfect entree into any spiritual scene that interested me, and could interview all the hottest gurus who came to town.[14]

Also, during the 1970s, a number of noncontroversial talk shows were launched, such as sports talk shows, which primarily attracted young males, and special interest programs, which proliferated especially on the noncommercial FM stations. I even had one of these programs myself on KPFA-FM, while I was at U.C. Berkeley studying for my doctorate in sociology. Since I had been a game designer before I started working on my degree, for about 6 months I did a show based on playing and creating games called *All in the Game*, which featured interviews with people in the games field, such as manufacturers of popular products.

In sum, talk radio in the 1970s helped to give voice to the swirl of new social developments. As people explored new social roles and personal identities at a time when the popular interest shifted from questioning society to questioning one's self and one's relationships, talk radio provided a forum for expressing these concerns.

success, disillusionment, and shock jocks in the 1980s

In the 1980s, the character of talk radio changed once again to reflect the new themes and attitudes of the times. While some of the programming of the 1970s continued strong, like psychology and self-help shows, there was a new emphasis on business success, reflected in a burst of how-to business programs—many hosted by authors or business/workshop seminar leaders seeking clients. In response, to support such special interest programs, a growing number of local stations and small networks of affiliated stations sprung up, which offered a host or producer the opportunity to buy time on the air. The buyer could then use that time to promote his or her own books or services—or could sell that time to guests or sponsors to do the same.

I even got on the bandwagon myself, after writing some books and putting on some seminar programs on business success and being involved with a number of multilevel marketing (MLM) programs in the early 1980s.[15] Seeing radio as one more way to promote these projects, in 1985, I started my own program on KEST, a pay-your-own-way station in San Francisco. Like many of these shows, it was basically a how-you-can-succeed infomercial, featuring interviews with people marketing various MLM products who paid the program's advertising costs, talked about the techniques they used, and pitched their own program, while I plugged my own books.

Other typical business programs were directed at the growing home-based business market, such as *Here's to Your Success* hosted by Paul and Sarah Edwards. It got its start locally in Los Angeles in 1987 on KWNK; went national on a new syndicate, the Business Radio Network in 1988; and evolved into a home business show that was eventually called *Working from Home* in 1992, corresponding to the name of the Edwards' book. The show featured interviews and comments on topics of interest to people just starting their business, such as how to market a product and discussions on how people in various small home businesses had made it.[16] In their early days, I was even one of their guests, talking about multilevel marketing.

the growing anger in america

But not everyone was caught up in the 1980s success mania—and some strongly rejected this emphasis on materialism. As a result, the political news/talk "gripe" shows that had begun in the 1960s continued to attract large audiences. In fact, some of these shows became even more aggressive and angry, setting the stage for the conservative advocacy, shock jock, and "hot talk" programs ranging from Rush Limbaugh to Howard Stern.[2]

The amount of anger was tremendous. Murray Levin, a political science professor at Boston University, measured this when he did an in-depth study of the anger and disillusionment with America that fueled these shows. After taping 700 talk programs in 1977 and 1982, he concluded that they reflected a strong skepticism, mistrust, and loss of faith in America, the result of numerous social and political shocks dating back to the 1960s. As he wrote, explaining this phenomenon:

> An unprecedented nationwide explosion of mistrust, an erosion of faith in America, was precipitated by repeated shocks such as the Vietnam War, the Watergate scandal, ghetto riots, the women's rights movement, the gay rights movement, the racial equality movement, inflation, recession, and stagflation. The country often appeared to be out of control.... Virtually every section of the country, every social class, and racial and religious group, experienced a precipitous falling away from traditional loyalties. There was an unprecedented crisis of confidence.[17]

As he found, many people experienced a tremendous gap between the day-to-day reality they experienced and the American Dream of equality and freedom based in the spirit of capitalism. For more and more people, especially minority group members, the "American Dream" wasn't working; and so they came to distrust government, business, and other institutions, resulting in a growing despair and anger, a growing crisis of confidence and belief in America.[18] It was a distrust that continued to grow, so by the late 1970s, one pollster, Yankelovich, Skelly, and White, reported that about 80% of all Americans believed that political leaders could not be trusted.[19]

Levin found this mistrust rampant on the two popular New England political talk shows—one liberal and one conservative—he monitored for 700 hours. People freely aired their dissatisfaction with society or government. In explaining why they called these shows, Levin suggested that many callers were lower-middle-class and working-class listeners who were more apt to feel a "natural estrangement" from society leading them to call to express their mistrust.[20] He also felt they might be more willing to vent their feelings in the absence of video, in that they were less self-conscious about their lower status position in American society. As Levin explained:

> Talk radio is the only medium that often provides an audience for working-class sentiment. And it is the only medium not dominated by established figures, romance, cops, and robbers, or celebrities.
>
> This working-class audience is preoccupied with the idea that America is increasingly unresponsive to its needs and weak in its commitment to social justice. The loss of political power is a common theme. The harshness and dangers of urban life are a common civic complaint. Callers are concerned with the debasement of daily life, the decay of manners and morals, the incivility of social exchanges.[20]

In particular, they complained about some of the same things that people still complain about today. For example, some of the callers' concerns included the following:

> The [callers] cite…their children's lack of respect for school and parents. They decry the sale of drugs in the local high school and the refusal to attend church. They are afraid to walk in their neighborhoods after dark, and they do not believe the police can be trusted.[20]

Other frequent topics included:

> the gap between the American Dream and reality … stories of unemployment and unequal opportunity, shabby living con-

ditions, inadequate police protection, the burdens of high taxes, and the pampering of welfare recipients.[21]

Levin also found that both the liberal and conservative shows attracted alienated listeners, although their reasons for being alienated differed. While the liberal disenchanted felt the hope of America had been destroyed by a corrupt business elite that exploited the poor, the angry conservatives felt the destruction of American society was the result of a meddlesome, inefficient government overly dominated by Democrats who hoped to turn America into an increasingly socialist-run society.[18]

Conservative and liberal types of listeners and callers were alienated. Both felt they had a lack of power that unfairly left them disadvantaged and open to exploitation, and called to express these feelings. As Levin observed, for many alienated callers,

> The issue is power, powerlessness, and the abuse of power. Oligarchy, governance by the rich, and widespread political corruption are the common complaints.[22]

Then, too, he found that many conservative callers, particularly those with a fundamentalist Christian perspective, were disturbed by what they viewed as a moral and ethical decline in American life. They were upset by the "decline of the Protestant ethic," complained the state was "promoting parasitism among welfare recipients" and "inhibiting self-reliance," and were angered by the "permissiveness of the courts, the destruction of the schools, the ease of obtaining abortions, and the debilitating effects of affirmative action."[23] Though Levin was writing in 1987, he could easily be describing the major gripes on the issues-oriented shows of today.

Likewise, many of the topics discussed on these shows of 15–20 years ago sound very much like today. Typical topics included:

- [ ] the rights of nonsmokers and gays
- [ ] the right to life
- [ ] the inequities of affirmative action
- [ ] the constitutionality of school prayer
- [ ] how to prevent child abuse
- [ ] how not to be cheated by auto body shops

□ how to make a million dollars
□ how to control pornography
□ the federal deficit[2]

Reading this list almost makes it seem as if we've been in something of a two-decade time warp, in which issues-oriented radio has provided a means to release feelings of anger, frustration, disappointment, futility, and powerlessness, like a national safety valve. However, not much seems to change, which is why the same topics evoke the same feelings today. We still feel angry and helpless and still don't know what to do to solve the problem of an out-of-control America dominated by increasingly distant, powerful, and distrusted elites.

For much of the 1980s, as in previous decades, much of the talk about political and social issues was on local or noncommercial radio, or was included in smaller segments on general-interest shows. It was limited, because station managers and owners felt a general audience could only absorb so much "sad and serious talk."

But then, at the end of the 1980s and the start of the 1990s, some hosts, like Rush Limbaugh, found a way to make political talk more entertaining. They used theatrical or confrontive techniques to make these programs more emotional and dramatic.

And some took the aggressive or insult approach to even greater extremes, applying it not only to strongly advocate positions on current politics and social issues, but also to talk about personal relationships, sexuality, and modern life-styles. For them, wild, outrageous comments and antics on—and sometimes off—the air became a key element of their fame. In fact, despite occasional run-ins with the law or station management, some hosts found that controversy helped their career. For example, after Mancow Muller lost his job in San Francisco because of several pranks, including stopping a van on the San Francisco Bay Bridge for 5 minutes, tying up traffic for miles, to protest Clinton's haircut on a jet, he ended up as a prime-time morning-drive talk show host in Chicago.

Certainly the best known of this "shock jock" type of host is Howard Stern, who started broadcasting in the mid-1980s in Philadelphia, later moved to New York, and began syndicating his program nationally in 1991. Even the FCC penalties against him and some of his stations didn't hold him back. In fact, the millions in fines were worth even more in publicity, helping to build his national reputation; he is now on more than a dozen stations in the biggest markets, with two best-selling books: *Private Parts* (Simon and Schuster's fastest-selling book) and *Miss America*. In fact, as of this writing, *Private Parts* is being filmed for a 1997 theatrical release, starring Stern and directed by Betty Thomas (*The Brady Bunch Movie*).

the growing power of talk radio

By the end of the 1980s, talk radio was becoming more and more powerful, both locally and nationally, helped along by new developments in technology and new avenues for promoting and marketing talk. Its growing power even inspired the 1987 film *Talk Radio*, inspired by the killing of Denver talk show host Alan Berg in 1984 by some right-wing fanatics. In the film, directed by Oliver Stone, based on a play by Eric Bogosian, talk show host Barry Champlain is a lonely, insecure guy with a "save the world sense of mission." He attracts equally lonely, insecure callers, who he then subjects to angry attacks that mask his own insecurities. But even so they still keep calling, drawn by the strong emotional appeal of making that safe, anonymous connection, despite the insults. Barry observes this himself in one of the climactic scenes in the film, where he rails at his audience: "I come up here every night and I tear into you, I abuse you, I insult you … and you just keep calling."[24]

Besides this emotional appeal, talk radio grew rapidly because of other economic and technological factors. One was that local radio was very inexpensive to produce, so almost anyone who wanted could start a show. For example, when I did my MLM show on KEST in San Francisco, the half-hour time slot cost only $125 (an equivalent slot today would cost about $200–225). And doing a radio show was even less expensive on noncommercial public stations—it cost from nothing to about $10–15 per half hour to sponsor a show. Also, on some smaller stations it was possible for one person to do a live on-air show, by monitoring both the control board and a single phone in a small studio—or one could tape a show with a high-quality tape recorder and later play the tape on the air.

For example, when I had my own show *Changemakers* in the early 1990s on KUSF-FM radio in San Francisco and broadcast it globally on Radio for Peace International to a million listeners, I invited guests to my home where I had a mike hooked up to a speaker/tape deck system. Then, as we sat on either side of a small table, I taped our conversation for the next half hour, only had to do a little editing required to insert some opening and closing music, and a few announcements. The whole project only cost about $50 a week for production and air time costs.

The 1980s was also marked by increasing possibilities for going national or international, such as through syndication services and satellite radio hookups with relatively low costs for individuals with a limited budget. For example, in the late 1980s, new satellite feed operations were launched so that an independent producer could upload a program, which a station could later download and insert in any time spot. As a result, a producer no longer had to mail copies of a reel or cassette tape—a time-consuming, slow, and expensive procedure. A simple upload could deliver the program instead, so increasingly producers turned to these satellite links for distributing programs.

Generally, all a producer had to do was provide a master-quality tape to a company that would upload the tape onto the satellite for broadcasting at a certain time. Then, those stations that wanted the program could pick up the feed and broadcast it live or tape it for later use, typically, on a barter basis—free to the station, but in return, the program producer included some of his own ads or ads from program sponsors. In turn, the more stations picking up the program, the more the program producer could get for these ads—or the more successfully he could use the ads for his own self-promotion.

In time, this satellite feed became a vehicle for some syndicators who created powerful national networks and eventually charged substantial sums for running a program. Meanwhile, many others used these time-sharing arrangements to get started with a low budget.

Some of these syndicating approaches worked quite well, and they helped to get more and more special-interest talk show radio programs launched. As a result, major syndicates expanded by signing up large numbers of stations nationally to create the big celebrity talk shows, like the Rush Limbaugh program, syndicated by EMI. Meanwhile, publications and directories like Radio and Record's *Radio Supplier's Guide* grew, and helped local stations know what shows were available on a pay-to-play or barter basis.

Meanwhile, as all of these talk shows proliferated in the late 1980s, resulting in about 225 issues-oriented shows and hundreds more on other topics, the talk show hosts began to organize themselves into the first organization in the industry—the National Association of Radio Talk Show Hosts. It was started by cofounders Jerry Williams of WRKO in Boston and Carol Nashe, then an administrator for Blue Cross and Blue Shield, and had its first annual conference in 1989 in Boston at Faneuil Hall, with about 75 participants. From the beginning the group promoted the populist, grass roots character of talk radio, which gave voice to the ordinary citizen. It was, as conference host and organizer Jerry Williams observed at the conference: "the greatest forum for American citizens in history," "a window on the world for millions," "the last bastion of freedom of speech for plain ordinary folks," and a place where listeners who feel "disenfranchised by government by the elite" can air their views.[25]

Soon, though, there was a growing backlash as talk show hosts gained a growing audience and more power to influence listeners. In particular, the more liberal members of government and the press became concerned about the conservative views of many of the radio hosts and guests, now that they were gaining more power. As of this writing, that reaction has become even more vocal, especially following the Oklahoma City bombing, since President Clinton and others have suggested that the talk on conservative radio helped to fuel the anger against the government that led to the bombings. It's a charge talk radio hosts hotly dispute, claiming the government and liberal media are trying to squelch freedom of speech because they disagree with the views expressed. In response, many in government and the press have attacked both conservative talk show hosts generally and the National Association of Radio Talk Show Hosts in particular, claiming it to be a group of more reactionary "hometown demagogues" with a "hidden agenda."[26] This liberal/government talk show battle is ongoing today.

Meanwhile, as talk radio has grown to about 2500 talk/news stations today and thousands of additional programs, so has NARTSH, so that by 1995, it had about 3000 members, and attracted about 400 participants to its annual conference, held this year in Houston, Texas. But even with its growing prestige and broadening membership, NARTSH evoked a storm of critical reaction from the media and government critics when it selected G. Gordon Liddy to receive its Freedom of Speech Award. The outcry occurred because on his show Liddy had suggested that if a federal agent begins invading your home and you have to defend yourself, you should aim at the head if you are a good shot or otherwise aim for the groin since these agents will be wearing bulletproof vests. As Liddy concluded: "When federal agents are going to make war against innocent American people, it is reasonable for those innocent American people to defend themselves. That is what the Second Amendment is all about."[27] Subsequently, Liddy's comments were widely interpreted as an invitation to shoot BATF or FBI agents, although Liddy was arguing for self-defense.

In any case, without supporting Liddy's particular comments, the organization argued that Liddy deserved the award, because its purpose was to recognize the individual's freedom to say what he or she wanted, even if it might not be particularly popular or acceptable to others. Though some board members were a little uncomfortable with Liddy's message, the majority vote was to support his right to say what he did; that it was important to protect even unpopular speech from attack.[28]

And so the popularity and power of radio talk shows of all

sorts has continued to grow. In the next chapters, we'll explore the types of programs and hosts that have become the most popular and powerful and the latest trends in talk radio today.

notes

1. "Talk Radio 1966," *Broadcasting*, June 27, 1966, p. 75, cited in Wayne Munson, *All Talk: The Talkshow in Media Culture*, Philadelphia: Temple University Press, 1993, p. 37.
2. Wayne Munson, *All Talk: The Talkshow in Media Culture*, Philadelphia: Temple University Press, 1993.
3. *Broadcasting*, 1966.
4. Wes 'Scoop' Nisker, *If You Don't Like the News … Go Out and Make Some of Your Own*, Berkeley: Ten Speed Press, 1994.
5. Nisker, p. 50.
6. Nisker, pp. 51–52.
7. Munson, p. 41.
8. Munson, p. 44.
9. Peter Laufer, *Inside Talk Radio: America's Voice or Just Hot Air?*, New York: Birch Lane Books, 1995.
10. Munson, p. 47.
11. Ward L. Quaal and James A. Brown, *Broadcast Management: Radio & Television, 2nd edition*, New York: Hastings House, 1976, p. 187, cited in Munson, p. 47.
12. Laufer, p. 74.
13. "Touchiest Topic on Radio Now: Talk about Sex," *Broadcasting*, March 19, 1973, pp. 118–119, cited in Munson, p. 48.
14. Nisker, pp. 134–135, 140–141.
15. *Success in Multi-Level Marketing* is published by Prentice–Hall; *Get Rich in Multi-Level Selling* by Self-Counsel Press.
16. Interview with Paul Edwards, July 14, 1995.
17. Murray B. Levin, *Talk Radio and the American Dream*, Lexington, Massachusetts: Lexington Books, 1987, p. 3.
18. Levin.
19. Yankelovich, Skelly, and White, Inc., "Trend of Anti-Business Sentiment 1968–81," cited in Seymour M. Lipset and William

Schneider, *The Confidence Gap: Business, Labor and Government in the Public Mind*, Studies of the Modern Corporation, New York: The Free Press, 1983, p. 21, reported in Levin, p. 8.

20. Levin, p. 16.
21. Levin, p. 19.
22. Levin, p. 20.
23. Levin, p. 21.
24. Munson, p. 127, quoting from film.
25. Munson, p. 94.
26. Munson, pp. 94–95, quoting Siegel and Williams at the conference.
27. Transcript of the G. Gordon Liddy broadcast provided by G. Gordon Liddy on April 26, 1996.
28. Interview with Carol Nashe, Executive Director and Co-Founder of the National Association of Radio Talk Show Hosts, July 20, 1995.

chapter four

the rise of radio superstars
from king to limbaugh to stern

hough radio was largely local through the 1980s, in the late 1980s and 1990s, as talk radio increasingly went national, a few radio superstars emerged. Others are now following in their footsteps. The big three are Larry King—the first to go national, who left radio in 1994 for CNN on TV—Rush Limbaugh, and Howard Stern, who besides radio have become something of media phenomena—with books, fan clubs, TV appearances, and other appurtenances of superstardom.

How did they break through? What accounts for their phenomenal success?

Part of it is, of course, personality. They each have a charismatic, unique quality about themselves that has contributed to their popular shows. And they each fashioned a program with something distinctive that attracted notice and was a first in some way. Larry King, who specializes in a very personalized, informal, spontaneous, unpredictable chat with interesting guests, from high-profile celebrities to people in the news, was the first to launch a national program. Rush Limbaugh, a master of explaining a confusing complex mix of world events in a simplified (some critics say simplistic) easy-to-understand way, turned talk into show biz and entertainment. He uses snappy phrases, clips, and music to liven up his commentary, commonly an attack on the latest excesses of government, and sometimes invited callers to join in. As for Howard Stern, well, he is just out there, with edgy, push the envelope, often explicit sex talk and biting commentary, giving everyone permission to get wild and crazy.

But, besides having powerful show content—and being the first, best, or most outrageous—other factors that contributed to the rise of these radio stars were the new satellite and digital technologies that permitted instantaneous national hookups. Both hosts and guests could be anywhere they wanted to be. Plus each of these shows was promoted by a strong marketing genius—an individual or company that masterfully coordinated signing national sponsors and setting up agreements with hundreds of radio stations all over the country to broadcast these shows.

Here I'll look at the stories of the big three—King, Limbaugh, and Stern. What are their shows like, and how did they become so big? All are now on TV, but they built their rise to fame on radio, and Limbaugh and Stern still have their strongest following there.

from miami to mainstream america: the rise of larry king

Larry King has one of those backgrounds that let you know from the beginning he was destined to be big in radio. Born Larry Zeiger in the late 1930s in Brooklyn, he grew up poor—and fascinated by radio. Soon after his father died, and his family went on welfare while his mother took in sewing to help pay the bills, King took to going out into the streets to escape. There, with a rolled-up newspaper as a microphone, he pretended that he was a radio announcer and spoke to the passing crowd, announcing among other things the passing cars. "Here comes a 1947 Chevrolet.... It's a 1949 Hudson.... Here's a 1945 Nash."

After graduating from high school, with grades so bad he couldn't get into college, King moved to Miami and found a job at radio station WKAT-AM. Though hired to sweep, he soon got a break when a disk jockey quit and the manager gave him a chance. However, first the manager changed his name to "King," saying that "Zeiger" sounded "too Jewish," at a time when discrimination against Jews was more open and widespread.[1]

It was the break King needed. He took to the airwaves immediately, combining music with a slick glib patter, in which he commented easily on everything, using his powerful memory for detail to talk about almost anything—from the 1918 flu epidemic to the feats of an all-American fullback. His active imagination helped too, since he used it to create elaborate scenarios that enthralled listeners, such as when he described how one corrupt police captain sold drivers revolving room lights so they wouldn't get traffic tickets.[1]

Then, when King got his own show, starting in 1960 and continuing through the 1970s, he discovered the formula that would later make him famous—interviewing and drawing out guests by asking questions. Part of his engaging style was that unlike many other interviewers, his approach was generally non-confrontational. He didn't even use a prepared checklist of questions. Rather, his style was simply to listen to guests and react to what he heard with more questions. In turn, his informal friendly style helped guests feel comfortable, so they could talk openly. He was much like a facilitator, leading the guest to talk about whatever they wanted to talk about. As King describes this approach in his account of guest interviews, *Tell Me More*:

> Before I begin an interview I often have no idea of the wealth of information I'm about to stumble across.... I listen and learn. That's the joy of it.[2]

Later in an interview with radio producer Evan Haning, King further explained his interview style:

> I ask good questions. I've been asking them all my life. I'm an interviewer.... I listen to the answers; I ask short questions. I leave myself out of it.[3]

Unlike many other interviewers, King's approach was and still is to interview the guest cold, without any advance research or preparation. This way, he could—and still does—approach the guest fresh, just like a member of the audience, with the same kind of questions that person might ask. As he told Haning:

> If you're really curious [you can do a good interview]. And I'm curious. I think you have to be intrinsically curious [to be a good interviewer].[4]

In short, his approach was to be the "hip, curious Everyman who asks the questions [his listeners] would most like to ask."[5]

Through the 1960s and 1970s, King perfected this style, and his success at it helped him become the first to go national—or at least the first known for doing this, since the first national show host, according to Peter Laufer, author of *Inside Talk Radio*, was probably Herb Jebco, whose show originated from Salt Lake City in the mid-1970s. But King was the first to build a broad national following. The latter story began in 1977, when C. Edward Little, president of the Mutual Broadcasting System, was searching for a new host for the late-night show that had been hosted by longtime radio talk host Long John Nebel, who had just died. King agreed to do the show, and soon after, Little suggested trying a national hookup.[6]

Up until then, talk radio had been highly localized, but Little felt the country was now ready for it, since the growth of the mass media had created a mass culture in which everyone throughout the nation was interested in the same thing. And so, King inked a three-year trial contract, and the show went national on January 30, 1978, starting on 28 stations. Within a few years, it was up to 430.[6]

Part of the magic of the show was its late-night time slot from midnight to 5:30 a.m.—9 to 2:30 a.m. Pacific time. It was the ideal time for King's informal, probing style that helped people open up. Also contributing to his success was the fact that the national hookup attracted nationally known celebrities and political figures, which began to read like a who's who of American society. For example, his guests included everyone from Presidents and ex-Presidents, such as Ronald Reagan, George Bush, and Richard Nixon, to noted authors like James Michener, Gore Vidal, and Tom Clancy, to controversial figures like Louis Farrakhan. In turn, King's ability to obtain such noted guests and draw out revelations from them helped turn what happened on his show into news, making his show still more powerful. For example, it was news when Frank Sinatra, who normally didn't do interviews, appeared and admitted that he trembled with fear whenever he performed.[1]

Thus, though King might efface himself in his interviews to showcase his guests, he soon became a high-flying media celebrity. For a while his high living (which included buying a new Cadillac every year, eating at expensive restaurants, gambling heavily, and seeing many women) brought him lots of personal troubles. He even went bankrupt in 1978 when he was $350,000 in debt. But despite his personal difficulties, his media career kept flying high, so that by 1990, he was reaching an audience of about 3.5 million people late at night five nights a week.[1]

His popularity led to a TV show in 1990, in which he became a kind of "kingmaker" in the elections, when Ross Perot decided to announce his candidacy on King's show. But that's another story, to be discussed in the chapters on talk TV.

In any case, King's breakthrough into national radio and later talk TV helped open the door for the many other national talk show hosts who followed. As Dallas talk show host Mark Davis commented, "He was the one that started it all. He prepared the way for the talk radio phenomena we see today."[7]

the rise of rush

Like King, Rush Limbaugh had a hard-scrabble background and was early on drawn toward radio. But where Larry made it by putting his own ego into the background to highlight his guest, Rush's formula was the opposite. He got rid of the guests, and instead rose to power on a show that featured what he thought about everything—along with the input of some callers, music, poetry, and assorted pizzazz. What made it work is he spoke to an audience that felt long forgotten; he expressed the opinions that a broad spectrum of the American public wanted to hear. And he did it with great showmanship that soon made his the nation's number one radio show, broadcast on over 600 stations.

beginnings

How did it happen? To read Rush's early history until about 1988, one might think he would be the last person to make it big.

As Rush freely admits in his books about himself and his show—
The Way Things Ought to Be[8] and *See, I Told You So*[9]—he had
already been fired from previous radio jobs seven times, and from
the time he was 21 to 32, he was on a "downward financial spiral,
earning less money each year than the year before."[10] Yet, he was
still struggling, "trying—desperately" to find his niche.

The strong incentive he grew up with to work hard to succeed
helped him find it. As told by Limbaugh, he grew up in Cape
Girardeau, Missouri, a child of the 1950s, whose parents incul-
cated in him the traditional values of achievement. But apart from
high school football, where he was the team's offensive tackle, he
never liked school, and after a few months as a freshman in
college, he dropped out at 20 to become a full-time radio disc
jockey. As Rush writes: "I had always loved radio and I was
convinced I could be successful without a diploma."[11] His father,
though, was deeply disturbed, convinced Rush would never
amount to anything without that degree.

Still, Rush plugged along in radio for about eight years earning around $12–15,000 a year. Then he briefly took a job selling
tickets for the Kansas City Royals. The job actually seemed to be a
step up to his father, who considered this a more secure job with a
good company. But Rush felt disheartened, not only because he
was making so little money, but because he found the work totally
unsatisfying. He even began to think of himself as "worthless," as
someone who could "never be attractive to anybody."[10]

But after five years of being unsatisfied professionally, economically, and socially, Rush decided to take a chance and get
back into radio, and convinced a Kansas City radio station to hire
him. But though he was back in radio, it was still a struggle, since
he was hired to be a disc jockey but never liked the kind of talk he
was supposed to do. He didn't because he couldn't candidly
express his own opinions or develop a style of his own. Thus, he
often found himself at odds with what management did want him
to do.

For example, when he worked at an FM music station, the
station management wanted him to stimulate questions on local
issues between records, urging him to be controversial and insult

people, like another local jock was doing with some success. Though Rush tried, he never liked doing this. He didn't like insulting people and hurting their feelings, leading him to think more carefully about what he really wanted to do on radio—and what worked for the people with long-lasting show business careers. He discovered that the long-timers didn't insult or mistreat the guests on their shows; and so when he got his first big break in 1984 to have his own show on KFBK in Sacramento, California, he decided to take this approach. The management wanted him to be controversial and stir things up, but he was determined to do so by expressing his opinions on the issues—not by putting people down. Rush described the decision that helped make his career, which took off a few years later:

> I finally knew who I was. And I had a clear idea of what I wanted to do.... My idea was to stir controversy in discussing substantive issues rather than with shock, rudeness, and insult. I was not going to go on the air just to be outrageous. I wanted credibility. I knew that was the key to having longevity ... *and* to securing sponsors.[12]

The other important decision Rush made was not to have any guests. Instead, his way to make his show unique was to be the focus of the show himself, giving his own opinions and views. As Rush explained:

> I wanted to be the focal point of the show. Why should I interview the same guests who were appearing on every other talk show in the country? How would that distinguish me from the pack?[12]

Ironically, no one thought this approach would work. They couldn't imagine that people would want to hear one person talking. But one radio consultant, Bruce Marr, backed him up, saying he was one of the few hosts who didn't need guests.[8] And so Rush's opinion-driven program began, and he soon built up a strong loyal following of listeners in the Sacramento area.

Another key reason his program worked, besides his ability to express his opinions in an interesting, personable way, is that Rush was tapping into a reservoir of conservative opinion in the

United States that was not being otherwise expressed. That's be-cause in the mid-1980s, most mainstream media—the newspapers, magazines, TV, and Hollywood—were dominated by a strong politically liberal voice, while mainstream AM radio was still largely music dominated, with a sprinkling of insult jocks in the larger markets. Meanwhile, FM radio was but a blip on the media screen, and largely dominated by specialty and public affairs programming. Thus, Limbaugh started his conservative opinion show at a time when there was nothing like it on the air—and he soon mined an untapped conservative audience hungry to hear someone speak to them.

going national

In January, 1988, Rush got a second big break that turned his popular Sacramento show into a national phenomenon. He was beginning the third and last year of his contract, when Bruce Marr, who had battled for him in the beginning, arranged for a key meeting with Ed McLaughlin. McLaughlin had just retired as the president of the ABC Radio Network and had started his own company to syndicate radio programs nationally—the first being the *Dr. Dean Edell* show, which became an early success. McLaughlin had already heard and liked the program when he took a trip to Sacramento to consider buying the station, and then Marr called to set up a meeting with Rush in San Francisco.

After a good meeting, McLaughlin pressed forward to start the syndication process. But would the show work? As when Rush started his show in Sacramento, there were skeptics, partic-ularly since the show was scheduled for the middle of the day. At the time, station managers believed that such programs should be local, because most listeners wanted to hear about local issues, hear calls from local people, and call local phone numbers them-selves. By contrast, managers were more receptive to taking on a national program at night, because there are fewer listeners and advertising rates are less, so there is less at stake, and it becomes "cheaper to take a show off a satellite than to hire a local host."[13]

But Rush's program was an issues-oriented program scheduled to run in midday. Initially the reaction from virtually all of the major stations McLaughlin contacted around the country was that syndicating such a program at this time was impossible. And many stations turned them down. But even so, McLaughlin pressed on and set up a deal that made it possible—by arranging for Rush to do two shows. He did a local New York show from 10 a.m. to noon, which enabled the show to get studio facilities, including engineers, telephones, and call screeners, at no charge. Also the New York base was attractive to sponsors. Then from this base, McLaughlin worked on finding stations around the country to air the noon to 2 p.m. show.[8]

It was a tricky bit of behind-the-scenes legerdemain. But it worked—and within a month, Rush was broadcasting to an audience of 250,000 people, about half in New York and the rest of them listeners of the first 56 stations that broadcast the show. The first local show aired on July 4, 1988, the day after the U.S. shot down an Iranian civilian plane in the Persian Gulf, so that was the first issue Rush talked about. Then, on August 1, the network show began.[8] It was hard going juggling the two shows, but once the show gained national popularity, Rush was able to drop the local New York show and expand the national show to three hours.

Probably if Rush had to depend on the New York audience to make it, he might have bombed, since he was not argumentative, and the New York audience liked argument, or as Rush put it: "Life in New York is one long argument."[14] But what really made Rush take off is the heartland. Many people there felt that Rush was talking to them, expressing their feelings and views, and fueled by some ingenious marketing and controversy that sparked national publicity, the show took off—up to 100 stations in three months.

For example, Rush used some early resistance in South Bend, Indiana, on station WAMJ to turn the reaction around and gain added popularity. The controversy began the first day the program aired, since Limbaugh's show was so different from what the previous host in that time slot, Owen Spann, had done. Spann did a friendly, lightweight, chatty show, talking, for example, about the origins of fruitcake. Then, boom, the next day, Limbaugh was on the air.[15]

The local uproar was instantaneous. The first day, the station was inundated with hundreds of calls saying "Get this guy off," and the station co-owner and general manager were quickly on the phone to Ed McLaughlin to cancel the show. But he persuaded them to give the show time, telling them that the show had been a big hit in Sacramento.[15]

Meanwhile, as the show's fate hung in the balance, Limbaugh appealed to the general public, determined not to lose the station, which might lead to still others bailing out. He announced on the show that "a concerted effort to censor this show has begun," pushed by a "few angry liberals" who were "calling the station demanding that this show be taken off the air." So Limbaugh urged his listeners: "If you love this show ... you must let the station know. Otherwise, we will be canceled."[16]

The results were immediate. The station was swamped with calls not only from people in South Bend, but from all over the "Fruited Plain" as Limbaugh puts it, and so the show was saved. And when Limbaugh met resistance in other cities, he similarly urged callers to call and show their support, which they did.

Likewise, he found ways to turn advertiser resistance around. For instance, in late 1988, after the owner of Woodie's Barbecue in Santa Barbara took offense when Limbaugh described some ardent feminists working for women's rights as "femi-nazis" and called the station saying he wouldn't advertise on a station that permitted someone to use this term, Limbaugh quickly responded. Though this was just a $250 ad, the next day he told his listeners that the advertiser was upset and he wanted to deal with the problem directly. So he urged people to go to Woodie's, since, he explained on the air: "I understand Woodie's food is great, and we need to show him that he's making a mistake by not being part of the EIB [Excellence in Broadcasting] Network revolution." Needless to say, people flocked to Woodie's, and business was so good that Woodie laughed off the incident. He even ran a local ad saying that Limbaugh had endorsed his restaurant.[17]

Other marketing coups for the show were built on ideas developed by listeners, which is how the hundreds of "Rush Rooms" around the country started—essentially places in local restaurants and bars where people would gather to hear Limbaugh's program during the day. After the first one started in Mishawaka, Indiana, just across the river from South Bend, the station owner and general manager started promoting the lunch hour on the air, calling the place where the gathering to hear Rush occurred the "Rush Room." And soon Limbaugh started talking about it, too, planting the seed for what would lead to the growth of hundreds of similar lunchtime Rush Rooms all over the country— about 300 by 1993, according to a *U.S. News and World Report* story, reporting on the phenomenon.[15]

In turn, such marketing efforts helped to further steamroll the popularity of the show. For example, after the *U.S. News and World Report* article about the Rush Rooms appeared, fans of the show began flocking there from around the world—eager to see the first Rush Room, have prime rib dinners there, and even get the Rush Room T-shirts which were now part of the phenomenon.[15]

Meanwhile, as the popularity of the show spread, Limbaugh helped promote it even more by going around the country speaking to groups, meeting people, and reaffirming their heartland values with his message of hard work, individual rights, the power of the people, and "patriotism and loyalty to American tradition." And to further build support for the show, Limbaugh developed a variety of related material that reinforced his basic conservative message. For example, in 1991, he started the National Conservative Forum, which sponsored meetings on conservative ideas with top name guests, such as former Secretary of Education Bill Bennett, Southern California Congressman Bob Dornan, and Judge Robert Bork. Though Rush might have aired the same kind of program on air, the forums were designed so everyday people could meet these well-known conservative spokespeople personally.[8]

Then, in 1992, Limbaugh launched a newsletter called the *Limbaugh Letter*, to provide listeners with information and advice about a variety of current problems, such as reforming the educational system, restoring family values, dealing with the environment, government, the economy, and foreign policy, and getting rid of unnecessary government programs. Today, the *Letter* has about 450,000 subscribers.[9]

And from time to time, Limbaugh turned everyday incidents into marketing and promotional coups, building further rapport and popularity with listeners, such as turning a listener's complaint that his wife wouldn't let him spend $29.95 for a subscription to the *Limbaugh Letter* into Dan's Bake Sale in Fort Collins, Colorado, in 1993. After Dan Kay, a former flea-market employee, called Limbaugh's show to report this, saying that his wife felt they couldn't afford it, Limbaugh briefly considered taking the easy "liberal approach" by giving Dan a free subscription as a gift, which he had done in other situations. But instead Limbaugh decided to send his listeners, as well as Dan, a message—that the liberal giveaway approach doesn't work—and support his own self-reliance, free enterprise approach. So he suggested that Dan might have a bake sale—as a creative entrepreneurial way—to raise enough money for the subscription "in the true spirit of capitalism." After Dan agreed to try, Rush provided him continuing promotional help, giving him a plug now and then to let people know about his sale.[18]

The results were amazing. Within days, an advertising company telephoned Dan and offered to put up billboards around Colorado. Other vendors called to say they wanted to set up booths, including a world class New Orleans restaurant that offered to send a top chef to serve up thousands of its special banana dishes. Then Limbaugh announced on his show that he would attend. In the end, about 65,000 people showed up from all over the country and the event gained massive publicity.[4]

Such promotional events and marketing know-how, along with Limbaugh's showmanship and conservative appeal, helped turn his show into the number one national talk show, with about 20 million listeners each week on over 600 stations. Building on this, in 1992 Limbaugh launched his TV program, now on over 200 stations, and his two books—*The Way Things Ought to Be* and *See, I Told You So*—have sold over 7 million copies. He has traveled to over 90 cities with his "Rush to Excellence Road Show," with crowds as high as 7000 people.[19] And he has done the inevitable TV circuit, including *David Letterman*, *20/20*, *Nightline*, *Meet the Press*, and *Donahue*. In 1995, the National Association of Radio Talk Show Hosts awarded him its Top Radio Show Host of the Year award.

the limbaugh reaction

But as much as Limbaugh has inspired this outpouring of support—sometimes called the "Rush to Rush"—he has inspired the most fervent antireaction as well. Some opponents have even called him "The Most Dangerous Man in America,"[20] a label that Rush has adopted since he finds it so amusing.

Why the fear? Because liberals are afraid he is offering people simplistic and distorted answers, creating a "cadre of robots" they call "dittoheads" because these fans call the station and agree with what Rush has said. Though Rush thinks he is doing exactly the opposite, getting listeners and now viewers to question accepted truths spread by the liberal media and government, liberals think he is dumbing down discourse, assuring his audience, for example, that if they listen to him everyday, "they will no longer need to read newspapers or watch TV."[21]

In any event, this upset over Limbaugh's message has spawned its own counterindustry. For example, in 1992, one critic started *The Flush Rush Quarterly*, devoted to highlighting Limbaugh's latest "lies" and distortions, and in one diatribe, he called Limbaugh "a pot-smoking, draft-dodging, homophobic, sexist, racist clown prince of the airwaves who is a danger to our environment, the animal population, and free-thinking people everywhere."[22] Even some fellow radio commentators checked in with their own criticisms, such as Howard Stern, who called him "a big, fat dope. Rush's mom named him that because he was always rushing to the fridge." And Larry King criticized him for "gay-bashing, bashing women, [using the term] 'femi-nazis', bashing blacks—I don't think that's funny."[24]

Numerous anti-Rush books have recently been published to point at his fallacies and foibles, such as *The Great Limbaugh Con ... And Other Right-Wing Assaults on Common Sense*, out in 1994 by Charles M. Kelly, who describes various Limbaugh "sound bites" and slogans, such as "wealth trickles down" and "government regulations equal communism, or, at least, socialism," to inspire readers to fight back "to preserve and protect ... democratic capitalism."[25]

Another such book is *The Way Things Aren't: Rush Limbaugh's Reign of Error*, written by an independent media watch group called Fairness and Accuracy in Reporting (FAIR). It catalogues a list of "over 100 outrageously false and foolish statements" by Rush, and next to each states "the reality" versus Rush's false claims. For instance:

limbaugh: Women were doing quite well in this country before feminism came along. [Radio; FRQ, Summer/93]

reality: Before feminism "came along" in the late nineteenth century, women couldn't even vote.[26]

In 1995, Ted Rueter brought out *The Rush Limbaugh Quiz Book*, which provides a somewhat tongue-in-cheek critique of Limbaugh and his philosophy, using a short-answer quiz format. But underneath the humor is Rueter's real concern about Rush's influence, for as he observes in his introduction,

> In the "Era of Limbaugh," it is every citizen's duty to learn as much as possible about "the most dangerous man in America."[27]

What for example? Here's a sample from the book:

Question #112: How did Rush celebrate "Earth Day" on his radio show?
- a. He conducted the program from the backseat of his limousine as he was driven aimlessly around New Jersey.
- b. He handed out styrofoam cups and plastic bags at a Burger King in Greenwich, Connecticut.
- c. He opened a chain of toxic waste dumps in Alabama.

d. He hired a pilot to start fires in Yellowstone National Park.

e. He played a tape of a chain saw cutting down a tree.[28]

The correct answer is "e."

The most recent book of this genre, *Rush Limbaugh Is a Big Fat Idiot and Other Observations* by Al Franken, was published in January 1996 and reached number one on *The New York Times* nonfiction best-seller list.

Much of this reaction has occurred because Limbaugh's activities have tapped a wellspring of conservative grass-roots sentiment that can translate into political action and votes. Additionally, Limbaugh is seen as leading the rising tide of conservative radio that has been gaining increasing power, since he opened the door to this kind of programming in 1988. His show was the first of its kind to go national, and it has since inspired hundreds of other conservative local and national programs, such as talk shows by G. Gordon Liddy, Ken Hamblin (who calls himself "The Black Avenger"), Michael Savage, Oliver North, and others. Limbaugh is the most popular and visible, so he is the easiest to attack.

But to a great degree, the attack on Limbaugh reflects a broader attack on conservative talk radio generally and its vision of America, since liberals are so afraid of this vision—and on the radio airwaves, the conservatives have been winning. So that's why the liberals are fighting back, sometimes with their own liberal hosts, like Alan Colmes and Tom Leykis, but more generally through other news media with a more liberal point of view— which ironically is what led Rush and other conservatives to use the airwaves to give ordinary citizens a voice they weren't finding elsewhere. It's a battle that is likely to continue over the next few years in the struggle for the airwaves and heart and soul of America. Meanwhile, on another front, Limbaugh's breakthrough in using showmanship and marketing to spread his show and spin-off products across America helped open the door to other big national shows—most notably to Howard Stern, whose show helped revolutionize radio in America, too.

howard stern and shock jock radio

Howard Stern also gained a huge following and made break-throughs in radio because he brought a uniqueness that attracted listeners. And like King and Limbaugh, early on he was deter-mined to make it in talk radio.

However, despite his big-name following, including the best-selling *Private Parts* and *Miss America*, Stern's program is contro-versial not only among radio listeners and the FCC, because of its often bawdy, outrageous, insulting, sometimes libelous content, but also among fellow radio hosts. Certainly his show has spawned imitators, especially in the competitive morning-drive time slot, because others are trying to follow his popular formula, while adding their own personal style. But many hosts have mixed feelings about the kind of image Stern is giving radio generally.

On one side of the spectrum, for example, Mark Davis, with the highest rated show in the morning slot in Dallas, feels a sense of relief to have Stern out in the vanguard. Though his show is issues oriented, not a shock jock show, his reason, he told me, is that: "Stern helps set the limits for what all of us can do. The regulators check out his show, and they target him first if anything is offensive. So that gives everyone else guidelines on how far to go. In a sense, Stern being out there makes it safe for everyone else."

But on the other side, many in the radio industry feel embar-rassed and disturbed by what Stern is doing. They feel his show is tasteless and gives radio a black eye. For example, John Leslie, a host of an international program dealing with world issues and commentary, feels that talk show hosts have enough trouble trying to have what they are doing taken seriously and have enough trouble gaining credibility without having someone like Stern acting out and making a fool of himself and others on his show on a regular basis. As Leslie commented:

> There are a lot of people in the broadcasting industry who
> have honed their skills and are very proud of what they do in

the business, and they look with a great disdain at Stern for giving our industry a black eye.... He's defining the limits ... and there are many, many morning personalities across the country that are pushing the envelope. They are saying things on the air that civilized society really doesn't want to hear, though they are doing this to get the audience.[1]

But whatever industry members and people in the community think about Stern and his show, his success has been based on many of the same factors that characterize the other big successes, like King and Limbaugh—a powerful drive to succeed, a hard knocks beginning, years of struggle in the industry, a strong show with unique content, personal charisma, and the marketing breaks to pull ahead of the competition.

getting started

So how did Stern do it? Here's how it began.

Born in 1954, Stern grew up on Long Island, and early on developed a fascination with music and radio, since his father worked as an engineer at a New York station (WHOM, which later became K-Rock—with the call letters WXRK-FM—where Stern works today) and used to tell Howard stories about working with DJs.[29] Then, when his father became part-owner of a Manhattan recording studio, where they taped cartoons and commercials, he took Howard to the studio from time to time, and the boy got to meet the voices behind his favorite cartoon characters. Stern also had an early introduction to the art of interviewing, when at seven his father took him and his sister to the studio and recorded a brief interchange about the U.S., the U.N., and then President Kennedy. After a short time, Howard became bored with the questions, and began making noises, to which his father admonished him, telling him finally to "Shut up! Sit down."[30] Given Stern's subsequent radio career, which included playing that tape on the air, his early reaction to serious questioning and authority proved to be a foretoken.

Thus, early on, Stern's goal in radio was set. As he reflects in *Private Parts*:

I was in heaven [visiting his father's studio]. Even then, I realized that I wanted to entertain people on the radio. My father would drive into Queens and we'd take the subway from there into the city. The driving part of the commute was horrible. We'd always listen to the radio on the way in, and if anything good came on, my father would get totally into it. It dawned on me that if you were half a mutant you could probably get on the radio to entertain people and to make them forget about the drudgery of that shitty commute.[31]

So Stern's goal to get into radio began early, and from the beginning he knew he wanted to talk, not be a DJ and play records, even though no one was doing wild talk shows at the time on a national scale. Ironically, he was extremely shy growing up, and in his high school classes he barely spoke and was something of an outsider, notably unsuccessful with girls and not a good student. But he did well enough to get accepted at Boston University, and from the beginning he worked toward getting into radio. He majored in communications, and soon after he graduated in 1976, he started at WRNW-FM, a small 3000 watt rock station in Briarcliff Manor, in Westchester County, a suburb north of Manhattan. It wasn't much—just $96 a week, and Stern's job was primarily to play music and not say anything, but it was a start.[32]

The next stop was Hartford, Connecticut, as the morning man on WCCC AM-FM. He got the job after responding to a station ad in *Radio and Records* for a "wild, fun morning guy," and it was there that Stern started experimenting with the offbeat characters, song parodies, and humor that came to characterize his show. He also began building the comedy team he would work with, starting with Fred "Earth Dog" Norris, a writer who did good impressions, whom he met in Hartford. And he began staging some of the wacky stunts that would become even wilder productions over the years. For example, in 1979, during the gas shortages, he promoted a "To Hell with Shell" boycott, urging people to drive with their lights on to protest the rise in fuel prices.[29] Very tame, Stern commented in *Private Parts*, but a start.

Stern soon tired, however, of struggling at a struggling station (earning only $12,000 a year at the time), and after two years he headed for Detroit in 1980 for a brief stay as a morning DJ before the station went country nine months later. Still, during that time he got some early recognition for what he was doing by being named *Billboard* magazine's top album-oriented rock personality for 1980,[32] and received national publicity for some stunts. For example, in one promotion he led hundreds of people who donated $1.06, the station's call numbers, to smash a Toyota, and donated the money raised to Chrysler, then in trouble along with the rest of the auto industry.[29]

Stern also began making the show wilder and wilder and crafting his wild public persona as a kind of bad-boy teenage adolescent—willing to humiliate himself as well as humiliate and insult others, and forever fascinated by sex and bodily functions. It was an approach of releasing his own and his listener's id as far as he could go. For example, in describing these days in Detroit, Stern writes:

> I did anything to get noticed. I entered a local Dolly Parton Look-a-Like Contest. I wrestled women (and lost!) on the front lawn of the station at 8:00 A.M. in front of two hundred screaming maniacs. When the Republicans came to town for their convention we organized a protest in support of the Equal Rights Amendment. It was "Burn your B-R-A for E-R-A" and again, I humiliated myself in front of hundreds of people, parading around in a bra and then collecting a few dozen others and burning them....
>
> ... And I got wilder with Dominatrix Dial-a-Dates with the Leather Weatherlady. One time, in the middle of another Dial-a-Date, I decided I was gonna drink and I got so loaded I passed out on the air during the show.[33]

making it

Then, having found his unique niche, Stern added a few more people to his team, pushing the envelope a little further, and looking for opportunities for better markets with bigger audiences. It was his formula for expanding until he made it big.

On his next job, on DC 101 (officially WWDC-FM) in Washington, DC, he met his partner Robin Quivers, a black woman, who had previously been a nurse and in the Air Force and had only recently gotten into radio. She was like a straight foil in a comedy act, and she went along with his teasing, even when Stern was, from the perspective of many women, acting like a male chauvinist pig—chiding her about her weight, her hips, her breasts, asking her about her sex life, and other personal details. Meanwhile, the show itself got crazier, bringing even more publicity and ratings, while Stern reveled in this bad-boy, break-the-barriers role. He even gloried in the outrage of critics—like the little kid who loves making his parents and teachers nuts. As Stern commented in *Private Parts*:

> I kept chipping away at management's archaic approach, and we began to assemble the program I had envisioned. We did parodies like Hill Street Jews. We did Beaver Breaks, bits where Wally made love to an inflatable doll or Ward got a sex change. I introduced God and had Him do the weather.... Then I had God reveal that he was gay and living with a guy named Bruce. I savored every letter of hate mail and read the best ones on the air. I even called the haters up and got them on.[34]
>
> I was pushing the boundaries all over. I didn't know how far I would go. Anything that happened to me became grist for the mill of my show.[35]

The approach worked, because no matter how tasteless some found the program, it gained Stern a notorious celebrity in Washington. After a year on the air, the audience grew fourfold, and when Stern went out to do public appearances, he and any team members with him were mobbed. Sometimes people even came up and tried to press coke or pot into his hands, though he turned them down.[29]

But despite success, there were continuing conflicts with management—this time, Stern says, because the station manager resented that Stern was getting all of the attention and praise for the station's success, not the manager. So Stern moved on. The next stop was WNBC in New York, where he became the afternoon drive-time personality for the next three years. Though again there were battles with management, as the station tried to rein in some of his perceived excesses, such as by sending him memos about what he couldn't do, such as "NO ... jokes or sketches relating to personal tragedies ... jokes dealing with sexual topics in a lascivious manner," Stern kept pushing.[36]

He even added more sex and scatology to the show at times, such as in one new feature called Sexual Innuendo Wednesday, in which he invited women to call in with their stories about sexual harassment, child abuse, or rape, and they did. In turn, Stern's popularity with the audience helped him get away with what he was doing. Management could see the ratings continue to climb. But eventually, in 1985, Stern finally did go too far when he did a Bestiality Dial-A-Date program, soon after the station's new general manager had asked him to "clean up" his act so they could get "better, more prestigious advertisers on the show." Stern did the Bestiality program anyway, and that was about the last straw. His show was canceled.[37]

But Stern was soon back on the air. Within a few weeks, while NBC was still paying Stern off for his canceled contract, he lined up a contract with the station that would take him national— K-Rock (or more officially WXRK-FM in New York). The station hired him for the morning slot, which put Stern head-to-head with the morning DJ on his old station, Don Imus. Stern gleefully saw this as an opportunity to "destroy" Imus and the station that fired him. And in effect that's what happened. Stern's ratings on K-Rock soared, NBC's share dropped, and after a few years, NBC sold the station at a loss.

going national

The next step was going national in 1986, soon after Infinity Broadcasting took over K-Rock. Stern headed to Philadelphia and eventually won a ratings war in 1990 with the rival station's DJ, John DeBella, who was doing a wacky but much tamer program called the Morning Zoo. But again, Stern's wildness won out, and he celebrated the win with a funeral for the "Zoo Keeper."[32]

Meanwhile, as Stern was building in Philadelphia, Infinity

was moving on to other markets, starting with Washington, DC in 1988, Baltimore soon after, and spreading to L.A. in 1991. But would Stern's style play outside of the East Coast? That was the big question, Infinity's L.A. licensee Greater Media asked. Could his East Coast style of humor, which worked so well in New York, Philadelphia, and Washington, go national? For example, would his ethnic and racial bits, like, "Do you want to go to The David Dinkins Speech School and learn to sound as white as Bryant Gumbel, O.J. Simpson, and Lester?" work elsewhere, or would they be misunderstood or considered too offensive?[38]

But, perhaps for the same reasons the *New Yorker* and *Spy* gained a strong national audience, Stern soon broke through nationally—at least in the big cosmopolitan cities like L.A. Within a year of his 1991 launch, Stern had taken his morning show from the number 21 to the number 1 slot in L.A. And since then, Infinity has taken his show on to other markets, including Cleveland, Dallas, Boston, Las Vegas, New Orleans, Pittsburgh, Phoenix, Rochester and Albany in New York, Washington, DC, and San Jose in California—about two dozen stations in total.[39] But in some cities, like San Francisco, after brief debuts, the show was pulled, because of local protests or concerns by the station management about local sensibilities. And stations in other cities simply declined the show at the outset.

But what may not have played in San Francisco or Peoria did help to build Stern a kind of cult following among those who wanted to let loose, including many people in traditionally stigmatized minority groups and on the margins of society—a following Stern often played up on his shows. For example, a representative show might feature everything from S&M leather goddesses, transvestites, and radical lesbian feminists to anarchists—very much a counterpoint to Limbaugh's conservative target market. Ironically, at home Stern was actually a monogamous, loyal, dutiful family man with his wife Alison, concerned with protecting his kids from inappropriate influences, including listening to his own show. In fact, when Barbara Walters interviewed him on *20/20*, he firmly asserted that he didn't think his show was appropriate for his kids; they were too young and he didn't want them to hear him talking about his own sex life (among other things). But in public, he plays his wild-man, let-it-all-hang-out persona to the hilt.

As a result, once he began his national show, he was soon the target of both the Federal Communications Commission (FCC) and right-wing religious attacks. But despite a $1 million FCC fine, these attacks only helped increase his publicity and popularity. In fact, Stern became something of a cause célèbre among free speech advocates and civil libertarians, even though many of them detest his message.

The FCC and religious attacks began in November, 1986, soon after Stern expanded to station WYSP in Philadelphia. A Mississippi-based group, the National Federation for Decency, headed by the Reverend Donald Wildmon, a United Methodist Minister, took offense after monitoring his show and alerted the FCC. But after the FCC responded by writing to Infinity, charging the station with obscenity and indecency, Stern turned this response into still another national media event. Among other things, he organized a protest rally supporting free speech outside the U.N. in New York in April, 1987, in which he made fun of the FCC and its stand. A highpoint was a crowd of about 5000 chanting "Fuck the FCC" on a national broadcast.[32]

Although Stern wasn't fined or otherwise penalized for this first round with the FCC, in November, 1990, the FCC levied $2000 fines against three of the stations carrying Stern's show, since it found Stern's Christmas show especially offensive—most notably when Stern featured a man playing a piano with his penis. The amount was like spare change, given the show's audience and the publicity value of the fine. But then in 1992 and 1993, the FCC imposed over $1 million in fines on Infinity—more than it ever has on any other broadcast organization for indecency, and Infinity eventually relented to pay the $1.7 million in 1995.[32]

In any event, the program and promotional activities surrounding it led to all sorts of spin-off activities, including *The Howard Stern Show* on the E! network on TV, which started in 1990, and is still on in about 50 markets, usually late at night because of its risque nature.[32] Basically, the show involves filming Stern's radio circus on TV. Other spin-offs have included Stern's many TV talk show appearances, his brief attempt at a campaign for New

York governor on the Libertarian ticket, and the *Private Parts* and *Miss America* book phenomena.

It's a popularity that continues today. Though Stern may not have wide numerical coverage, the two dozen or so stations that do carry his program are in many of the largest markets, like New York, L.A., and Washington, DC, giving him millions of listeners and keeping the phenomena going. The paradox is that many in radio find him an embarrassment in their own efforts to be taken seriously, while at the same time many hosts have copied some of his techniques because they build ratings. And Stern's ratings remain high. In fact, much like Limbaugh has created his own community through Rush Rooms and other events appealing to the heartland, Stern has created another kind of community, primarily in the big urban markets among people who like the chance to be wild and crazy or who are already living on the margins of mainstream society. Stern's program gives them support for being who they are.

summing up: the appeal of the big three

Thus, in various ways, through unique programming, charismatic personalities, and powerful marketing and promotion, the big three of radio have led the field for many years.

Perhaps a reason they have gained such popularity is that each in his own way represents a powerful part of the self that draws a different type of audience from the community as a whole. For example, Stern's program appeals to the child, id, or unconscious in us all. It gives full vent to the liberty-loving, ever-adolescent, "don't want to grow up" self. At the other extreme, Limbaugh's opinions, advice, and reassurances are like the parent, superego, or superconscious speaking to us, telling us what is right and wrong, and what to do. Then, in the middle, there is King, whose interviewing style as the friendly, supportive facilitator is like the adult, ego, or conscious part of ourselves, which wants to understand, investigate, and explore, ever curious to ask about and learn more.

In a sense, these three masters of radio (one of whom has

since become a TV superstar) reflect the three major streams of radio today—the more opinionated political and social issues programming of Rush reflecting the parent; the freewheeling comedy, theatrical, and playful programming style of Stern reflecting the child; and the more neutral want-to-understand-what's-happening style of King reflecting the adult. These are broad characterizations, but as seen in these terms, the big three are talented leaders who have sculpted these three types of radio, and subsequently brought their radio style to TV. In turn, because they have been so good at doing and marketing what they do, they have gotten where they are. And now numerous competitors are following behind them, seeking to get to the top of the mountain themselves, and perhaps unseat these kings in the process.

notes

1. Lynn Rosellini, "All Alone, Late at Night," *U.S. News and World Report*, January 15, 1990.
2. Larry King, *Tell Me More*, New York: G. P. Putnam's Sons, 1990, pp. 205, 219.
3. Peter Laufer, *Inside Talk Radio: America's Voice or Just Hot Air?*, New York: Birch Lane Press, 1995, p. 103.
4. Laufer, pp. 103–104.
5. Rosellini, p. 54
6. Laufer, *Inside Talk Radio*.
7. Interview with Mark Davis, July 21, 1995.
8. Rush Limbaugh, *The Way Things Ought to Be*, New York: Pocket Books, 1993; Simon & Schuster, 1992.
9. Rush Limbaugh, *See, I Told You So*, New York: Pocket Books, 1994; Simon & Schuster, 1993.
10. Limbaugh, *See, I Told You So*, p. 33.
11. Limbaugh, *See, I Told You So*, p. 32.
12. Limbaugh, *See, I Told You So*, p. 35.
13. Limbaugh, *The Way Things Ought to Be*, pp. 9–11.
14. Limbaugh, *The Way Things Ought to Be*, p. 12.

15. D. Howard King and Geoffrey Morris, *Rush to Us*, New York: Pinnacle Books, 1994.

16. Limbaugh, *The Way Things Ought to Be*, p. 15.

17. Limbaugh, *The Way Things Ought to Be*, p. 16.

18. Limbaugh, *See, I Told You So*, p. 113.

19. Ted Rueter, *The Rush Limbaugh Quiz Book*, Kansas City: Andrews and McMeel, 1995.

20. Limbaugh, *The Way Things Ought to Be*, p. 23.

21. Limbaugh, *See, I Told You So*, p. 24.

22. Rueter, *The Rush Limbaugh Quiz Book*, Kansas City: Andrews and McMeel, 1995, p. 96, citing *The Flush Rush Quarterly*, 1994.

23. Rueter, 1995, p. 104, citing Paul D. Colford, *The Rush Limbaugh Story: Talent on Loan from God*, New York: St. Martin's Press, 1993, p. 225.

24. Rueter, 1995, p. 104, citing *The Rush Limbaugh Story*, p. 174.

25. Charles M. Kelly, *The Great Limbaugh Con … And Other Right-Wing Assaults on Common Sense*, Santa Barbara, California: Fithian Press, 1994, p. 14.

26. Kelly, p. 51.

27. Rueter, p. x.

28. Rueter, 1995.

29. Howard Stern, *Private Parts*, New York: Pocket Books, Simon & Schuster, 1994.

30. Jim Cegielski, *The Howard Stern Book*, New York: Citadel Press, 1994, p. 4.

31. Stern, pp. 133–134.

32. Cegielski, *The Howard Stern Book*.

33. Stern, pp. 160, 164.

34. Stern, p. 172.

35. Stern, pp. 177–178.

36. Stern, p. 197.

37. Stern, p. 227.

38. Cegielski, pp. 59–60.

39. Howard Stern FAQ, updated and posted on CompuServe's BP Forum on January 21, 1996, by Lewis Rosenberg.

the voice of the people
what people are saying coast to coast

N ow that news/talk has become the most popular format, up from number two in 1992, with over 14% of the over-12 population from 6 a.m. to midnight, according to industry ratings,[1] the question is why? And what makes particular shows so popular? How do the hosts get people to listen and call?

the power of personality and participation

Though people listen or call a talk show for lots of reasons—feeling part of a community, getting information, feeling plugged in and connected to others—a key factor is the personality of the host. Again and again, talk show hosts I interviewed told me this—the hosts with the most popular shows achieved this because they "build a relationship with the audience"[2] or "establish some kind of rapport with their audience."[3]

Another key factor in making a show popular is audience participation and emotional involvement. Unlike television, where viewers generally passively watch a screen, many radio listeners like the opportunity to interact or to vicariously experience others like themselves interacting. Though a few TV hosts like Larry King invite call-ins, the callers play a much more limited role than the listeners in radio. Much more of the interaction comes from the members of the studio audience or guests; only a few calls from home viewers get on the air, in contrast to the radio call-in program built around attracting many callers.

Still another big element in radio's appeal is the sense of equality that comes with everyone being just a voice. As a result, the signs of status and celebrity are largely stripped away, unlike on television, where a few minutes of airtime can create an instantly recognizable national celebrity. Instead, on radio, the relationship of host and guests is more like everyday people talking, and many people are drawn to this quality.

The spontaneity and uncertainty of what will happen on the show is also a powerful attraction. Though some stations use a seven second delay to edit out any potential problems with defamation, copyright infringement, and obscenity on the air, the trend is to broadcast live radio and let the host disconnect a caller as soon as he or she perceives a problem. So radio has that unpredictable give and take of ordinary conversation—unscripted, unplanned.

The appeal of controversy is also a pull on some shows, where it makes the interaction and emotional involvement even more stimulating and involving. On such shows, not only are the topics discussed controversial, but many hosts up the emotional impact by taking a strong—and sometimes unpopular—position inviting listeners to call in to express their support or disagreement. Either way callers have a chance to air their own strong opinions and gripes in a place they can get support, or at least attention, from the host and the larger listening audience—like a national catharsis of the air.

For example, in trying to explain the growing appeal of news/talk radio in *Brandweek*, the industry publication for advertisers, Mark Hudis had this to say:

> Talk radio ... doesn't care if you're offended. It doesn't care if you disagree.... All talk radio cares about is that you listen. And what keeps people listening? Personality.... Controversy makes talk radio interactive. Talk radio audiences like the interaction, they're tied into the show.... And the more

interesting or infuriating the chat, the more audiences love to love or love to hate the show and its host.[4]

the anatomy of a talk show

What helps to build this love-and-hate relationship? How do hosts create community? To explore such questions, I monitored a sampling of different types of shows closely. I was even on a few shows myself.

building a community: on the air with duane garrett

I saw the powerful way a radio talk show host can build an on-air community myself when I was on a show with San Francisco host Duane Garrett in February, 1995, taped one of his shows in early July, and witnessed the outpouring of sympathy in the local press and on his station KGO when he killed himself about two weeks after the show I taped.

I was on the show originally because I had written a book on how and why people lie—*The Truth About Lying*[5]—and at the end of the book I had included a test I developed—the Lie-Q Test—in which people can score and compare themselves to others on how much they lie. Garrett was fascinated by this test, and he invited me to be on the show he was handling for KGO host Ronn Owens, who was then working out a contract dispute with the station. My interview was a good example of the community building that goes on in talk radio between the audience and on-air hosts. That's because not only was I going to be on to talk about the book and test, but Garrett had also invited KGO afternoon news/talk personality Rosie Allen to take the test on air—and during the show, he had Ed Baxter, Allen's coanchor, call in take the test. Also, Garrett began the show by describing quite honestly how he had taken the test himself and the results, and then for most of the show, I read off questions from the test—about 150 of them—while Allen answered with yeses, nos, not sures, or 0 to 3 ratings of how much she lied in various situations; and for part of the test, Baxter answered too.

In turn, the informal conversation about the test, the results, and why each person gave certain answers made for very personal radio, helping to humanize each of the on-air personalities, as they revealed details about themselves in taking the test or made comments about each other. Their responses contributed to building a sense of relationship or rapport between the host and audience.

For example, as we proceeded, with the questions about lying in different situations (i.e., to get a job, promotion, have a better relationship) Allen made revealing comments, such as noting that she might lie to pay less for something. And after a brief break, when Garrett observed that "We caught her in a lie in one of the answers," Allen acknowledged making an "unconscious" lie, when she said "I'd never accept an engagement unless I planned to be there." As she explained: "I'd tell the person 'I'd love to, but unfortunately I can't make it.' And the 'I love' is a lie, though maybe sometimes I might 'love' to do it." Then, she added a few more personal revelations, such as noting that her boyfriend was a cop, so she wasn't sure how to rate her score on lying to cops—in general or to her boyfriend? And after comparing scores with each other, Allen and Baxter talked about their experiences in growing up and being taught to have strong values.

And then when Garrett opened the phone lines for a few questions and feedback, this was a chance for the callers to relate their own experiences and react to what was said, thereby feeling more connected and part of this personalized radio community themselves. In turn, Garrett helped the callers feel like equals, in that any listener could call and express an opinion, and Garrett gave their opinions as much serious consideration as he did my own, even though I might express more opinions. For example, after one woman called to describe how she thought her boss often lied about things at the office, such as telling her to tell a caller "I'm not in" though he was there, which her co-workers considered mere exaggeration, Garrett asked for her opinion and she proceeded to describe how an employee can be a buffer for the boss.

Only after she finished stating her view did Garrett turn to me as the in-studio "expert" to comment on her comments.

In short, the hour I was on the air was a classic example of the way a talk show host builds a sense of closeness and community with the listening audience in various ways, such as personalizing himself and others on the air, using humor and light banter to create an easy comfortable atmosphere, and bringing callers briefly into this on-air community created by these other techniques.

Later, when I taped Garrett's own show, I saw more examples of how he did this using a more serious political topic.

politics and community on air

A key way to build rapport and community is by sharing personal experiences, and in talking politics, Garrett was really good at this, because of his own experience running campaigns. Thus, instead of simply talking about the issue of women running for vice president in the upcoming presidential campaign, he began with memories of how he had run the campaigns for several women. Then, he aired some callers who shared their own reminiscences of these campaigns, followed by a few callers with questions or comments. As in many talk shows on politics, most shared his viewpoint—which is common because with mutual agreement, they could reaffirm their own beliefs and bond with the host and with thousands of unseen listeners through their connection with the host.

To illustrate, here are some examples from the program I taped on Wednesday, July 12—just two weeks before Garrett's suicide on July 26, 1995. It starts off with Garrett's reflections to personalize his view about women before he goes to some callers:

garrett: [After mentioning several names of people he worked with on several campaigns, including chairing Dianne Feinstein's successful campaigns for the Senate in 1992 and 1994, he goes on to state:] So I've been somewhat involved with it [women in politics]. Let me take a few minutes and describe what it was like ... in our selection of Gerry Ferraro.... We felt we had very little chance of cracking through any significant number of states in the South ... and in order to win, we had to win the West Coast.... So our pollster Peter Hart came up with a pretty clever idea. He said, "Let's not take a political poll at all. Let's take a poll that asks people about a bunch of trends in American society ... and then let's ask the question, buried in this poll, do you think from a historical standpoint it is a positive step or a negative step, a good step or a bad step, to have a woman vice president.... " And ... we found ... people thought it was an important step as compared to a wrong step by about 2 to 1.

Then Garrett went on to explain the results, and how they discovered younger voters were especially receptive and so targeted their campaign to them, and eventually the nod went to Ferraro. Then Garrett went on to describe some behind-the-scenes reasons why, such as she "was more hot-blooded ... probably stronger on the stump," and invited callers, many of them old-timers, to share their own reminiscences of those days. So between his own accounts and those of his callers, Garrett built that connection between himself and the callers, and between the callers and listeners and each other through their memories. Also, using first names helped to add to that feeling of personal closeness, such as in this exchange:

woman caller (barbara): Hello Duane. I remember very well when Mondale announced that his running mate would be Geraldine Ferraro. I was thrilled. My daughter was thrilled. I'm 68. I'm no kid.

garrett: Oh, you're a pup.

barbara: And even more thrilling was when she was nominated at the convention and the place just went bananas. I just loved it.

garrett: It really did. I was there ... It was one of the most emotional crowds ... and you know we made history that night.... I'll never forget it.... My daughter was the youngest person on that stage the night Gerry and Fritz were nominated ... And Gerry Ferraro went up and hugged her, and I have this great picture of her and our youngest daughter who was just one year old at that time. And I think I treasure that picture more than anything else that I own. It was a wonderful historical night.

Then, after exchanges with a few more callers and a brief commercial break, the tone shifted, from emotional reminiscing and bonding to Garrett sharing inside information he had as campaign manager, reflecting another important role of radio talk, namely, helping people feel like they are *inside* otherwise far-away, distant events. For example, after one caller wanted to know the real truth about why Mario Cuomo never accepted a nomination he could have had and "probably could have won," Garrett replied with his inside view:

> I assume that Mario Cuomo, somewhere deep in his soul had an ambivalence that he revealed. I've never bought anything about this notion that there's some hidden ... secret or something of that sort.... The New York press is so aggressive ... and it had a twenty-year shot at this guy and it never found anything. I think deep in Cuomo's soul he had reservations about wanting the job and about wanting to go out and campaign with the day-to-day intensity that it takes.

And so the dialogue continued for the hour, with Garrett using his own opinions, personal experiences, and insider insights to involve listeners and evoke strong emotional feelings and connections. In short, he helped to humanize the discussion by making himself a personal part of it, so it was more than just an intellectual-style political discussion based on reason and opinion. In turn, his approach made the discussion feel more immediate, more alive; and it helped listeners and callers feel more involved, more connected to the host, and through him to one another.

death and the radio community

This personal sharing and community building is what made it so emotionally wrenching for everyone—not only those who knew Garrett at KGO but the community of callers as well—when they learned of Garrett's jump from the Golden Gate Bridge in San Francisco soon after his body was discovered in the bay.

The official news began in the newspapers on Friday, July 28, once the news of Garrett's death was confirmed, with a straightforward reporting of the details. "Political Guru Apparently Kills Himself; Duane Garrett's Body Recovered Under a Bridge," read the *San Francisco Chronicle* headline.[6] Meanwhile, on the air, the news was spreading with shock ripples, and the other talk show hosts soon began sharing their feelings about how much Garrett had meant to them, what a great guy he was, and how they couldn't believe he'd committed suicide, since he had so much going for him. Ronn Owens, whose show Garrett had taken over while he was gone, was especially broken up, and in a news cutaway for his reaction, he sounded like he was about to start sobbing on the air.

The following day, not only were hosts sharing their feelings, but they invited listeners to call, and those who did similarly described their feelings of care and concern for Garrett, along with shock at his death. Many of the hosts took over Garrett's evening time slot, and besides recognizing him on their own programs, they turned Garrett's show into a radio memorial or eulogy for him. At times during the day, KGO also rebroadcast Garrett's past shows, including the last show he had done.

This response was a process of grieving that went on for a couple of days after his death, and it spread beyond the bay to other broadcasters, which included comments on the Internet and on on-line forums shared by talk show hosts and producers. For example, some of the comments on CompuServe's BP Forum (for Broadcast Professionals) were these reactions:

> Even though I don't agree with his views, his shocking loss will be felt by the Bay Area broadcast community as a whole.... Just like that—he's gone.[7]
>
> Duane left a wife, two kids and thousands of friends.[8]

In short, just as Garrett had created a radio community through his years of being a talk show host, so in death, that community pulled together to honor him and express its sorrow at his loss. Not only the people who knew him personally or worked with him felt this grief; so did the thousands of people who only knew him as a voice on the air. For Garrett had become much more than a host providing a forum for information and ideas; for some, he had become like a beloved member of their family, and you could hear that sentiment in their deep sorrow when they called to express their grief.

sound off: providing an on-air forum for gripes, grievances, and political advocacy

Besides providing a sense of distant community, much issues-oriented news/talk or political radio provides a place for people who feel disenfranchised to air their gripes and grievances. Sometimes the hosts—or even the callers—urge listeners to take some action to right the wrong.

Right-wing and conservative talk radio in particular has gotten this reputation. Some even call it "hate radio" or believe it is full of "unsubstantiated propaganda" posing as information, such as Peter Laufer, author of *Inside Talk Radio: America's Voice or Just Hot Air?* As he argues, the hosts "regularly present information as fact without bothering to rely on accepted journalistic devices for ascertaining that the information presented comes from reliable sources." Also, he asserts that "some hosts are flat-out not interested in pursuing truth, but only seek to stir up the audience in hopes of generating increased ratings."[9]

While this may be true in some instances, when I monitored several dozen hours of programming, in general I observed something quite different on these shows on either sides of the political spectrum—from impassioned liberals to conservative shows. While some hosts and callers did express anger and hostility, it seemed they were not so much sharing hate and misinformation, as giving voice to a strong frustration, disillusionment, and dissatisfaction with the way things were. Plus they were expressing deep-seated fears about having lost or losing control—and not being able to resolve the problem as a result. In turn, these programs enabled them to gain a feeling of validation and support for their outrage from the host and other callers who held their views. And generally people did get support, since they typically called hosts who largely shared their own outlook, in that upset liberals called the liberal hosts, while angry conservatives called the conservative ones.

But more than creating community bonding among the host, listeners, and callers, I found that issues and political radio often sounded like a political party meeting where people could not only feel support and sympathy after they expressed their feelings, but could also feel there might be some effect on the powers that be in Washington or on the state level, as well. Then, too, this kind of radio sometimes stirred up the excitement of a battle or prizefight, such as when a hostile caller challenged the host and callers to a verbal slugfest. In the end, the host ultimately won, either with a better argument or by simply hanging up on the caller. But in the meantime, emotions rose as the caller had a chance to try for a round or two before the host finally decided he had had enough.

To illustrate, I taped two examples of this kind of political breast-beating on radio—Michael Savage on the right (aired nationally and on KSFO in San Francisco) and Bernie Ward on the left (aired locally and sometimes called San Francisco's "lion of the left").

appealing to fear and anger: the savage nation

Whether or not Michael Savage's last name is his real one, the name of his show—Savage Nation—certainly expresses his general approach of spotlighting wrongs in the "savage" world out there. It's a world where officials are corrupt, taxes are too high, immigrants are impoverishing the nation, and crime is rampant. While much of this may be true, Savage's show, like many of these accuse and scare shows, highlights the worst problems so that it seems the world is on the verge of collapse. In turn, most of his callers seem to feel similarly angry, frustrated, and afraid because of this threatening "savage" world out there.

For example, here's a typical exchange from June 29, 1995 about how the wrongheaded liberals in government are trying to rip off the taxpayers for unnecessary funds to support unworthy, irresponsible college students[10]:

Caller: There's a phony Proposition 13 assessment. I want to tell everyone, every property owner in San Francisco that they have to write in before July 13 to oppose this or they're going to raise the taxes.

Savage: Now what's the purpose for the taxes—to give more money to the colleges? I'll tell you what they're going to do, they're going to remove graffiti. The animals they let into college these days. All they do is spray graffiti on the walls.

Caller: Yeah, graffiti removal, urine abatement, parking lot improvement …

Savage: The college students are urinating on the walls these days. So the barbarians are not at the gates. The barbarians have crashed through them…. You know, the old-line tax-and-spend liberals, they can never change their tune. Their mentality is eat the rich, tax and spend, tax and spend…. Redistribute the wealth, all power to the people.

But perhaps even scarier than out-of-control college students is crime, and Savage invites callers to express their outrage at how it is spreading and how there seems to be little anyone can do. To illustrate and trigger calls, Savage gives an example of a couple who drove into a project area by mistake and the woman got raped. Soon the first caller responds, a Muni bus company driver, who has had some personal experience with the problem, and Savage helps him bring out the horror of driving a bus in the city today, building the image of fear in a collapsing world—a little like the film *Road Warrior* about a disintegrating society. Here are some excerpts:

Caller: I drive the 19-Polk. Everyday I go through those projects at Hunter's Point and at Potrero Hill. The things I see as far as the dope dealing and everything else. It's incredible. There are no cops around there.

savage: There's an open market in that area in other words. They're afraid to go there.

caller: That's it. They won't touch that area ...

savage: So ... what do you think about this rape? Why did they do this to the couple? Was this just a random incident or is there more involved here?

caller: There's more involved. Those kids up there. They have nothing better to do. They do it for kicks ...

savage: I think they should put warning signs up for tourists at San Francisco International Airport saying "Beware of Certain Areas" because they're dangerous.

caller: I'd love to see them get more cops up there.... When these crimes do occur, the police come out in force. Then, three weeks later, they say: "Well, we showed the city that we did our job."

savage: ... Now how do you survive up there? Do they bother you, these kids?

caller: Well, I try to stay out of their way. One of the drivers was driving through the projects and he wasn't familiar with that run. While these guys are dealing their dope, they're parked in the middle of the streets, so you can't get by them. He blew his horn to tell them to move. They threw bottles at the window. They shot at the coach. He called for the cops and they didn't arrive till a half-hour later. Everybody jumped off the bus and they ran.

savage: The cops were probably busy going to an affirmative action class ... on how to be sensitive to somebody's race from Guatemala ... or how to treat a criminal with sensitivity.... Meanwhile, Henry, you're life is at stake ...

caller: Well ... at one time, when I started working for the Muni about six years ago, I used to carry a piece with me, a .38 ... I'm not supposed to carry it.

savage: I know the story, but you ought to carry it.

caller: I know. And you know at night, which is the worst time, I had it in my pocket. And it was fully loaded all the time. Thank God I never had to use it. But there were times where I had my hand on the gun.

savage: I don't blame you ... There's been a big change in the city, as there has been everywhere else in the country. But I think it could be turned back if we got a mayor with a little fiber and we got rid of our police chief who's a politician ... We need a tough-talking, tough-dealing police chief, not a politician ...

caller: Yeah. I think we have a bunch of clowns that are running this city. Not only in the police department, but down in City Hall.

savage: Well, keep listening. We need you ... And as you're out there driving, run 'em over ... Use your buses as a tank.... No, actually, I'm not recommending that. I'm recommending that we have compassion for these wild youth. They've not had proper guidance ... I'll be right back.

Was this just a chance to gripe? Or might the program have some influence? Apparently, in this case, it could, because when Savage returned, he had a brief exchange with Mayor Frank Jordan's press secretary Noah Griffin, about how they were dealing with the incident. He assured Savage and his listeners that the woman who had been beaten and raped was going to press charges and the D.A., with the mayor's backing, was going to press charges, too. In addition, the mayor was doing a press conference to urge a curfew, because if it had been in effect, the cops would have had a reason to pick up the kids and maybe they could have prevented this incident. Then, after some more discussion about the efforts of the mayor's office to combat crime, Savage concluded the exchange by pointing out how important radio was in getting the story out and giving the average citizen some hope of fighting back against crime and corruption. As he commented:

Well, I'm glad that you broke the story on the *Savage Nation* ... so we can tell the people to calm down about this, that the city does not just ignore this kind of heinous crime and turn the other cheek ...

So you see, this is what makes this an important medium. You heard about the couple that was attacked. The girl is going to press charges and so is the boy. You heard it first on KSFO. You heard it first on the *Savage Nation*.

Then, after another brief break, Savage was back taking calls and faxes from people who wanted to share their own outrage over what had happened and reaffirm the need for new priorities to protect society with more cops going after the violent criminals. As one brief fax Savage received put it:

My heart goes out to the young woman who was assaulted by the predatory animals.... I also feel deeply for the young man who was with her. He will have to live with the abrogation of his divine duty to protect the woman who had placed her trust in him for the rest of his life.... Notwithstanding any law made by man, when I am with my wife, I'm prepared to defend her to the highest level of threat that I believe exists. If that would have been me, two or three of those bastards would be severely injured or dead. My wife would most likely be safe, and we would disappear. No elected official is going to tell me I cannot defend my loved ones.

It was a view Savage quickly echoed:

Thank you for putting some fiber into the *Savage Nation*. Because the people will not stand for this. The people are not going to stand to see their wife raped and victimized and the police not appearing. We don't care about why. We don't care about how ... We care about survival.

Then, the hour was up. And while this time listeners might feel something would be done about an especially disturbing incident in that charges would be filed and prosecuted, mostly the program was a chance for listeners to vent their feelings of fear and outrage, learn that others felt the same way, and feel a little better as a result.

Likewise, shows on immigration, affirmative action, the Oklahoma bombing, and other hot topics of the day, gave people a chance to air their concerns about an America gone terribly wrong and think about what to do to bring back a renewed, stronger, more innocent America.

the other side: anger and fear on the left—late night with bernie ward

But not just conservatives and right wingers are mad; liberals are too, though about a very different agenda. For them, the big problems of America center around the evils of big business, a justice system that picks on the average person, especially those who are poor or members of a minority group, and the decline of government services hurting everyone, particularly poor and minority group members. In turn, since the identified problems are different, the prescription for cure is different. And once again, the talk show provides a venue to gripe and gain support.

To illustrate, I taped several segments of the late-night Bernie Ward program on KGO in San Francisco. With a background as a high school teacher, who among other things teaches ethics, Ward has been doing his show on KGO for about two years, and has become well-known for his irascible, preachy, teachy style, with deep suspicions about those with power or money. The "lion of the left" some call him.

On one of the shows I taped, people were griping about the recent crackdown on flag-burners—arguing that this was a violation of American civil liberties, initiated by right-wing patriotic types who were wrongly involving the justice department and police in persecuting individuals who were just expressing their rights. On the second show, people were complaining about a managed health care proposal that looked like a ploy by big business, insurance companies, medical firms, and lawyers to control the average citizen and get more money. As on Michael Savage's show, the callers largely agreed with the position of the host—they were calling to give and gain support and feel better that at least here was someplace they could go to get solace and maybe some advice, though things were bad and getting worse.

As is typical of these issues shows, Ward began with a synopsis of what he wanted to talk about and his viewpoint, so callers could decide if they agreed or wanted to oppose him. First up was the flag burning amendment, and Ward argued that it was an erosion of individual rights, in contrast to conservatives who wanted to protect the flag as the symbol of America. As he introduced the topic, he used ridicule, paradox, and other techniques to support his view and discredit those who believed otherwise. He was a little like a boxing referee setting the ground rules before the contenders stepped into a ring.

For example, to set the stage for the debate, Ward began with these words inviting agreement or battle[11]:

> You have that wonderful patriotic group, the House of Representatives that passed this anti-flag burning amendment to the Constitution. They want to amend the Bill of Rights for the first time in the history of this country … other than perhaps prohibition and limiting the president to two terms … and what do they want to do with it? They want to take rights away …
>
> What constitutes a flag? … Around the 4th of July, every newspaper prints a flag … So if you've got a flag on a newspaper, and you put that in your barbecue to light your charcoals, have you desecrated the flag? … What can you do? Is it okay to spit on the flag, just not set it on fire? Can you defecate on the flag, as long as you don't set it on fire? …
>
> I want you to tell me tonight what it means to desecrate a flag…. First, you've got to tell me what constitutes a flag. Secondly, then what is desecration? … And why on earth would you want to amend the Bill of Rights for the first time in the history of the country to take freedom away? … And what should the penalty be? … Should somebody go to jail for this? Should they lose their job? What kind of social havoc do you want to wreak on someone for doing this?

In short, Ward's position against the amendment was clear, and most callers agreed, and sometimes Ward used their comments and questions to bolster his argument that this was a terrible idea—another example of conservatives in government gone amok. For example, to one caller on a car phone, Ward responded like this:

caller (bob): It's like you have said … it's a symbol … We don't need to protect it … A lot of the states already have laws to protect it …

ward: Yeah … and if Congress passes this, I'd like to know how it adds one job. I'd like to know how it increases the wages of one worker. I'd like to know how it helps the day care for one child.

Conversely, when one caller attempted to support a position Ward disagreed with, protecting the flag and what it symbolized, Ward was quick to attack him. And when the caller argued back, Ward did what many hosts can do in this situation—hang up and move on to the next caller. For example, when Mike in Fairfield called, here's what happened:

mike: The flag burners are bashing the country …

ward: … But now you're going to pass a law that overturns the very symbol of freedom, you become unfree. Don't you see the irony? … The flag is the symbol of freedom in this country. Now you're going to turn around and say that if anyone harms the symbol, which is not the country, you're going to put them in jail! …

Mike kept trying, but again Ward was quick to put him down.

mike: Burning a flag shows great disrespect for what this country stands for … I just don't think people should desecrate the flag.

ward: So you want to make a law that says if someone desecrates this great symbol of freedom they go to jail and lose their freedom? … And who gets to define disrespectful? … Is it disrespectful to make a flag bathing suit?

Then Ward proceeded to give Mike a series of examples, almost like a cross examiner trapping him into a web of confusion and illogic, so that soon Mike seemed to waiver, no longer sure of his original position. And eventually Ward hung up feeling a sense of triumph, as if he had once again bested a disagreeing caller—a tactic many hosts use to show who knows best. For example, Ward's exchange with Mike ended thus:

ward: So if I make the American flag into a piece of clothing is that desecrating it? … How about if it's upside down?

Meanwhile, in between Ward's many hypotheticals, Mike's answers were a series of weak and uncertain responses: "I don't know … Yeah, maybe upside down." Then Ward bore down for the kill:

ward: Upside down is desecration. So we're going to put someone in jail for putting the flag upside down.
mike: Maybe a small fine …
ward: … What if I roll it up into a ball, and we throw it to each other? Is that desecrating it?
mike: I'm not really sure that making the law should be that big of a thing, but I don't know.…

At this point, the exchange was virtually won. Ward concluded with a few more remarks making fun of Mike's position: "Wait a minute now! You've gotta have a penalty. You can't pass a constitutional amendment without a penalty! Somebody's gotta go to jail. If this thing's that important as you say it is, people ought to go to prison, don't you think?"

Finally, Mike retreated to his original unsupported statement: "Well, what bugs me is that so many people are showing this high outpouring of support for people who would desecrate a flag."

But it was over. Ward's logical rhetoric had shown up Mike's unthought-through emotional feelings about the flag, and it was time to move on. "I appreciate the call," said Ward. Then he was on to the next.

help me: solving personal problems and resolving conflicts

Another major role for radio talk shows is providing help for personal problems and interpersonal disputes by on-air advisors, many of them professional psychologists or therapists. The response is quick, usually about five minutes or so to explain a problem and get an answer. This is one complaint of critics, who feel such radio advisors have taken over the in-depth counseling role provided by face-to-face discussions with religious leaders, counselors, and family and friends. But many who turn to these on-air advisors find the quick fix helpful—and many like getting some fast feedback and advice, and they feel more comfortable sharing even the most embarrassing of problems because of the anonymity of radio. Then, too, many listeners feel better about themselves when they hear others share their problems, through knowing that others have problems too, often even worse than their own. And if someone else has a similar problem, the advice given may help. So turning to the radio advisors is a little like looking to the newspaper columnist for advice, except the response time is faster and there's a chance for some questions and answers.

Yet, since the program is still entertainment and any response necessarily brief, there is no way to deal with really complex problems. Still, if the issue lends itself to a quick fix—through useful advice or just giving the caller a feeling of support and validation by knowing that others are listening and interested—on-air therapy can work very well.

There are two basic types of help programs. One is the more traditional Dear Abby-style on-air psychologist or counselor who deals with personal problems from a psychological perspective. The other is the spiritual or psychic adviser, who often combines giving readings to resolve problems with an uplifting message about how to live a more satisfying, prosperous, harmonious life.

the psychologist is in

While many therapists in face-to-face sessions are primed to spend a lot of time listening and helping the person make his or her own decisions about what to do, the talk show advisor is generally more directive, and typically expresses a more clear-cut model of how people should act. On the air, there is no time for in-depth reflection and analysis, and besides, the listening audience wants to hear the advisor giving advice, not listen to someone uncertainly grope about to discover his or her own answers as is often the case in traditional therapy sessions.

Hence this "What's the problem?," "Get to the point," and "Here's what to do" approach. At times, this approach can seem harsh and confrontative, when the host directly tells the caller it's time to wake up, stop doing the wrong things creating the problem, or otherwise change his or her behavior—say by taking responsibility, making the first move, letting go of an attachment to someone, or otherwise doing things differently in the future.

It's an approach well illustrated by the Dr. Laura Schlessinger show, which is syndicated nationally. Like many other hosts, she starts off with a brief introductory monologue to stir up interest, and then invites callers to share whatever is bothering them.

The night I tuned in, on July 11, 1995, she was talking about "bad words," noting that New York had the dubious distinction of being the most "foul-mouthed" of cities in the nation, as researchers had recently discovered. It "rivals only prisons and the armed forces in its penchant for profanity," she said, quoting a *New York Times* article of a few weeks before.[12] Then, after she described some other findings, such as the growing use of profanity in the U.S. generally, the calls began to come in.

Her first caller, Dean, had a custody and commitment problem. He basically wanted to continue to have a close relationship with his girlfriend's kids and wanted to keep living together, yet didn't want to get married. And complicating the picture was the fact that his own kids were living with his ex-wife who was across the continent. Though he seemed to want sympathy from Schlessinger, it was soon apparent he wasn't going to get any, no matter how much he protested. Instead, Schlessinger wanted him to clean up his act and learn to make the appropriate commitment— a theme she commonly expressed in supporting the basic principle of having a committed monogamous relationship and providing responsible parenting for kids.

As the following excerpt shows, after Dean described his situation, Schlessinger soon had him on the defensive, as he tried to argue that he wanted to build ties with the kids without making a firm commitment to his girlfriend. Yet despite her stinging criticisms of him, like most callers in a similar situation, Dean continued to let Schlessinger rail at him and put him down for doing things wrong. And eventually, like many callers, he acceded to her point of view, as the following highlights of their dialogue illustrate. After he briefly described his situation, Schlessinger asked a few clarifying questions, and soon had him on the hot seat defending himself.

Schlessinger: Dean, welcome to the program …

Dean: [explaining the problem] Okay, I'm 36 years old, recently divorced for three years. I have two sons that live with their mother in Pennsylvania. I'm living here in Las Vegas. I've met a woman and have been associated with her for several months now. She has two small children … Now she wants to move forward. We have a relationship in which I admire her, I like her. We have common interests, and I absolutely adore her children. Her children have become the children that I can't really associate with because they're so far away. You understand? … And now she wants to move forward. She wants a commitment of sorts …

Schlessinger: What do you mean a commitment? She wants to get married now?

Dean: Well, she wants me to move into her apartment.

Schlessinger: [disapprovingly] She wants you to move in? She has two little kids and she wants you to move in?

Dean: Uh-huh.

Schlessinger: How does she explain the benefit of that to her children? Do you think little kids need to have a guy living there to see if he's going to work out, and then if he doesn't work out, then we dump him and we do the next one. Do you think little kids benefit from that?

Dean: No, I don't think so.

Schlessinger: No, I know so. So that's a no, whether or not you want to get closer and closer to her.

Dean: But I love these kids.

So now the situation is basically laid out, and Schlessinger is quick to respond with her own view of what's right and wrong and what Dean is doing wrong. As she quickly points out, his current life and hopes for the future are full of contradictions. For a minute or so Dean resists, but the force of Schlessinger's argument based on assuming responsibility, making a commitment, and taking care of the kids overwhelms him. Finally, like many of her callers he backs down, acknowledges her point of view, and the call ends with Schlessinger essentially scoring another victory over one more wrongheaded caller, as well as having dispensed some advice. Here's how Schlessinger leads Dean into this realization and retreat:

schlessinger: [firmly interrupting] You can't love them when you're not there. Love is a behavior. It's not a sentiment one has in absentia. That's a romantic notion, but it doesn't hold water with someone who needs hugs and interaction. So of all the options you did not give me, the one I'm giving you is you move to Pennsylvania and don't find surrogates for your own children, but be there for your kids.

dean: I see what you're saying.

schlessinger: And tell your girlfriend that she shouldn't bring men home to live with her little kids. That's wrong.

dean: Well, it's not like we just met yesterday!

schlessinger: [Forcefully] It doesn't matter. You two are not committed! Until you marry, you ought not to be living with the kids. What do you want to teach them? Shack up and see how it goes? Do you really want your 10 year old daughter to think she should just shack up and not think anything about marriage and make a few babies with a bunch of different guys? Do you think that would be in her interest, the kids' interest, or in society's interest?

dean: Oh, you put me on the spot. None of the above.

schlessinger: Well, then, don't denigrate something that's really an important part of the foundation of a society. And that's order and organization around children. So no, you cannot move in.

dean: So basically, what you're saying is if I want to continue this relationship, continue it as is ...

schlessinger: For another year, a year and a half. Then, if you guys decide this is a match, fine. But I think you should ask her to move to Pennsylvania with you to resume the relationship. You know it breaks my heart, because I can imagine if I was one of your kids listening to this phone call with you saying: 'You know, I love these kids. I don't have mine because they're in Pennsylvania, so I'm just gonna love these as though they were mine,' that would be like taking an axe right to your kids' heart.

dean: [Regretfully] I never looked at it that way.

schlessinger: This is a new beginning.

Then with a quick cutaway from Dean, indicating that the quick advice session is over, Schlessinger provides a quick reminder of who she is—"I'm Dr. Laura Schlessinger"—and she's on to the next caller and the next problem. This time it's Andy who has trouble feeling motivated about what turns out to be a very mundane and uninspiring job. Again, Schlessinger is quick to zero in on the problem, show Andy what he's doing wrong, and what he has to do to fix up his life. It's the same basic "face reality, change, and move on" approach—and again it works. Some highlights:

andy: My problem for about the last year is a lack of motivation in my job ... I'm still making ends meet and doing okay. I just don't seem to be happy. I just don't seem to be able to get into the pace of work I used to have ... I'm only doing what seems absolutely necessary to get by. And I'm not satisfied with that.

Then, after Andy explains that he sells and installs doors and windows, and though the work is available, he has lost his aggressiveness, his "desire to go out and really conquer," Schlessinger begins zeroing in on what's really wrong.

schlessinger: You're saying in no other aspect of your life are you showing this ennui … What's your purpose?

andy: Right now it seems to be just to pay bills.

schlessinger: Well, no wonder you're kind of bummed out … You're feeling a little hostile cause it's all going out and nothing's coming in …

andy: But I just have a hard time setting goals …

schlessinger: You talked about setting goals. I talked about you feeling hostile, cause it's all going out and nothing's coming in, and you went back to goals … Let's stay with being hostile! Talk to me about being mad!

Then after some discussion of why Andy hasn't been putting out much effort to sell doors and windows recently, Schlessinger comes to her overall conclusion and diagnosis of what Andy needs to do:

schlessinger: I don't know how excited you can be about doors and windows … How excited can you stay your whole life about that? You have to redefine what your challenge is … And you haven't redefined it. Right now your challenge is: "I've got to feed the ex-wife and the kids." … But you have to redefine what your challenge is …

[Then after relating a personal story she concludes] So it's all in the attitude and what you set as the goal. If you're setting as the goal simply to make more money, I don't think that's impressing Andy anymore … If you're going to come up with some interesting way to either market or create different kinds of doors and windows, or do a totally different thing, then you're going to be enthusiastic, because there's something creative in it. Right now you're a worker bee. And you're bored.

What exactly should Andy do? Schlessinger leaves the specifics up to him.

andy: But how do I do that?

schlessinger: That's your job … It has to come to you, it's your creativity. What you're going to do with these doors and windows is unique to Andy. Laura can't come up with that …

andy: So I hear you. So basically what you're saying is it lies somewhere deep inside of me?

schlessinger: I don't know how deep it has to go … But there's gotta be something unique that you can now proceed with. There's something different that you have to do. You're at the jumping-off point for a new idea.

andy: [Enthusiastic] Goodness. I'm excited. How do I …

schlessinger: Call me and tell me what it is, when it happens. I'm Dr. Laura Schlessinger …

And so on to the next. The basic structure of each call is the same: the problem, some brief clarification, getting the caller to face down what can sometimes be an unpleasant truth, and making a resolution to change and move on. This approach seems to work for the callers—and for the listeners as well, who can empathize with each caller, as well as think about how their problem and Schlessinger's advice might apply to their own lives.

calling the psychic hot line

In the case of giving psychic advice, the host uses a reading and counseling based on certain conceptions about reality to help callers solve their problems. Generally, the host starts with just a brief outline of the problem to do a reading, much less information than the on-air psychologist usually wants to start talking about possible solutions. Then he or she talks about what he or she perceives about the problem, what the caller might do, sometimes claiming these insights are coming from channeling or spiritual guides. Though these readings often sound fairly general and applicable to many people, the callers generally feel the advice applies to their own situation, and report a sense of relief or direction at knowing better what to do or at least feel better for the emotional support from the psychic and feeling other interested listeners are out there.

Meanwhile, before or between callers, the hosts commonly talk generally about how to have a more satisfying, successful life, using a psychic or spiritual approach, such as seeing the universe filled with love and energy and following the universal spiritual laws. Typically, too, on these shows, which are usually local and self-produced, the hosts appeal to prospective clients to contact them for counseling and extended personal readings.

For example, one representative psychic show I taped was led by cohosts Marlene Caldes and Moria on KEST-AM in San Francisco. The day's topic was being psychically ready for love and money.[13] Mixed in with a general discussion about how to change the way you look at love and money to be more successful, the hosts gave a few callers readings with advice on what to do. For instance, here's one of the hosts describing the spiritual approach to love and money:

host 1: How much do … multiple hindrance attacks keep you from getting what your ideal is in life where love and money are concerned?…. Money really is a form of energy. And of course love is a form of energy … So what it comes down to is … being willing to be present and aware and to allow the energy in our bodies to truly flow through us … You'll find that when you look at prosperity in the truest sense that it is a form of energy. Who doesn't want to have that? What an incredible blessing it is … And that's how you can attract it to you. By really giving the subconscious the message that it's great, this is a terrific thing and if you have it, people will bless you.

And then, the second host does a reading:

host 2: So now let's go bless Susan in San Francisco.

To do so, she draws a card from a Tarot deck, and uses this to tell her what the next year will bring. And instead of the more confrontative approach common on the psychological self-help shows, the approach on these psychic shows generally is much kinder and more supportive, emphasizing the basic message that everything is going to be okay. You just have to have a positive outlook and channel your energy to achieve the happiness and prosperity you deserve. For instance, as the host told Susan:

host 2: I think this is going to be a pretty positive year for you. You have some remarkable tools that will be made available to you as you move through the next few months. I think you either have an excellent education or skill or some intuitive knowledge ... that's really going to help you channel your energy creatively and open up a future to a much more expensive place for yourself ... And one of the things that makes that happen for you is that you think you deserve it ... Your subconscious is now aligned for you to open up and allow that abundance, that light, that understanding to come into the light ...

Needless to say, Susan is very pleased and reassured, and thanks the host enthusiastically for the good news. Similarly, there is reassuring news for Sophia, who wants a reading dealing with marriage and money. As the host tells her:

host: Marriage and money. Well, you can see that you've got a lot of growth happening this year ... And I see you going in a new direction ... Where marriage is concerned, we can see that you are willing to make yourself available to that ... You are wonderful marriage material. Somebody will, indeed, marry you ... And ... prosperity is a natural by-product, just because you're doing the right thing. You're applying yourself to breaking through the obstacles that come up. And so I would say that you have a very well-aspected year in front of you.

But to learn who might marry her and when, the host suggests that Sophia needs a longer reading—so for that she or other listeners should call the show's 800 number.

Meanwhile, between callers, the hosts chat about how individuals should act and feel to have a more satisfying life based on following universal laws. For example, as one observed:

> When we look at love and money together ... It's like a food chain ... As we begin to raise our consciousness ... as we reach each level of fulfillment ... we have room in our brains to think about other things besides just foraging around, looking for food or looking for money. And so once we have that taken care of, we have an opportunity to really open ourselves up to the other aspects of life that surround us and that can make us happy ...

I even tried calling a psychic advice show myself—*The Paranormal Connection*, sponsored by the Academy of Psychic Studies in Berkeley, featuring the Reverend Sandi Sandhu and the Reverend Rick Greer. After listening to them chatting back and forth for about 20 minutes about things like how to get more relaxed, have better relationships, and clean out the past, and how their own workshops might help ("It does take a ... decision to bypass your conscious mind and enter into that quiet serene space. And you can learn how to do it in these trance workshops that are coming up," "I'm going to be teaching a prosperity workshop ... This is really going to be about learning how to receive, learning how to count your blessings"), I decided to call.

"What might the future bring?," I asked as the first question that came to mind, and the Reverend Sandi gave me a quick outlook, speaking the psychic language of energies and spiritual development:

> I see two things going on for you. One is ... a trip coming up for you in the near future ... So in the next few months or so you're going to take a little physical journey and change the vibration you are in, so you can make it real—like saying, "I'm letting go of the past and I'm moving on to new things." ... And it looks like you have some ideas about starting a business ... or the business you are involved in now is going to thrive more than it has before ... You're going to have a lot more energy freed up for the kind of things you'd like to do.

I thanked her for the reading, which fit, though it was so general, it could fit many others, too. But in either case, it was some quick useful advice, a key basis for the appeal of such self-help shows.

taking the political pulse of the nation: talk radio left and right

Besides giving listeners a chance to sound off and feel part of an on-air community, many shows, particularly those focused on current political issues, provide a way to take an on-air straw poll to see which way the political winds are blowing. Some hosts even take their own polls by asking callers to give yes/no opinions on various issues. Though polls can't be completely accurate, since callers only represent about 1–2% of the listening audience and they tend to be more vocal and passionate about a particular issue, at least the polls give a general impression of what callers think. And although liberal callers tend to call the shows with a liberal slant, and conservative callers tend to call the conservative shows, some opposing callers weigh in, too.

Besides dealing with particular issues, these shows give listeners a chance to reaffirm and gain support for their political philosophy from like-minded hosts and callers. In fact, the repetition almost becomes ritualized, reaffirming a shared point of view like a religious ritual—such as the repeated liberal mantra about the threat of big business and the need to help the downtrodden and the conservative refrain of the need to fight off big government, decrease taxes, and crack down on crime. Radio helps to shape, clarify, or reaffirm these positions—and in doing so, it increases political interest and intensity.

To illustrate, following is a sampling of excerpts from several shows on different sides of the political fence.

a chance to express the liberal perspective: dealing with drugs in the classroom

Here are some examples from the Michael Krasney show, taped from a nonprofit station in the San Francisco Bay Area—

KQED, which generally features a liberal point of view in its programming.[14] The subject is freedom and drug testing, in response to a recent court decision permitting the drug testing of student athletes. Krasney has a few guest commentators who seem to share this liberal perspective. And callers quickly go beyond the topic to express their general views about resolving the drug problem by looking at root causes and increasing government programs for drug prevention and education. From time to time Krasney jumps in to sum up the general view or trigger related questions for thought. A few samples of how this underlying liberal perspective helps shape the dialogue and creates a consensus view follow.

betty: What I'm concerned about is what's missing in this whole discussion [about drugs in the schools] which is what are the root causes? ... Why are the teenagers turning to drugs? Let's get to the root causes, let's figure it out, rather than policing our high schools.

maria sheedia (president of the california interscholastic federation): I would agree wholeheartedly with the last two callers and the point of view that the schools are a microcosm of our society ... And until we can attack the larger problem, we're going to continue to have problems in our schools.

ed chen (staff counsel for the northern california aclu): Well, the first thing we need to do is increase our drug prevention and education programs ... There's a lot of research out there about the best way to run these programs.

carlos: ... We have yet to do anything to address the real problem or the people who have the power to bring these drugs into our country. We pick on Hispanics, the black kids, the poor kids, who don't have the same amount of justice that these big people have who are really the troublemakers ... the people who have the power to bring in the narcotics.

bob: I want to get back to root cause issue. This [the decision to test for drugs] seems to be yet another kind of quick fix approach to a very complex problem.... I don't really think its going to be effective to ... test everybody and everyone who tests positive we're going to throw in jail or deny them certain rights and privileges. I think that's taking the wrong direction. What we have to do is address the issue of what are the real effects on people's lives from using drugs and who are the people who can comment on this intelligently.

Thus, while the debate may be about drugs, it is also a chance to bring in notions of getting to root social causes, expanding government efforts to heal the problem, and the unfairness of justice in America toward minority group members—all reflecting the liberal point of view.

a chance to express the conservative/libertarian perspective: legalizing marijuana

By contrast, a debate about drugs on a show with a conservative/libertarian orientation on a station with this general view—the *Tom Camm Show* on KSFO in San Francisco[15]—takes a different slant. It focuses on the problem of too much regulation in the case of marijuana, and the general consensus is the government should leave people alone, not create more programs. In turn, this will be good for business and capitalism, since people can profit from the sale of marijuana and products derived from it. Following are some excerpts illustrating this more conservative/libertarian view.

steve: The vast majority of pot smokers, drinkers, even gun owners don't go out and kill people. However, there's the more pressing reason to legalize it, and that's the caller who says he was making $300–500 an hour from this stuff. He's doing that once a month and is depriving the state of about $300–500 a year in state taxes ... This could be big business ... You could spawn a whole new era of entrepreneurs, horticulturalists ... and I think it could really expand the economy and help the state out.

tom camm: So you're in favor of it ... I understand economically what you're talking about, but do you think that outweighs any greater risk?

steve: Well ... It's a matter of choice, because the vast majority of users really aren't a problem to society ... And you really can't protect people in society from every contingency, and I don't think that's the purpose of a law anyway. I think the purpose of a law is to be fair ... and I think people are sick and tired of having to build new prisons to put people away in jail who do petty things like this.... I don't think personally growing marijuana is a crime.

melissa: Like everything, used in moderation, you can have a successful life [using marijuana]. I smoke it maybe once every three or four months and I live my life. I think it's just like alcohol. Anybody who drinks everyday to excess, will no doubt have their life wind down. The same with marijuana. So I don't see the danger in legalizing it.

ned: I don't smoke marijuana and never did.... But if they'd legalize marijuana, we'd get the old hemp back again, rope, oil, etc. If they'd legalize it, we'd be able to get all the by-products back out of it.

Only one caller at the end of the show expressed concern that legalizing marijuana might open the door to legalizing other more dangerous drugs. But otherwise, the general consensus favoring legalization was clear—and for conservative reasons: less government regulation, stimulating private enterprise, and promoting individual choice and responsibility. So again, besides providing a forum for opinions on particular issues, the program helped reaffirm the more general political orientation of listeners.

reacting to and venting about current issues

Besides their other functions (such as community building, support, and validation), issues-oriented shows allow listeners and callers to vent their feelings—which usually means opposing or griping about something that recently happened. These critics usually call for the same reason that customers typically write or call stores to complain, not because they have gotten a service or deal they expected. So, since callers tend to call like-minded shows, liberals typically call liberal-oriented shows to complain about what conservatives have done; while conservatives gripe about liberals on conservative/libertarian shows. In turn, expressing these opinions and releasing pent-up feelings can help callers feel better—and vicariously, listeners who identify with these opinions and feelings, can feel better, too. Even opponents can gain some release by using their disagreement with the views expressed to clarify their own views, as well as feel a surge of excitement which is stimulated by their opposition to opposing views—much like the challenge of battle helps charge up a fighter before a fight.

Again, I taped a sampling of these shows to illustrate.

judging the schools

Here's an example of how one host, Shann Nix, filling in for Jim Eason at KGO-AM in San Francisco,[16] triggered an outpouring of feelings after describing an incident at the public schools and using it to launch a discussion of public versus private home schooling. It was clear she personally supported the parent who took his child out of the school to tutor him at home, since the public schools weren't teaching him to learn. Here's a bit of her intro, followed by a few responses from callers:

shann nix: [providing an opening intro to set the stage] What would you do if you found out that your 13-year-old child was failing all five classes? Would you tutor that child? What would you do if after you brought that child's grades up, you were then convicted of violating a school code? ... It actually happened to Charles Hayden in Pittsburg, California ... He learned his 13-year-old son Chris was in danger of flunking ... so he started tutoring Chris, and he worked with him every day for two hours ... Eleven weeks later ... Chris actually passed with an 85% average ... Now here's the strange part. Instead of congratulating Charles Hayden for being what we all want parents to be ... administrators in the ... school district charged him with illegally taking his son out of study hall … Now just today, he was actually convicted of … violating the state school code … and fined $22, though the judge suspended the fine since she thought he had good intentions in tutoring his son.

Then, after noting the current emergency in public schools resulting from reduced budgets, poor teachers, and overcrowded classes, she asks listeners what they think. Would they do what Charles Hayden did? Do they think he was right or wrong?

Now listeners get to sound off, mostly echoing and expanding on Nix's point of view, as in most of these shows, building a supportive consensus of listeners, so everyone feels a little better in the end. For instance:

John: … I have to congratulate the father for what he's done for his son … and I believe the school and the state are trying to get off the hook from … professional jealousy. The father has done a better job than the school and the state have done. So they're trying to punish both the father and his son …

Nix: [agreeing and expanding on what the previous caller just said] Right … And what I find interesting is that the state law has a compulsory attendance provision. Now why?

When one caller expressed disagreement, arguing that a parent shouldn't pull a child out of school, since the father could tutor him after hours, Nix deftly argues him around to her view, noting:

Nix: I would say that at the point at which the school had defaulted on this child's education, they no longer had any right to apply laws to him.

calming fears in a crisis: talking about the unabomber

Talk radio can be especially good in a crisis in informing people about what is going on and enabling them to express fears and feel some reassurance. That's what happened when the Unabomber threatened to blow up an airplane in California if his manifesto wasn't published in a major paper. His threat was the number one topic on many talk shows, as people called in to let off steam about how one person was disrupting modern civilization and suggest what to do, such as on the Tim Dunbar and Fred Wygant show on KGO-AM in San Francisco. Their guest was former *Washington Post* publisher Ben Bradlee, talking about whether a newspaper should publish the manifesto or not. Here's a sampling:

host 1: So should his manifesto be published, and if it is published, would you read it?

bradlee: [after describing how some newspapers published and others didn't when several Croatians hijacked a plane in Chicago in 1976 and threatened to blow up the plane if the newspapers didn't publish] Today I'd play it very carefully, and I wouldn't dismiss it out of hand. But right now I'm undecided.

host 2: So the question is, would you read it, if they do publish it? Mary Ellen Geiss … has been asking people that question …

geiss: [calling in to the show] In San Francisco, most people I talked with said do not publish the Unabomber's manifesto. They didn't want to read it, and they didn't think it should be published.

Why? Geiss read some of the responses:

male subject: I don't feel they should publish the manifesto … because it's catering to terrorism, and we should not allow any maniac to indulge in every whim they might have.

female subject: Absolutely not. I wouldn't give him a s***. He's a crazy man.

And so after airing a range of views, on to the next topic.

better understanding the issue: talking about the v-chip

The talk radio format can also be ideal for explaining in more understandable terms what a fairly complex issue is all about. In an age when 80% of the population gets its news from TV rather than from newspapers, this ability to explain can be particularly important, since the interchange on radio provides a depth of coverage not generally available on TV—except for a few selected top news stories that get wide coverage. Such issues can range on everything from the O.J. Simpson trial to the Whitewater hearings, and the talk format is especially suited for considering the latest technological developments and their impact on society. Take for example what happened with the V-Chip proposal for regulating violence on TV. One talk show host who discussed this topic at length because of strong caller interest was Ronn Owens on KGO in San Francisco.[17]

OWENS: [introducing the topics for caller discussion] Here's your chance to get right on the air. Want to talk a little bit about O.J. Simpson, about Hugh Grant, about the V-Chip, about anything else on your mind? We've got lines available.

Peter: Good morning Ronn. I work for a TV manufacturer. I want to talk to you about the V-Chip … That's what bothers me. If instead [of censoring violence] we were to, say, put a chip in the television that gives the parents the right to say what the kid can watch—say from 8 to 10 on Channel 6 … —then the parent has control. And that's wonderful. But when you say, who gets to decide which show is violent, which show is not, then you really do have an issue of Big Brother.

OWENS: Maybe so, but … just because the V-Chip is on doesn't mean it's activated. The parents would be activating the V-Chip … So therefore the parent might have the responsibility of sitting down and saying, "Okay, I'm going to watch this series and decide whether or not it deserves a V rating." It might be a little bit more work for those of us who have kids, but that's fine. I'm more than willing to do that.

And so the discussion went on—clarifying what the V-Chip would do, how, and the role of parents in activating the chip, with Owens finally summarizing the function of the chip:

OWENS: It'll be more of a C-Chip—C being for choice. In other words, any objectionable programming could be blocked. You would have the right to pick a program and just block it.

Then, the role of the V-Chip explained, callers chimed in with their own views—mostly that it wasn't necessary or that the people in the media should look more deeply at what they were putting out. For example:

brian: Why do you have to legislate the chip? ... Why can't a manufacturer just make it on the market and sell it as something a parent can buy and attach to their TV set?

unidentified callers: I think the V-Chip would really be a failure unless they really think through the whole ratings system ... Maybe there should be multiple levels of ratings for violence, sex, and language ...

Thus, while one common criticism of talk radio is that it is filled with uninformed opinions and hate—a view emphasized in Peter Laufer's recent book *Inside Talk Radio* (for instance, he states: "Uninformed opinion is championed as thoughtful commentary. Groundless innuendo gets the same respect as investigative journalism. Hate is heralded as a valid response to problems.")—I didn't find that to be the case on most of the programs I listened to, though it might be true of some. Rather, as on Ronn Owens' program and many other issues-oriented shows, both the host and guests seemed to share a serious interest in gaining a deeper understanding of the problem.

Sure, from time to time misinformed or uninformed callers got on the air who had strong emotions invested in a position they took. But typically, I found that the host would quickly correct their misinformation or lack of knowledge, because the host had already prepared him- or herself on the subjects he/she planned to talk about or had a knowledgeable guest to do that. Or if the host or guest didn't correct misinformation, other callers would. So there was a kind of mutual informing or reinforcing effect on these shows that raised the level of general debate.

learning from the experts: shows featuring guests with special knowledge

This informing effect is further maximized on shows with expert commentators, book authors, or other specialists with knowledge of a subject. While many such informational programs are on noncommercial public service and educational stations, typically on FM, a growing number are turning up on commercial and AM stations.

Certainly, some "experts" may be misinformed themselves—and some callers may call in to question, even insult, their claims to knowledge. But generally, I found the experts relatively well-informed and the callers relatively respectful of their knowledge. So I think it's wrong of some critics to broadly slam talk radio as filled with hate, misinformation, and alienated, angry callers. Yes, some radio may fall in that category. But much does not. In fact, during the period when I was monitoring shows, much of the talk by experts was about the O.J. Simpson trial and related criminal justice issues, and these experts—mostly lawyers—helped to add a note of serious analysis to what was often a media circus on TV. And sometimes, the hosts, by extensive reading about a topic, made themselves into experts on that issue.

For example, on KPIX-AM in San Francisco, one host, Brian Butler, responded to Cochran's complaints of racism after witness Robert Heidstra claimed he heard what sounded like a black man talking to another person, by demonstrating how one could tell one's race as well as other characteristics about a person by voice alone. To illustrate, he invited listeners to call and he would tell them about themselves. As he explained:

> **butler:** Of course you can tell someone's race and their heritage when they talk on the phone or on the witness stand. I'll prove it to you tonight. It's not racist … An accent is but an open book to a person … You can tell somebody's race, their demeanor, if they're nervous, probably something about their family background, maybe their level of educational attainment, how well they might lie on the stand or anywhere else, their acting abilities, language skills, written and spoken. You can even tell somebody's physiology in their voice…. I'll even go as far as trying to tell you your age, your height, and your weight.

And for the next 10 minutes or so, Butler did.

> **butler:** You're white.

vicky: I am white.

butler: … You stand about 5′7″ tall. You weigh 163 pounds. And today you are wearing blue.

vicky: [surprised and laughing] I AM wearing blue! Very good.

butler: And I can tell all that because I was listening to your voice. It's a matter of experience.

Then he continued with a few more callers, scoring an accuracy rate of about 75%. The callers were suitably impressed.

the host as expert and advocate

Sometimes the host *is* the expert as well as an advocate, particularly on the political shows, and this role raises concerns. That's because people on the opposite side of the issue fear that the host's power will unduly and unfavorably sway voters and possibly change the outcome of an election. And possibly it will.

The most powerful shows of this type generally reflect conservative politics, and they have come under the most attack, especially after the Oklahoma bombings when Clinton publicly denounced many conservative radio talk show hosts as being "promoters of paranoia." As he noted in an April 24, 1995 speech at the American Association of Community Colleges in Minneapolis: "They spread hate. They leave the impression, by their very words, that violence is acceptable."[18]

But for most radio talk show hosts, these opinions and debates are just part of the national dialogue, protected by free speech. Yet as experts and advocates, some have extremely powerful influence over their listeners.

The Rush Limbaugh Show is, of course, the most prominent of these shows, reaching out to about 20 million listeners through about 650 stations around the country. And often Limbaugh does alert his listeners to political dangers so they can perhaps take some action. For example, on the show I taped, he was warning listeners about the dangers of the trade deal with Japan and about the problems with an economic theory that claimed the deficit is good for the economy by protecting taxpayers and workers against market fluctuations.[19] Whether one agrees with his analysis or not, he presented his views in an authoritative, persuasive way.

And in a similar way, Michael Reagan urged listeners of his show to take action themselves. For example, at the beginning of the show I sampled, he began his intro by stating:

> This is where we talk about the issues, get your comments and concerns on all that is going on across this great and wonderful land we call the good old U.S. of A … And as always, get out a piece of paper and a pencil, because during the course of the hour, there are probably some phone numbers, maybe even a bill number I'll throw at you to have you write down, because you might want to call your representative or call somebody and let them know what is going on back in Washington, DC.

Then Reagan began profiling the major issues to be concerned about, such as the Administration's backdown on blocking Russia's sale of nuclear reactors to Iran, Medicare's Federal Hospital Insurance Trust Fund, and an outcome-based education bill coming up for a vote in the California Assembly. He viewed these upcoming bills as a danger to America, and he described and discussed with his callers what was wrong with them, while urging listeners to take action, too.

When you consider the millions of people listening to these nationally syndicated shows being asked to act, these hosts have tremendous power—which can be used favorably or unfavorably, depending on your own politics and point of view. They have this power because they can make a direct appeal to the listener/caller/voter—and to varying degrees their appeal is working. It's helping to create a more aware, informed electorate, which has contributed to the conservative revolution that swept the House and Senate, since most talk radio is conservative. In turn, this power is a reason there's a growing political struggle for the airwaves today. So far the conservatives are winning, but a growing number of liberal shows have gone into syndication featuring hosts like Tom Leykis, and they are seeking to counterbalance this trend.

summing up

As this review of the major types of talk radio illustrates, characterizing talk radio as primarily entertainment or as mostly hate talk by a largely ill-informed populace is misleading. For talk radio takes so many different forms. Yes, much is entertainment; some is comedy and parody; and much of it is used to inform, provide an emotional release, clarify understandings on issues, and motivate political action.

Plus many other programs serve many other purposes—such as programs for kids or teens; special interest programs on health, money, guns, and other topics; and religious programs providing spiritual guidance and worship. Now radio is even expanding beyond the radio waves onto the Internet and audio soundboards of computers. And for many talk show hosts, FM is the next talk radio frontier because of FM's stronger signal.

What do talk show hosts think about these developments? How do they develop and promote their own shows? What do they see as the major trends in the near future? Those are some of the questions I'll deal with in the next chapters.

notes

1. Mark Hudis, "Gabber's Gift: No Ads Shift," *Brandweek*, Vol. 4, No. 18, May 3, 1993, p. 28.
2. Peter Wilkinson Thiele, CompuServe comment on BP Forum, June 28, 1995.
3. Kris Earl Phillips, Statement on CompuServe, BP Forum, June 28, 1995.
4. Hudis, p. 29.
5. Gini Graham Scott, *The Truth About Lying*, Petaluma, California: Smart Publications, 1995.

6. Susan Sward and Susan Yoachum, "Political Guru Apparently Kills Himself," *San Francisco Chronicle*, July 28, 1995, p. 1.

7. Raymond Chuang, BP Forum posting under the category: "Duane Garrett, RIP," July 27, 1995.

8. Doc Searls, BP Forum posting under the category: "Duane B. Garrett, RIP," July 28, 1995.

9. Peter Laufer, *Inside Talk Radio: America's Voice or Just Hot Air?*, New York: Birch Lane Press, 1995, pp. 221–222.

10. Michael Savage, *Savage Nation*, June 29, 1995.

11. *Bernie Ward Show*, KGO, June 29, 1995.

12. Dr. Laura Schlessinger, July 11, 1995, 12–1:30 a.m., on KPIX-AM (155.0) in the San Francisco Bay Area. Syndicated on other stations nationally.

13. Marlene Caldes, KEST-AM, June 29, 1995.

14. *Michael Krasney Forum*, KQED-FM, June 29, 1995.

15. *Tom Camm Show*, KSFO-AM, June 29, 1995.

16. Shann Nix, for Jim Eason, KGO-AM, June 29, 1995.

17. *Ronn Owens Show*, KGO-AM, San Francisco, July 12, 1995.

18. Todd S. Purdum, "Shifting Debate to the Political Climate, Clinton Condemns 'Promoters of Paranoia,'" *The New York Times*, Tuesday, April 25, 1995, p. A19.

19. *Rush Limbaugh Show*, KNBR-AM, San Francisco, June 29, 1995.

chapter six

talking to talk show hosts

the talk radio reaction

given the increasing attacks on talk radio and its growing popularity, especially its conservative programming, talk radio is at something of a crossroads today. While some critics, like Clinton who described talk radio as a medium that breeds "cynicism ... negativism ... pessimism," are disturbed by its power, radio hosts see talk radio as "a form of democracy in the media" (to quote talk show host and current presidential candidate Pat Buchanan).[1]

In response, some angry listeners have urged the FCC to bring back the fairness doctrine, and since 1993, some members of Congress, urged by the Clinton administration, have explored reimposing this doctrine. However, such efforts haven't gotten very far because of the strong national sentiment against further government regulation.[2] Perhaps a more likely outcome is the growth of a liberal counterreaction in the form of a growing number of liberal talk shows on local and national TV. For example, some of these shows include the Bakersfield-based Tom Leykis show, now in syndication, and several out-of-office liberal politicians now launching their own shows. Among the latter are Mario Cuomo, former New York governor; Gary Hart, former presidential hopeful; David Dinkins, former New York City mayor; and Jerry Brown, former governor of California.

Meanwhile, this controversy over talk radio has bubbled up

in the industry itself, including in a recent book on talk radio written by Peter Laufer: *Inside Talk Radio: America's Voice or Just Hot Air?* He accuses the largely conservative talk show hosts of being caught up in the rush for ratings and greed, and he or his interviewees characterize these hosts as "manipulative ... sensationalistic ... demagogic ... quasi-journalists ... unprepared ... a radio version of tabloid newspapers ... self-centered ... infantile ... blowhards ... in the business of personal attack ... phonies ... who spew lies ... glib ... [with] out of control egos ... liars ... selfish" and so on. Likewise, Laufer or his interviewees characterize the listeners and callers of these shows unfavorably, calling them "masochists ... malcontent ... gullible and naive ... losers ... liars."[3]

In turn, other radio professionals, unhappy with this characterization, call Laufer an out-of-touch disaffected liberal who wasn't able to successfully program his own radio show back on WRC in Washington, DC and was fired as a result. As one network talk show host, Ted Byrne, writing in *Talkers* magazine, a preeminent radio talk show publication, puts it: "Peter Laufer is a frustrated man, and frustration oozes out in so many ways: sometimes as contempt—sometimes as anger ... and sometimes, as in *Inside Talk Radio*—both."[3]

This pro and con controversy eventually hit the National Association of Radio Talk Show Hosts, the largest organization of such hosts in the United States, at its seventh annual conference, when it gave its Freedom of Speech Award to G. Gordon Liddy, because of his outspoken comments on his show. Though the board itself was divided on giving him the award, since some objected to his comments about firing at government agents, the majority felt he deserved the award because of his "courage" in speaking out. They felt the principle of free speech should support even controversial, confrontational, provocative, blasphemous, crude, or otherwise unpopular speech.[4]

Yet, for all of this talk about conservative talk radio, this is just part of the picture. These conservative shows may be the most visible and controversial part of talk radio, and some conservative hosts like Limbaugh, Liddy, and Bob Grant have the highest ratings. But if one looks at all of the talk radio programs on the air (perhaps around 10,000 when one includes shows on small stations), these shows are just a part of the overall talk show picture.

Accordingly, in interviewing talk show hosts and asking about their programs and trends in talk radio today, I spoke to a sampling of hosts with different types of programs. For apart from the glitz, controversy, and big names, much talk radio is very local; it still represents grass roots radio; and it is still possible for almost anyone to get a program on the air—and even get it in national syndication. Even kids, such as 12-year-old radio host Evan Roberts, are able to do it, as was magazine writer Tom Gresham, who within four months had over 50 stations syndicating his program on guns for sportsmen, *Gun Talk*. We'll meet them and the others I interviewed next.

serving and promoting the talk show hosts of america: talking to carol nashe of nartsh

First stop on the talk show host tour was Carol Nashe, the cofounder and now executive vice president of the National Association of Radio Talk Show Hosts (NARTSH), with a membership of nearly 3000. These include both talk show hosts and those involved in the industry, such as publishers, equipment suppliers, and many talk show guests. The organization has a number of purposes, which include promoting and publicizing talk broadcasting, helping members with careers and job placement, and raising funds to provide fellowships and scholarships to young people interested in joining the industry. But perhaps most important is its primary mission, which according to Nashe is "protecting the First Amendment which we all know is freedom of speech."[5]

This is what led to the organization to give Liddy its Freedom of Speech Award. In the wake of the furor over the award at the recent NARTSH convention, Nashe many times had to explain and defend the choice to the media, and she was quick to explain NARTSH's position to me:

> Why did we choose Liddy for the Award? Mr. Liddy lives in the United States of America. We believe firmly in the First Amendment, and because the government was trying to interfere with a program on the radio, we felt very strongly that Mr. Liddy's freedom of speech was being interfered with. We did not in any way agree and do not to this day agree with some of the things that he may have said or allegedly has said. We think that those things were taken out of context. But he has the right in this country for free speech, and if you don't like what he says, switch the station.

By contrast, the choice of Rush Limbaugh as the Talk Show Host of the Year Award was not at all controversial—it was more like a coronation of the recognized king of talk radio. As Nashe observed:

> The criteria for the award is the information that's put on the show, the entertainment of the show, the impact of the show ... Rush does a political issues-oriented show and is also a fabulous entertainer ... He has in fact had the greatest impact of any talk show host in the entire United States on the industry.

Nashe also had a few final observations on the major trend in talk radio—toward "more political and more issues-oriented talk"—and she felt it was likely to become even more conservative since "the whole country is becoming more conservative. Where goes the country, so goes the media. That means the electronic press, the pencil press, and talk radio." As to who had succeeded or would succeed, she felt success depended on a combination of having a good show with "very wise marketing."

> It's pretty obvious that there is a group of people behind these people who have become very successful who are out there talking to stations and marketing those particular hosts to be on those stations. Rush is on more than 600 stations. That does not happen easily. It means that there is a team out there selling and marketing.

the transformation of radio talk through technology: a talk with lynn dystler of comrex

But even more than selling and marketing, the popular fast-paced interactive talk shows of today have been made possible by the new technologies that permit national and international hook-ups via satellite. With these technologies, hosts can be anywhere they want to do their shows—in their own home or out in the field, as well as in the studio.

To better understand how this all worked, I spoke to Lynn Dystler, the vice president of marketing and sales for the Comrex company in Acton, Massachusetts, which manufactures the program transmission equipment used by just about every radio talk show host today. Her company is one of three or four manufacturers currently making such equipment. She had recently returned from being an exhibitor at the recent NARTSH convention, and she gave me a brief introduction to how these technologies work:

> Basically, this program transmission equipment is used either on the regular phone lines, or increasingly radio talk show hosts are using the new switch digital telephone lines.... Today, most radio talk show hosts are syndicated through various satellite up-links which offer programs from a major syndicator like Talk America or Major Talk, or through about a half dozen of these digital telephone networks.
>
> The advantage of these digital networks is that the hosts can be anywhere in the country or in the world for that matter. Then, they use our equipment to dial into these central facilities, and they send their own voice out on the network and get the caller's voice sent back to them. In effect, what these satellite up-links and digital phone lines do is they give the host a very long microphone cord and headphone cord that reaches out anywhere. And it's all happening live, so people can call in and connect from wherever they are.

The whole process operates much like a regular phone call—except with a much higher, studio-quality audio, which is increasingly going digital and converting to the ISDN (Integrated Services Digital Network) standard. So hosts today can increasingly operate outside of studios. As a result, this technology has helped open the doors for many newcomers who can now put together their own shows with a few thousand dollars of equipment and then transmit the program through a national carrier service directly to the listening audience, without even needing a syndicator to do this. As Dystler explained:

> The hosts can simply dial up from wherever they are. For example, there's one host in Boston who does a major morning talk show, and he does most of his shows from his house, and he often sits by his pool doing his show. He just dials in and it sounds like he's sitting right in the studio. Then he can chitchat with the callers and with his cohost, who may or may not be in the studio, since she also has the ability to dial in from her house....
>
> In fact, some hosts have used this new technology when they've had a problem so they can't get to the station, such as if they've been hospitalized for something.... So the hosts, cohosts, callers, and stations can be anywhere now, because the technology makes it possible.

At one time, this new technology had contributed to the rise of the big national syndicates of radio programs today—Talk America, Major Talk, Talk Radio, World Radio, and several others, making increasing inroads on local programming in some areas. At the same time, it opened the door for the individual to use self-syndication, by working through the sales representatives of the satellite delivery services. How? Dystler explained how it was possible to launch one's own program:

> A person who wants to syndicate their own show can do their own production work, buy time on these satellite delivery services, and then do their own selling to the stations that might want to pick up their show....
>
> It costs about $2500 in actual equipment costs, and then about $200 to the phone company to set up and install an ISDN phone line. Afterwards the monthly phone bill would be about $50 a month.

I mentioned that when I had my program on KUSF-FM in San Francisco and sent it to Radio for Peace International for world-wide broadcast in the early 1990s, I had sent it on a cassette tape. But now, Dystler explained, that was no longer mainstream. Certainly, some people still did use cassettes. But increasingly, as she observed: "With satellite delivery and every radio station having a satellite receiver in their backyard, people are going for live programming."

In some cases, some stations do pick up a program off the satellite or digital phone hookup for taping and later replay. But as I noticed myself in several weeks of intensive radio listening, the trend was definitely to live, call-in, and immediate response programs. And the new technology helped to make this possible— and relatively cheap and easy to do. So now, just about anyone can launch a program—even though a few powerhouse syndicators are sweeping the nation—and a few of the people we'll meet in this chapter did just that.

the role of the producer

Though host/producers may be common with small-scale launches, where the host does everything, for most programs, the producer is the behind-the-scenes person who variously organizes the show, gets the guests, finds advertisers, markets the show, and sometimes acts as call screener. To find out more, I spoke to one producer, Nicole Weber, currently producing the Blanquita Cullum and the Fred Barnes shows in Washington, DC. She had been involved in producing for three years, before recently taking over as producer for these shows.[6]

She explained that the producer's role was quite different in doing a taped show, such as the one for Fred Barnes, and a live show, as she did for Blanquita. As she explained:

For a taped show, like Fred's, I help think of the topic, I invite the guests, I get the guests set up in the studio, and then when everything's ready, I run the board for the program, while the host talks to the guests. I also tape the show, and after everybody leaves, I mix it. I add music, edit it, and send it out all over the country.

For a live show, like Blanquita's, I book all the guests, many who will be connected during the program by phone, so a lot of my work is done over the phone. Then, during the show, I'm in the control room, and I work the phones when calls come in, and hook up guests outside the studio. Also, I do a "Man on the Street Interview" each day, which we play on the show.

How did she feel about doing the two types of shows? Any preferences? Weber went on to make these distinctions:

> Which is easier? A lot of people ask me that and I go back and forth. There are good points to each. With the taped show, one advantage is that it doesn't matter if you make a mistake, because you can edit all that out. So the program sounds flawless when it goes out. It's tedious to get it all prepared, and there isn't the excitement of the live show. Sometimes you really don't feel like you're reaching anybody, because the program isn't going out over the airwaves, and you don't have callers calling in.
>
> By contrast, with a live show, it's instant gratification. You work hard all day on the show, and then it's on the air and people are calling in. So you know right away it's doing well. And it's exciting because you know you are reaching people, whereas with a taped show you never get feedback except in letters.
>
> But compared to the taped show, doing a live show is a little more stressful. There's no stress involved with a taped show because if anyone makes a mistake, say someone stutters, I can just edit it out; though it takes quite a bit longer to do the taped show—perhaps about 2 hours for each half-hour show—about 45 minutes for taping, and an hour or so for editing. But in a live show, I'm in the control room and people are calling in right now. Plus we're trying to edit in other things, like laughter, applause, sound bites, "Man on the Street" interviews, and other things. So it can get a little hectic at times. But if you have a good team and everyone works together, the program can go like clockwork.

Today, as Weber noted, most shows nationally are live. But with a live show, what happens when there are no callers? As on other shows, both the host and producer have to be prepared with backup alternatives, such as topics to discuss in the studio or announcing a poll on some topic of current interest to encourage calls.

It's hard to know what will provoke calls or not. Sometimes an exciting topic can result in few calls because people just want to listen. As Weber commented:

> The more I do a live show, the more often I will throw up my hands and say, "You never know." Because we do one topic, and I will think this topic won't get any calls, and all the phones will light up. Then, I've gone the other way, where I think some topic will bring in a million calls and we get just a few.
>
> For example, one time about a week ago, Blanquita happened to mention at the top of the hour before we were going on to another topic that there was some discussion at the Miss America Pageant on whether the contestants should wear bathing suits or not, and they were going to do a poll to see if the bathing suit contest should be eliminated. She wasn't even planning to talk about that more. But then our phones just lit up! For two hours she talked about this. We didn't really want to talk about this, but people kept calling up and were really interested in the topic. And, as it turned out, most wanted the bathing suits kept in. They basically said "Gimme a break … This isn't the Miss Mensa Pageant. It's the Miss America Pageant. It's a beauty pageant."

Yet, while it was hard to predict which particular topics might provoke callers or not, the topics that people felt affected them day to day or were very controversial seemed to be the main draws. Weber explained:

> Money is a big one—Mr. and Mrs. America's money…. If it's about a tax cut, Social Security, Medicare, all of that always gets calls, because that affects everyone … And something that is a very extreme issue, such as Ruby Ridge where ATF agents came in and shot a mother while she was holding her baby, that triggers calls. It's clear-cut, it's black-and-white, and people will call in to express their views. Then every once in a while we try to do a light topic, because people don't want to be in serious conversations all the time … We try to pick something that people talk about over water coolers.

So who chooses the topic? The host? The producer? Or both? On the smaller and local shows, the host might typically be in charge of everything. But on the national shows on which she worked, Weber found that she came up with many of the ideas.

> On the Blanquita show, we both review the latest news, and the topics are chosen by pretty much whoever comes up with something first before the daily deadline for the show. So it's pretty much about 50–50, and that's the same with Fred's show, which we tape. He'll say: "Do you have any ideas about shows for next week." And I'll say: "Yes, this and this." And he'll say, "Great." … He's so busy, so the more I can do the better.

But in the end, though the producer might suggest, it was the host who had the final say on what topics were actually discussed, since it's the host's program. He or she is the one who's on the air.

Then, typically, once the topic was decided, if there were any guests, it was up to the producer to find them. How? Like other producers, Weber used a variety of different techniques:

> I get some guests from friends. I ask people who know people. I use my rolodex. I have lists of well-connected people in Washington. I have other friends in the media business, who may give me a number. The newspaper is great. I've called information and gotten people's numbers. And the Associated Press is a big help when it comes to tracking people down.

If possible, the preference was to have the guest come into the studio. "Because it's better when you talk to somebody face to face than on the phone. For one thing, it's a little more conversational when they're in the studio together." But otherwise, given the distances, most guests were typically handled through phone interviews.

I also wondered about who owns these national shows. The host? The producer? The company or syndicate that hires the host or producer? Weber described a little bit about the process of how the big national shows get on the air.

Usually a company gets an idea for something. Then, it gets the host for it and all the staff. They build the show around a name, a talent, the person who's going to be on the air. But often ownership of the show varies. It can be the syndicate, or sometimes the host can be a partner in the show with the company, or sometimes the host owns it outright. For example, Fred doesn't own his show. Radio America does and he just comes in, and does it. But with Blanquita's show, she owns it outright, since she owns her own network. But that's very rare. The majority of radio shows heard across the country are owned by the big companies like Westwood One. Still, the host has some say in the format and who's on.

But whether the show was owned by the host or a big company, the big money was reserved for the big superstars and shows. As Weber explained:

There's not as much money in radio or TV as people think, unless you're huge.... If you have name recognition like Rush Limbaugh, you can get a big-time salary, and the people who work on your show will get a pretty decent salary, too. But until you are a familiar name to all Americans, you get much less.

Building name recognition, though, is the hard part, which is why the preference in the industry is for already known names. For example, when Fred Barnes started his show, he already had a following, since he had been involved with the *McLaughlin Group*, a political show on NBC Sunday mornings hosted by John McLaughlin, and had been on *CBS This Morning*. Plus he was a writer and editor on other national magazines, including *The New Republic* and *Esquire*. "So with Fred's show it was just a matter of letting people know that the show is available. He's already a known journalist."

Weber also talked briefly about getting a show out to the stations. The live shows, of course, went out instantly through the live satellite. But in the case of the taped shows, the show was not only made available by satellite so the affiliates could pick it up from that, but Weber also took the original show master to a distributor to make copies on a cassette tape to send to the stations. And, despite the satellite technology, most still used the cassettes.

"I would think that the tapes were the old-fashioned way of doing it," I observed.

"And I would, too," Weber agreed.

> I would think it would be easier to get the show off the satellite and then run it in the appropriate time slot. But apparently not. Maybe that's because the station feels more comfortable with the cassette. I know one of our big affiliates tried taking the show off the satellite and found there was a big problem with the weekend staff getting it off the satellite. Somebody always screwed up. So they just stick to the cassette copy.

But the stations taping the live show for a future broadcast have no such backup. They just record it directly from the satellite and play it later.

Finally, Weber explained a little about how these shows are packaged so they fit into local station time slots, and can include the commercials from local or national advertisers. Increasingly it seems the economics of the business has dictated more and more time for commercials, except on the programs on noncommercial radio, resulting in about 40 minutes of program time for every hour on the air. As Weber told me:

> Unfortunately, radio talk shows in general have more and more breaks for local news and commercials. Basically, with the *Blanquita Cullum Show*, which is one of the top 25 radio talk shows in the country, we have a top-of-the-hour break for about 8 minutes and then four breaks of 3 minutes each during the hour. So that's about 20 minutes break-time altogether.... We give the local stations our clock, and then they get to put their local commercials at specific times during the hour. Other times they have to play national commercials that we have and are playing from our control room.... So basically, the 20 minutes of commercial time is apportioned between the national advertisers and the local advertisers. You can come up with whatever clock you want for this—but the norm is taking breaks about every 15 minutes.

Usually this local–national advertising split is how the programs are financed, since the vast majority of programs are aired on a barter basis, meaning that no money changes hands. The station simply runs the commercials that are typically paid for by a national sponsor (unless a host or producer is sponsoring the program); then it has a few minutes during breaks in which to run its own commercials. In turn, as the program builds up more and more stations nationally, it can charge more for advertising.

"So that's generally where you make your money," Weber told me. "The bigger your show is, the more you can charge for advertising, and the more money that brings in.... Then, the better your advertisers and the more you are charging, the more money you are going to have to make the show better."

For example, with 650 affiliates in mid-1995, Rush Limbaugh's show cost advertisers $14,000 for a 60-second commercial, with a weekly potential of $1.26 million for 18 commercials during his 3-hour show. But other shows made far less. The then second-ranked G. Gordon Liddy Show with 243 affiliates was charging $1500 per 60-second commercial—a weekly potential of $202,500—while most other shows were averaging around $200–500 per 60 seconds, for about $18,000 to $45,000 a week.[7] In addition, some big-name programs, like *The Rush Limbaugh Show* and *The Howard Stern Show*, can get bonus payments from the stations that air them, too.

Under the circumstances, those starting a show generally have to start small and locally, with small advertisers, and gradually, if their show takes off, they can get bigger advertisers and spread their show to other stations. Typically it's a process that takes several years or more. For example, Rush Limbaugh was on for about 11 years before he went national. But there are exceptions. For example, Blanquita went to being among the top 25 shows with 40 markets in two years, while Radio America launched the Fred Barnes show with a single mailing to every news-talk station in the country and had the show up and running on over 100 stations within a few years, because he already had name recognition. But otherwise it's more like five years to make it, if at all.

Finally, Weber had one more comment from the producer's perspective on what it takes to make a good successful show:

> A very important aspect of success is how well the staff works together. I'm fortunate not to have to deal with egos with my hosts. But sometimes producers dealing with big name people, especially with big name guests, have that problem, and that's not conducive to making a show work well. But when you don't have to deal with egos, you don't waste time, and you can get down to work and make it a great show.
>
> Besides, if somebody really has a big ego, they're not going to sound very good with the host on the show.... They'll be so stiff and they can't go along with the discussion. So it doesn't make good radio.

And with that, I thanked Weber for her time—and she went back to searching for guests for the next Blanquita Cullum show.

hosting a national show

Like many national shows, Blanquita's show deals with current issues and politics, and blends a mix of talk, guests, and call-ins. To get a sense of what it's like running such a show, I spoke to Blanquita and several other national hosts, reviewed the press packets sent by the show producers, and tried to pick a sampling representing a spectrum of political opinion—Cullum a little right of center, Jim Bohannon and Bruce DuMont in the middle, and Tom Leykis on the left.

The first stop was an interview with Cullum, a long-term veteran of radio and television. She got her start in the early 1970s cohosting a morning drive show on KITE in San Antonio, Texas, following her first job on a country western station writing commercials. After kicking around on radio in San Antonio for awhile, she ended up in Washington in 1989, working at the Census Bureau, and then served as the White House Liaison for FEMA. These experiences helped her develop the Washington connections that were so helpful in launching her Washington-based show, the *BQ View*, in 1993. It went into syndication the following year, and now is in about 40 markets. In a year, the show grew so quickly that *Talkers* magazine and *USA Today* named Cullum one of the 25 most influential talk show hosts in the nation. She became a board member of NARTSH too.[8]

What made her show work so well so quickly? One key seemed to be building those important Washington connections, which opened doors to getting top guests. These connections also gave her insight into what was really going on as a Washington insider, and the show soon attracted well-informed "plugged-in" listeners, as Cullum described them, who read the papers, watched C-SPAN, and were very much up with current events. As Cullum explained:

> The show deals with a lot of politics and the issues that are breaking everyday ... Due to the nature of this town, we look at politics like a spectator sport ... I like to have guests from both sides of the topic, to keep it balanced, though I am more right of center. I go right to the sources, too. Plus I include the listener. Callers can talk directly to the guests, as well.

Her few years in government helped make those connections. As Cullum noted:

> I was working as a Marketing Director for Coors in San Antonio when I was offered a kind of grunt position as Marketing Director at the Census Department. I arrived with my children in Washington—not in a limo but in a Ryder truck—and for about a year I worked at the census. It was terrible. I thought I had died and gone to hell, it was so horrible. The bureaucracy was a nightmare. But I wasn't going to give up, and I was determined to work for George Bush who was then President.
>
> Finally, I got a job offer to be the White House Liaison at FEMA [Federal Emergency Management Agency] starting in about April, 1990. And it was there I learned the ropes about Washington, DC. The man I worked for, Jerry Jennings, had survived numerous administrations. He had survived Watergate, he worked with Reagan, he had been a CIA agent and an FBI agent. He had done everything. He told me how the town worked. He said to me: "You look to me like a pretty smart gal. But you play checkers and I'm going to teach you how to play chess."

What that meant was Cullum needed to learn who was who and understand Washington protocol—the key to gaining that insider familiarity that made for exciting talk with guests and callers about current issues. And that's what helped her gain her show as well. As Cullum told me:

> You have to understand Washington is a town with a pecking order. When you go to a party, they don't ask where you're from; they ask you where you work. If you have a political appointment, how high a level of appointment is it?
>
> So I learned how the town works and some of the rules of Washington, DC—such as in this administration, "You destroy the evidence." Or another important rule is "You follow the money." ... Then you see the way in which people are chosen or vetted for different appointments; and in the process, you see people go on the offensive, sometimes try to destroy others, because they want their own person to get the appointment. It's a truly brutal process....
>
> But I learned all these things about how Washington works, and it really made a difference. It gives me an unbelievable edge, because when someone is talking to me about a piece of legislation, an appointment being considered, some action that's going on in this town, I know what's happening. You can't fool someone who has been there. You can't fool someone who knows how things work. So I cut through a lot of the bologna, a lot of the "PR spin" put on what appears to be happening–and what is really happening. And my listeners really like that. They feel they have an insider's view.

Cullum's connections also meant that from the beginning, she could get powerful players in Washington on her show, even though she started on a small station in Richmond, Virginia, which was only, as Cullum describes it, a "5000-watt daylighter which goes off before sundown." But she knew the right people who would come on the show.

> When I started the show right after Clinton won ... I had a few members of Congress and friends and Cabinet secretaries that had been in the Reagan and Bush administration I knew. I started getting them on the show, and they liked the type of in-depth interview and discussion I was doing. So I started developing a reputation around the hill in DC in which people said, "Well, you know she's conservative, but

she's fair." So it was this little show on a small station. But I soon started getting anyone on the show I wanted, because they respected the way they were interviewed. They loved it. So the show started growing in popularity ... Even though it was a small 5000-watt station, I began getting a lot of phone calls. The lines were jam-packed with callers.

Of course, being close to the capital helped, and as the show gained a following, Cullum gained other sources, including information from investigative reporters discovering and breaking stories all over the country. All that helped her show stay very much on top of—and inside of—the latest news, which helped to further build interest.

Cullum gave some examples of getting the news out first. At the time of our interview, the big news from Washington was the Whitewater and Foster hearings, along with the FBI/ATF investigations; and she pointed out how early on she talked about some pending developments that later came to pass. [For example, one concerned Bill Clinton's close friend, former associate and attorney general Webb Hubbell, who was convicted of tax fraud and false billing to clients of the Rose law firm; another was airing an early criticism of the appointment of Larry Potts (since fired) to be Deputy Director of the FBI, because of objections in the way he handled the Ruby Ridge and Waco issues.]

In addition, with her connections, Cullum was able to bring an insider's perspective to some of the breaking crime and scandal stories coming out of Washington—another big audience draw at a time when the country seems to be fascinated with crime and scandal. For example, as Cullum told me:

> One issue we have talked about is Vincent Foster ... The circumstances surrounding his death are very curious ... What we have talked about is why Vincent Foster was taking trips to Geneva ... Why was he scheduled to go to Geneva, two weeks after his death? ... What was the purpose? Was he setting up bank accounts? What was he worried about? ...
>
> We've also looked at an issue that's been investigated in Arkansas involving the drug kingpin Dan Lassiter and whether laundered money from Arkansas was used in the campaign ... Who benefited from it? ... And why did the

political aides and Bernie Nussbaum check Vincent Foster's files? What was in his files? …

There are all these interconnections … and they raise questions about what happened when Vincent Foster allegedly committed suicide … What kind of can of worms was he concerned about opening? … And what about these other unusual facts, like why would he use the hand he didn't even write with to shoot himself? … I've raised these questions since they first happened on the air … And I've had a lot of heavy-duty investigative reporters on the show giving me information …

I go the extra mile to get the information … on this and other issues. For example, I've had people doing ballistics tests send me information about the Oklahoma bombing. I've had people who are getting documents from their Congress people on certain issues send me copies. For example, people that send me the newspapers from Little Rock, Arkansas.

In fact, Cullum sees this outpouring of listener contributions as part of the new, more grass-roots and participant-oriented relationship of the individual with the medium. As she observed:

Many of the people who listen to my show are very brilliant, connected, involved. The mainstream media doesn't understand this. There's this image of the angry, alienated listener. But that is not true. What's happening today is like the industrial revolution in talk radio. For example, when people watch television, they are essentially getting one network and three echoes. You basically see the same information at the same time. You get the same kind of sound bites and you get nothing in depth. People feel like they're getting propaganda news; they feel like it's filtered information.

But when they are listening to talk radio, they believe they are getting an underground sort of unfiltered news. And we're able to give them a depth on issues not covered by the major networks. In some cases, we deal with stories the network media don't want to touch.

They give you O.J. because that's pretty easy. But other stories are complicated and also very controversial. So they don't want to get their hands dirty, so to speak. But we talk about it…. It's a different kind of radio now. We understand the responsibility that goes with discussing these issues. There are some talk show hosts who are a bit more colorful and dramatic in their approach. But there are many who

understand what they are doing, and they are very responsible.

It was encouraging to hear Cullum say this, after hearing talk
radio criticized from so many quarters, and I got much the same
perspective from the other hosts I talked to. They were not just
attempting to offer up entertainment and hot angry talk to bolster
the bottom line. But they were making a serious effort to promote
awareness and understanding that was helping to create a more
informed America at a time when, as many hosts felt, the mainstream media, and particularly TV, were creating a bland sound-
bite diet leading people to want more.

continuing the tradition

While building a following from scratch with the help of
powerful connections is one way to launch a national talk show,
another is inheriting the mantle by taking over the time slot of a
host with a major following when he steps down. That's what
happened when Jim Bohannon, who now has the number two
radio show with 400 stations, took over from Larry King. He had
already been filling in for King from time to time for 11 years when
King decided to leave radio entirely for his TV show in January,
1993, so in effect Bohannon succeeded King.

Even so, he developed his own more middle-of-the-road approach. Or as Bohannon told me: "I consider myself a militant
moderate. I've always had the view that extremes are given influence out of proportion to their numbers or their justification in our
society." So he's part of the new wave of more moderate hosts
trying to take a more balanced approach to the day's news and
current trends.

His format is similar to many other news/talk issues-oriented
shows: interviews with prominent guests from different walks of
life ("entertainers, politicians, sports figures, authors, you name
it"); calls with questions and comments for those guests; and open
lines so callers can share whatever's on their mind. But in Bohannon's case, his daytime producer has to find the guests—unlike

many shows where the host lines up some or all of the guests. One reason is that Bohannon really can't do this because he works late at night—not a good time to call up prospective guests, say at three in the morning.

Taking over King's time slot, in turn, meant virtually instant success, since as Bohannon noted: "I inherited around 90% of Larry King's stations. On the other hand, I didn't lose any either." In fact, after two years, he added a few stations.

Bohannon gave me a quick overview of how hosts and producers work callers on a national show.

> Typically, only about 1% of a talk show audience has ever tried to call in. On my show or any other show. But what's interesting is that the callers tend to be about 70% male, even if you have a female-oriented show, like you're talking about breast cancer.... It's surprising because I would think the woman's place in the subservient position is long since gone, and we encourage women to call.
>
> Like most shows we have a producer who does some screening to make sure the calls are germane to the guest or at least the caller tells the producer what he or she wants to talk about and it's an interesting or relevant topic. On the open phones part of the show, we're not as picky about it. We pretty much take the calls as they come, while I play short-stop. You never know if the next call is going to be a line drive, a high hopper, or a pop-up, which is part of what keeps the calls so interesting for both me and the listeners.

Like Cullum, Bohannon disagreed with the popular perception of the hate-filled angry audience. As he observed:

> I don't think that talk is necessarily all that conservative or that hateful. In fact, surveys have indicated that despite the popular conception, the audience tends to be considerably more conservative than the host in general.... Also, I think there may be a lot more moderate talk shows out there than people think. They don't tend to get a lot of publicity, unfortunately. There's the popular notion that every talk show is spewing ideologically extreme positions and hatred. But that's an exaggeration. In fact, few shows do that....
>
> Why is talk radio so popular now? For one thing, a lot of people feel out of touch with the powers that be. There's a feeling of some alienation with not only the government but

what is also seen as the government-influenced media. There's a feeling that if you get the news through Brokaw, Rather, Jennings, or the other major media sources, somehow it's filtered through some kind of liberal filter that isn't the truth....

Secondly, a more enduring and powerful source of its popularity, I think, is that we don't talk to our neighbors like we used to except maybe in the smaller towns. But not in the urban areas. You've got the dead bolt locks and chains on your door, crime, and people don't know or trust their neighbors. We're also a more transient population.... And I think in many respects talk radio has become a safe, sanitized space for talking, like over the backyard of your neighbor once used to be. It's safe, because if you don't like the person to whom you are talking in talk radio, all you have to do is hang up the phone.... Talk radio is a new community and maybe it's a poor substitute for getting to know people personally, but it's better than nothing.

True, some callers might feel more lonely or alienated than the average person. But as Bohannon observed:

If the callers do in fact reflect the American public, we are a lonely and alienated society sometimes. But don't forget that loneliness and alienation are two of the most compelling reasons to call. If you are basically happy with life, you may just enjoy listening to talk radio and you may not be motivated to call. But if you are lonely, that's a motivation. If you are angry, that's a motivation.

That's part of why I think you tend to have more conservative callers. Angry people are those who have been out of power for years, when the Democrats ran Congress, and now Bill Clinton is in the White House. So there has been this feeling of alienation on the part of the conservatives. And now if a Republican is elected president in 1996, one wonders: "Will the liberals become the angry motivated callers then?" I don't know.

Yet while many talk show hosts, particularly those doing issues-oriented shows, are seriously interested in informing the public and fostering a true dialogue, owners and management still have a strong bottom-line concern. If information and dialogue is what people want, if that will bring in listeners and rating points, which will draw more advertising dollars, fine. But if the host needs to add or turn the show into entertainment to keep up the ratings, they believe he or she should do that. Thus, as much as hosts may want their programs to be informative, educational, or in "the public interest," they still have to think of their programs as entertainment and think of themselves as performers and talent, too. As Bohannon observed:

> There is certainly little sense of obligation, public spirit, or public service on the part of the owners. Their approach is whatever the public wants ... I see little of the ethical or moralistic approach to broadcasting. It's whatever the public wants. We'll serve it up. If they want topless serial killers, we'll give them topless serial killers ...
>
> But I think that's the nature of the beast. Talk radio is a market driven thing and I subscribe to marketplace economics myself. It's a method by which more people have received prosperity than any time in history. But at times I think it can tend to prostitute a profession. And I think that you do get something less than stellar programming sometimes as a result.

Take, for example, Howard Stern's show. While some hosts I spoke to at least appreciated Stern's out-there approach as setting guidelines for how far they could go, Bohannon was quite critical of the show as an example of pandering to the lowest common denominator of public taste. As he put it:

> Howard is very successful ... Maybe if I asked Sandra Day O'Connor or Senator Kay Hutchinson if she's wearing panties ... I'd be getting much more of an audience myself. Howard's approach is ... very sophomoric, and he panders to the lowest common denominator ... But Howard will not let his own daughter listen to his show. When you will not let your own children have access to what you do for a living, that may be some reflection on what you do.... To be honest with you, I think he's an embarrassment. I really do. He ... sprinkles bodily functions and bodily parts on the radio. I personally don't care for it.

And Bohannon didn't like what G. Gordon Liddy said either, feeling "it's ludicrous to reward that kind of behavior ... when a guy tells you how to blow away your friendly neighborhood federal officer." He felt Liddy should not have been honored for his speech by NARTSH, though Bohannon has since joined the board. But regardless of what he might think of Stern, Liddy, or any recognition they get in the industry, like virtually all talk show hosts—those I interviewed and others—he strongly supported the freedom of speech principle, the foundation of the industry.

the power of talk radio to influence

Bruce DuMont is another of those "raging moderates" now helping to shape public opinion—and in some cases influence political action. At least, that's how DuMont characterized himself during our interview, and that's how he thinks most members of the listening public consider themselves, despite efforts to characterize radio by its extremes.[9]

> Perhaps given the fact that talk radio is first and foremost an entertainment medium, there may be a tendency to go for the more bizarre and outspoken, the more opinionated commentator who clearly fits neatly in a category either right of center or left of center. But personally, that's not where I am. I don't think that's where the American people are. The game of life and the game of politics are really played between the 40 yard line and that's where I am. I am a raging moderate.

It's a formula that has proved popular, and since he went national in 1991, DuMont has built his Sunday evening show, *Beyond the Beltway*, dealing with current national news and featuring guests (typically a mix of elected officials and constituents) and callers, into a strong national presence—on 29 stations with perhaps 150,000–200,000 listeners. He started on a local public radio station in Chicago as a 13-week experiment in 1980, and after he built up a following over the years, his station WBEZ began sending out an announcement that his show was now available by satellite. In 1992, when the number of commercial stations carrying the show equalled the number of public stations, WLS radio, the dominant station in the American Midwest, took over the program and it went totally commercial.

Interestingly, DuMont reported, he didn't only get alienated, angry, or fearful listeners calling the program to gripe about something. Instead, many people were solution-oriented. They wanted to talk about what they could do to solve a problem—sometimes on a local level, in other cases nationally—and in some cases, the discussion on his show might have helped influence policy.

DuMont gave some examples. In one case, a program dealing with recent base closings in a community helped reassure people that the job picture wasn't as bleak as many feared. As DuMont noted:

> Sometimes we'll reach out to a particular community … such as several weeks ago in northern California, when the Base Closure Commission was about to announce its recommendations for base closure. The Public Information Officer for the Commission happened to be in Chicago one Sunday night, so he was my guest and explained the issue with the panel. Then, we spoke to the political reporter in Monterey, California, who had written about the closure of Fort Ord.
> We talked about what really happened to a community when the bases get closed, and we found out that the fear was never as bad as the reality, and the number of people that lost their jobs with the closing of Fort Ord, which was the largest base ever to close in the United States, was really less than 100 people. That's because most of them had either gone to civilian jobs or had moved to another military installation that picked up some of the slack from Fort Ord … So this helped to put the issue in perspective.

In another case, DuMont used the show to illustrate the importance of people looking after their neighbors and to encourage everyone to show more concern for one another. This occurred in response to the heat wave in Chicago that caused about 200 deaths. As DuMont pointed out:

> The mayor had just announced in a press conference two hours earlier that over 210 people had died … and I began the program by talking about what was happening in the city … I said: "What does this say about being a neighbor? … Are we at fault? What is the role of government?" … I pointed out that we have some cooling centers in Chicago, and I asked: "Is that a proper role for government, to have cooling stations

for people?" So we talked about that, and about the concern that many of the people who died had been senior citizens.

Why did they? We spoke about some of the factors. For example, senior citizens may not open the door even if somebody knocks on it. There were stories that people died who had never turned on their air conditioning, because they were probably fearful of the bill ... And we talked about how we should probably be celebrating the hundreds and thousands of people that were saved because neighbors did do the right thing, rather than feeling guilty about the 100 or 200 people who died, because in reality maybe there was no way to have saved them...

So it was a chance to talk about what people could do and should do, say if something like this happens again here or anywhere.

In addition, as DuMont illustrated, the discussion on his program contributed to some extent to the eventual decision to liberalize trade with Vietnam. It added to the mix of popular opinion showing that people were ready to accept this. It was an example, DuMont explained, of how talk radio has some power to influence political action. As he noted:

The week before the President was going to make his decision about recognizing Vietnam, I had Senator John McCain of Arizona on the program. He explained his vote, which was something of a surprise, since he was a former POW and a conservative Republican, that he agreed with Bill Clinton that it was time to end the embargo and open up diplomatic relations and trade with Vietnam.

...Then, during the questioning, I asked him whether, since so much of the negative press coverage had dealt with the issue of how much money was going to be made by this trade with Vietnam, if he was bothered by the profiteering aspect of this trade. He said he was, and I asked him if he would consider the idea of earmarking dollars gained from the trade relationship with Vietnam to helping Vietnam veterans and their families ... I asked him, "Can you support such a program conceptually?" And he said he could.

Then a couple of days later, there was something in the *Chicago Tribune* about it, and the following day the Washington *Hotline* which features all these inside scoops ran something on it. And soon after that, I got a call from Oliver

North's program and I was a guest on his program the next day. Oliver North endorsed the idea, and I urged his listeners to call Senator McCain if they thought that it was a good idea. Then I called my own senator, Senator Paul Simon, and I spoke to a couple of editorial writers in Chicago as well ... So maybe out of this new trade with Vietnam, there will be some legislation or a tariff or some voluntary action that will help the lives of the Vietnam veterans. And that started as a preamble to a question to John McCain.

So talk radio, even on a grass-roots level—not just by radio's superstars—can influence the political process, as ideas expressed on the air are spread and expanded through other channels. This is a good sign, in that people seem to be increasingly turning to talk as a source of positive action—not just a place to air gripes and fears. DuMont commented:

> I think that talk radio is definitely a sounding board. But I feel strongly, because I've been doing talk radio for over 25 years, that the American voter is demanding more than just using it as a blame game against elected officials. I think that the American people want solutions to problems, and I think that they want solutions from their elected officials ... I think they are frankly tired of just a reciting of what the problem is. I think they are looking for answers. They are looking for new ideas. They are looking for people who are trying to solve a problem and not just get into a partisan battle ... And that's one of the things I try to do on my program—provide a forum where people can talk about solutions and get feedback about what works and what doesn't work.

And like DuMont, more and more talk radio today is doing just that—both nationally and on the local level.

notes

1. Donna Petrozzello, "Clinton Criticizes Media for Message," *Broadcasting and Cable*, July 4, 1994, 26–27, p. 26.
2. Jorge Morales, "Air America: Conservative Talk Show Hosts Exercise Their Right to Free Speech Over the Airwaves," *The Advocate*, May 2, 1995, 42–43, p. 43.

3. Ted Byrne, "Book Review: Peter Laufer's Inside Talk Radio," *Talkers*, July 1995, p. 11.

4. Gene Burns, "Freedom of Speech Awards," *Talkers*, July 1995, 16–17, p. 17.

5. Interview with Carol Nashe, July 20, 1995.

6. Interview with Nicole Weber, July 24, 1995.

7. Rate Sheet for Radio Talk Shows provided by Thomas C. Porter & Associates, Advertising and Marketing, West Des Moines, Iowa, on July 24, 1995.

8. From an interview with Blanquita Cullum, July 22, 1995.

9. Interview with Bruce DuMont, July 25, 1995.

Chapter Seven

In the niche
from local to specialty radio

While much of national talk radio has moved in the direction of political and current news/issues talk, other types of talk have focused on filling a particular niche. Some have focused on local concerns, especially the morning and afternoon drive-time programs and the local public service and educational stations. And many national and local programs have targeted an audience with special interests—such as doing a money talk, legal talk, gun talk, or kids talk show. What makes this possible is the relatively low cost of putting together a radio show combined with the technology. One can go national or international with relative ease and low expense.

For example, that's exactly what I did with my own show *Changemakers*. I started with a small independent station affiliated with the University of San Francisco, where I got my J.D. in law, and to apply to do the show, I used a few sample interview tapes that I recorded at home with a simple microphone and tape setup. I didn't even have the music introduction or conclusion that I used later. Then, once I got the show, after recording a few interviews in the studio at the station, I did most of them at my home with two mikes connected to three high-quality cassette decks. After the interview was taped, I had a student engineer mix in the opening and closing music and commercial announcements. He was also able to make occasional minor edits for mistakes in the interview.

The cost was about $10 a program for about $1\frac{1}{2}$ hours of engineering work. My additional outlay as a local sponsor was about $15 for each half-hour program.

Then, with a program on tape, it was an easy step to go national, since after I submitted some samples, Radio for Peace International picked up the program for broadcast on worldwide satellite radio to about 1 million listeners. Thereafter, I just had to send a cassette copy of my original mixed tape to Radio for Peace along with a check for airtime—about $30 a week. So for about $50 a week, I had my own international show—truly a grassroots undertaking only possible with the economics of radio.

This low cost is what makes possible the wide variety of niche programming and makes radio still very accessible for almost anyone today. Yet, at the same time much niche or local radio can still be very big business (such as the big drive-time local shows or the syndicated specialty shows that go national or international).

I spoke to a sampling of hosts and producers handling such shows to learn about their programs and how they did it.

hosting a local or regional show

The local shows, especially during drive time, are a particularly good example of the grass roots speaking, or "democracy in action," as some hosts say. In some cases, these might be more accurately called regional shows when the station has a powerful transmitter, about 50,000 watts or more. A typical mix of topics may include some hot national issues (like the OJ trial or the Oklahoma bombing story when these were front-page news). But rather than having experts give their opinions, the hosts emphasize getting local reaction from callers. In fact, many call in on cellular phones on their drive to or from the office. Also, many of these shows feature local issues, local guests like city officials involved in a current city problem, and often every 10 minutes or so, the shows spotlight local traffic with the station's helicopter pilots calling in their reports. Sometimes a mix of music and news is thrown in as well, along with lots of commercials on the big audience drive-time slots—with the peak times 8–10 a.m. and 4–6 p.m.

I spoke to two hosts handling shows that include some of this drive time: Mark Davis at WBAT in Dallas, Texas, and Tom Becka of KFAB in Omaha, Nebraska, both doing shows from 9 to noon.

getting the pulse of the community

Mark Davis, whose show in Dallas beams out over a 50,000-watt station is an example of a local show gone regional—and still proud of its local community character. Before getting the show, Davis, now 37, had been doing local shows for 13 years, mostly in small cities in the South, including Jacksonville and Tampa in Florida and Memphis, Tennessee.[1]

For him, the key to making the show work was honing in on the issues that people were talking about in their community. As he explained:

> A Mark Davis show is about 80% topics that I choose or the callers bring up and some of them catch fire ... I look for things on a given morning that people are going to be talking about around their dinner table that night. Or maybe they've talked about it around their dinner table last night. I never want to be more than 24 hours old with stories. I want to be talking about things that people are talking about around their water coolers at work today.

The reason people called in, he observed, was because many couldn't discuss these topics enough with others in their daily life—a theme echoed again and again by the hosts and producers I talked with. As he continued:

> We don't get to talk to each other very much anymore. We've become a busier, more intense society, that leaves less time for recreational conversation ... So I think if people can drive around and listen to a talk show, it's the next best thing to sitting in a room full of people talking about the issues of today. It's a little less personal. But if people want to get more personal, they can easily pick up the phone and call me...
> The way I see it is talk radio has become the equivalent of

sitting around the old cracker barrel or community forums of one time. Today, talk radio has become the electronic town hall for the United States of America.

Like many hosts, Davis got into the talk host business by being in the right place at the right time when the station he was on went talk. While he was at the University of Maryland in the late 1970s studying for a journalism degree, he got some experience at the university radio station as a DJ, news reporter, and sports announcer. Then, after graduating in 1979, he sent sample tapes to radio stations all over the country, started in West Virginia as a reporter and newscaster for two years, and did the same job when he moved on to Jacksonville, Florida. Soon after, the news director got fired, and at 24 he took over that slot. A few months later, the entire radio station went talk, and after becoming part of the ABC talk radio network, the station had an opening for a morning show. So that's how Davis got started, and he loved the show business pizzazz of it, explaining:

> It changed my life immediately. I discovered that I could have the journalistic thrill of interviewing newsmakers. Yet it was an entertainment, show business job, while being a news reporter can sometimes be kind of dry.

Like many local hosts, Davis found the caller-driven show especially popular, since it leant itself to more variety and diversity, in part because local shows have more difficulty getting the high-profile guests who more commonly do the national talk-show circuit. So the hosts have to come up with more diverse ideas to keep up local interest. As Davis observed:

> I could say tomorrow I'll never have a guest for the rest of my life, and the show would do fine ... Most guests are boring and useless. Say out of 100 guests, 90 of them will bore you to tears. They will be authors who are not engaging speakers. There will be people who are interesting for 5 minutes, but certainly not for the hour they are kept on the radio. One thing that a guest does which is harmful to a radio talk show is guarantees that 10 minutes from now or 20 minutes from now or 40 minutes from now, you'll be talking about the exact same thing ... But with callers, you can have more variety.... You can talk about whatever happens to catch fire that day.

What catches fire? Like many hosts, Davis tried to get a mix of opinion—both agreement and disagreement—that triggered more calls, using a screener to help him select his calls. He described the process:

> I'm a pretty conservative show … But people that disagree with me know that liberal calls will be treated with great respect and civility. And I crave disagreement … It makes for a more interesting show, and I don't think I serve myself well by beating people up on the radio … Everybody knows where I stand on things, but they also know that if they disagree, they'll be glad they called, because they got their point across … And even if I'm conservative and most of my listeners are conservative, we can still disagree about a lot of things, like which GOP presidential candidate is most on the ball and the kinds of subjects there are lots of disagreements about, like school prayer and abortion…
>
> In any case, I try to move callers that disagree with me to the top of the line. As the calls are screened, they're put on the monitor that sits here in the studio in front of me …I see them chronologically. But no talk show should ever take calls in the order in which they come in … To make a talk show interesting, you need to put it together like a work of art. You need to determine which is the best call you can take next. Whether it's been somebody on hold for 40 minutes or somebody on hold for 40 seconds. I'm moving people up in line all the time.

In particular, Davis moved up the callers with a difference of opinion. He explained:

> In deciding on who to pick next, number one is disagreement with something I've said. Number two is disagreement with what another caller has said. Number three is someone who has a point that is different from one that people have heard 500 times already … I want the point of view to be distinct and interesting, a little off the beaten path.

As for timing, the typical caller was about two minutes, much like the approach on most music radio stations, where disks are typically about two to three minutes. Though some callers might stay on longer, in our fast-paced, low-attention-span age, quick on and off is the rule. As Davis put it:

I'm usually looking at two minutes per caller. At the end of two minutes, if people have said pretty much what they need to say, I'm looking to wrap them up. If they're really giving us great new fresh insights, stuff you don't usually hear, I'll keep them on longer. My show features the shortest calls you'll ever hear and the longest calls. It's completely determined by content.

Finally, Davis had a few thoughts on why conservative talk radio was the most popular format today—and where he thought talk radio might be heading. Conservative radio was hot because conservatives were still the outsiders, and so conservative shows could be more edgy and exciting. As he commented:

Even though we've had a long period of a Republican presidency, and we now have a Republican-dominated Congress, make no mistake, the social force that has held sway for half a century in this country is liberal. It still pervades our educational process. It still pervades our popular culture. Those things will always be more powerful in our lives than politics and who's in Congress. For that reason, conservatives are still outsiders. We are trying to make change from the outside, and that will always bring with it a certain irreverence ... and ability to critique the status quo. It brings a kind of bad boy mantle to use that is a much better springboard for humor...

So ... if a show is a little more exciting, a little more edgy, and a little more fun, that's going to be better radio, and that's going to attract more listeners. So that's why stations all over the country are seeming to tilt conservative.

As for what's next, Davis, like many other hosts, felt the next wave will be FM talk, attracting a younger audience.

The next big thing you're going to see is talk shows on FM.... AM radio tends to skew a little more mature, and FM tends to have a younger audience ... .Right now there is a glut of music format on FM and a lot of stations with one or two or three shares that want to increase their listenership. A lot of them are going to become talk radio ... So you're going to see dozens and dozens of new FM talk stations between now and the year 2000. And as they come on line, they'll bring their younger listeners with them ... As the appeal of talk radio broadens, you'll see different shows reaching out to these different groups.

And so Davis was very much part of this growing trend toward local, fast-paced, conservative—and hip—radio.

making it entertaining

Since a key to a successful radio talk program is making it entertaining, Tom Becka, host of the morning show out of KFAB, Omaha, found having a stand-up comedy background was a big help. After a short stint as a radio DJ and sales manager in the 1970s, he was on the road doing comedy for years. Occasionally, he appeared on TV, and when he started his show on KFAB, a 50,000-watt AM station, heard in five or six states, he incorporated comedy bits as well. As he pointed out:

> I formatted the show like a party in the kitchen. When you're at a person's house, often the best part of the party is people hanging around in the kitchen. That's because they're talking about politics, sometimes talking about sex, relationships, jokes, whatever. Sometimes they'll be in a very serious mood. Sometimes the topic will be ridiculous. Sometimes people will get in heated arguments. Sometimes you just flick someone off. And that's the kind of feeling I wanted to get in my program. You never know what you are going to find. We're topic driven, and I try to talk about whatever is in the news or on people's minds so they can relate to it.

In many ways, his program sounded much like Davis's—an opening monologue highlighting some major themes of the day, a screener making sure callers were on topic, limiting callers to two to three minutes unless they had an especially interesting point to make, even the preference for callers who don't agree ("If everybody calls up and says, 'Hey, I agree. You're great,' that's boring. I'd rather have people not agree with me."). Also, Becka felt talk radio provided listeners with an electronic community that had become "what the backyard used to be" for talking to neighbors.

But for Becka, in part because of his comedy background, keeping the show entertaining was especially important, and so, as appropriate, he mixed in a light touch and sometimes humor, even when the discussion was about something serious. Becka gave an example, a local issue involving the mayor. The discussion began with some serious comments about how the major had angered a lot of local people, though he had many good ideas, because he was not a smooth talker and had made some blunt comments that left hurt feelings, though he subsequently apologized in a press conference. For about an hour Becka led a discussion about what the mayor could do to soften his image, and the conversation soon veered into humor and some wild suggestions for the mayor. Yet, Becka felt the comedy incorporated some real truths about how the mayor might change—showing the power of comedy not only to amuse but also to help one discover some truths about an issue. As Becka observed:

> For an hour we talked about how the mayor could soften his image. We had callers talking about things like: "Well, he could walk around with a cardigan sweater, holding a pipe in his hand." And then it got wild. Somebody called up and said: "How about if the mayor walked around in bunny slippers?" Another suggested: "Maybe he could make balloon animals for the kids, because you can't be mad at a guy who's making balloon animals."
>
> So there were suggestions along those lines. It was all very tongue in cheek. Yet through that comedy, we also got to the heart of the matter, which is how important it is for the mayor to be smooth or be effective.... It became very interesting and entertaining, because we took a humorous angle and poked some fun at the mayor. But it still had that serious point to make underneath too.

In Becka's view, this emphasis on personality and entertainment would be a continuing trend in talk radio over the next few years. In fact, he felt the power of entertainment was a major factor in Limbaugh's success—not just his conservative message. That's because, he emphasized: "People want to be informed. They want to get a perspective on things, but they also want to be entertained." Becka went on to explain:

> Rush Limbaugh made it because he was entertaining, not because he was conservative. The message he had to say was a message many people wanted to hear. But the bottom

line was that he was entertaining ... He did all sorts of things. He added a lot of elements to talk radio that hadn't been there before. Sound effects, music, song parodies, humor.... He took the approach that we're going to poke fun at the opposition. And we're going to do it with songs, with jokes, with sound effects, and so forth. He took all the elements of a very successful morning radio program, such as a DJ uses, and he took it into the talk radio realm....

And ... that's one of the things I bring into my show because of my stand-up comedy background. It brings entertainment value to the program. Not everything we talk about is a joke. We do talk about serious issues and have some interesting serious conversations. But because of my stand-up and entertainment background, we can add a lighter touch to something ... Because that's what people want— information and a point of view, and being entertained as well.

In fact, Becka had a few especially appealing comedy bits, such as his weekly Friday feature called the "Butthead of the Week." Becka described it thus:

On Fridays, people call up and nominate whoever they think is the biggest butthead of the week ... And that includes both local and nationally known people. For example, this week, some people called to nominate the mayor as a butthead. Also, typically somebody will call and bitch about his next door neighbors. Many people call to nominate their spouses ... The husband or wife will do something stupid, and the spouse will complain.

As for nationally, this week we had a caller suggesting Charlie Sheen for spending $53,000 on hookers with Heidi Fleiss. Another proposed Susan Smith. And as always, callers usually propose Bill Clinton. The particular nominations depend on whatever is in the news.

Given his humor perspective, Becka had his own humor-related angle on a reason men were more likely to call than women. Besides other factors, they were more willing to appear foolish. As he commented:

Though I've got a very strong female listener base with this show, men are usually the ones to call ... I think that's because men are brought up to be more involved in things, like politics, current events, and civic issues, whereas women have been more involved in things having to do with the home, though this has been changing now ... Plus a lot of the issues that are talked about on radio tend to be more male oriented, such as talking about militia groups ... Though when we talk about issues more likely to appeal to women, such as domestic violence, we got a lot of female calls.

Then, too ... women traditionally, I think, are more afraid of making a fool of themselves than men. And when you call a talk radio station, you take the risk of making a fool of yourself. That's a real risk for some people, which men are more willing to take.

Finally, Becka had some thoughts on the influence of talk radio, feeling it was more a reflection of current thoughts and feelings, than being able to motivate someone to do something he didn't want to do, particularly since it was just one source of information for most people. As he noted:

I think talk radio can give people a point of view and help them think a certain way. But it can't motivate them to think a certain way. It's like advertising. You can advertise all the cigarettes in the world, and I'm not going to smoke. I hate smoke, and I'm not going to smoke again, no matter how many ads I see.

So I don't think talk radio has that influence some people claim on the nuts and kooks, the marginal people in society, to go out and do harmful things ... We have had bombings before we had talk radio. We had murder before talk radio. We had all sorts of civil unrest before talk radio ... To suddenly blame all of this stuff on talk radio is wrong, though some do because talk radio has become such a phenomenon ... But there's nothing talk radio is making people do that they haven't done before.

Rather, it was more of a place where people could express their fears, because as Becka commented:

There's a fear in society that maybe we haven't had before. People are afraid of losing their jobs; they're afraid of dying; they're afraid of drugs; they're afraid of a lot of things ... And sometimes they can use talk radio to dump their fear, which is a service we can provide. But I don't think we can motivate anybody to do anything.

Besides, Becka emphasized, talk radio was only one small part of the media explosion:

> There's so much information out there … Talk radio is just another angle, another perspective. But it's no more than an electronic editorial page, where people can express themselves like they used to do in their backyards … At this point in time, talk radio is the most exciting thing going on in radio. Because it's personality, it's human, and it's real. It's not the same ten songs over and over again. It's something fresh and different everyday, and that's what makes it exciting to be a part of … But motivating people to go out and do something they wouldn't do otherwise—no, I don't think it can do that.

bringing the world together through talk

While one direction for talk radio has been to go local, some hosts and producers have taken the opposite approach, i.e., going global. This is still considered a specialty approach, but the numbers become awesome—millions of people listening through a satellite hookup, which can result in having more listeners than the most widely heard programs in the country.

For example, according to John Leslie, who is host and executive producer of the internationally oriented program *World Radio*, the show may have up to about 80 million listeners on 300 stations around the world, although they are out of the mainstream of radio in the U.S. He got the idea for this global talk approach when there was still a Soviet Union. At the time, Leslie had been in the radio business for over 25 years, starting in the early 1960s, when in 1987, he did a series of 32 features on the Soviet Union for Stoner Broadcasting Systems, which has since merged with American Radio Systems of Boston. He was the first American journalist allowed to travel freely through the Soviet Union, right after Gorbachev cracked the door open with Glasnost. Then, in the spring of 1988, he did the first talk show between the USA and the former USSR—broadcasting to all 15 republics of the Soviet Union and on 210 radio stations in the USA. Leslie describes how the program led to *World Radio*:

For the first time ever, Americans were allowed to talk freely and openly, uncensored, to Soviets. The program was received so well and won so many awards that I decided that the world needed to be brought together through the power of radio.

Eventually, in 1993, he left American Radio Systems and started the new venture to create a one-world audience, working with a broadcast group called Enterprise Media that provided the distribution equipment and much of the financing. This way they could send out their program from Binghamton, New York, near Leslie's home, via an uplink to an ITT satellite and then around the world. As Leslie told me:

We set out on a venture to entertain literally the world. We wanted to do everything, to investigate every area of interest on the face of the earth. And now to do that, we have a three-hour Saturday morning program, where we have nine guests from every reach of the world...and we talk about everything from politics to people who can turn themselves invisible to routine, day-to-day, family and life-style matters.

The way Leslie described it, these programs were a way to promote world understanding by showing people that regardless of differences in politics, religion, or culture, we all have some basic interests in common, "things that interest virtually everybody." And so far, Leslie has been in about 20 countries broadcasting on-site to show the life-styles of people all over the world. It isn't always serious politics and world news either. For example, Leslie described one program that might be a typical lighthearted morning drive-time program in the USA.

We went to Munich, Germany, and talked about what was happening there, what was interesting to the people of the city. Not national news, not international news, but what are the people in Munich worried about right now? And the topic of interest turned out to be that the cleavage on the picture of the woman on the Oktoberfest poster was too revealing. So the whole town was in an uproar. It was great, because that was the most important thing on their minds right then ... And it was amusing to the whole world as well.

Leslie also explained the procedures for getting stories—which sometimes involved global networking using the Internet and its 14,000 or so newsgroups.

> We have people who have a full-time job of Monday through Friday surfing the Internet finding interesting people. They put out announcements—they check the discussions. And when they find people who seem interesting, they ask them if they'll come on the program, and it's amazing how many people are excited about being on the radio for 10 or 15 minutes.

In fact, as we were talking, Leslie was preparing to take his next trip to interview some people in the Crimea for a program on the oil wells and gold mines of Far Eastern Siberia. Besides himself, he usually took a half dozen people with him on these trips—including engineers, producers, and translators.

Ironically, not only did Leslie use the Internet to find prospective guests and topics, but recently he had discovered there was even a newsgroup about the program. People shared information about it and discussed their views on what they heard.

So how was Leslie able to tell how many people were listening worldwide? Where did the 80 million figure come from? Leslie was the first to admit it wasn't easy, because globally there is nothing equivalent to the Arbitron rating used to determine the popularity of programs at home. So it was more of a rough guesstimate; but then the Arbitron rating was not so exact either. As Leslie pointed out:

> It's hard to know where they [Enterprise Media] come up with that figure for the number of listeners, because there are no Arbitron ratings … I think they take a map and look at the population—how many people actually live there and how many radio stations service those areas. Then they come up with a ballpark figure that seems reasonable.
>
> By contrast, when Arbitron rates markets in the U.S., they rate the major markets four times a year, the medium markets two times a year, and the very small markets one time a year. In any given market, they send out around 3000 requests to families inviting them to participate in a 1-week

rating period during a 12-weeks' rating period. Every person in the family 12 years of age or older gets a diary, and they are asked to keep accurate track for one week of all of the stations they listen to from the first thing in the morning to late at night. And you're even supposed to indicate if you listen when you're showering, while you're driving to work, and when you switch stations or turn the radio off.

But even that isn't totally accurate. The people who agree to do the ratings have every good intention from the start. But after one or two days, people are busy. They don't keep careful track of their listening habits. Then they may try to figure out what they did later … Or they may indicate they listen from when they get up in the morning to when they go to bed—say 6 a.m. to 10 p.m.—with an arrow from the top to the bottom. But they are not listening at many times, say when they do various things like shopping.

So the system isn't terribly accurate. Yet it is the only rating system that's out there currently. And it's so important to the radio economy that in major markets, one-tenth of one point increase or decrease can mean over a million dollars of revenue for that station. The ratings affect ad rates, tell you how many people are supposedly listening, in what age group, and at what time of day. And of course, morning drive is always the biggest audience, and the most desirable age segment is men 25–54, so everybody targets to that.

By contrast, in tapping into the world market, there was no way to get such precise figures. The best Leslie and his network could do was estimate based on the potential listening audience and the number of stations receiving the program.

As for the future of world radio, it fit in with what Leslie saw as a continuing trend toward more network radio—part of a growing trend to concentration throughout the world, in radio as well as in business. It was a development in which strong personalities, powerful companies, and big promotional dollars were all contributing to create a more standardized world—except for the specialty shows and specialty markets. As Leslie commented at the end of our interview:

> Radio formats swing back and forth like a pendulum. The cycle is about 15 years. Back in the 30s, 40s, and early 50s, the

local affiliates were all serviced primarily by networks. And that's what's happening again. In the late 50s and early 60s, the pendulum started swinging the other way and radio stations started hiring local talent. They almost put the networks out of business, and we went through the rock and roll era of the 50s and 60s.

Then, in the 70s, when songs started getting longer, four, five, six, seven, eight, nine minutes long, there was less and less emphasis on talent and more and more emphasis on music. So the radio station ownership started thinking, "Well, why do I need to pay high price talent when these songs are so long?"

So that went on through the 70s and late 80s, when Limbaugh, Larry King, and my program *World Talk* came on the scene. All of a sudden, people started liking personalities again. But they weren't coming from the local stations. They were coming from the networks. So now the pendulum is swinging in that direction where the networks are now servicing local stations. Generally, most AM stations still have a morning drive personality—but from about 10 a.m. on until 6 a.m. the following morning, most stations have network or syndicated programs run by computers.

In turn, he felt these networked programs, including his own specialty program, had a powerful appeal to prospective callers. It expanded their scope of influence—nationally, or in his case, globally as well. As he observed:

> Radio is a great equalizer. People can be themselves. They don't have to be gorgeous, important, powerful. Nobody sees them and they're anonymous. They can participate in something big from their small place in society and maybe have an impact in society at the same time.

And in the case of his program, heard around the world, the impact could not only be national, but also global—showing the power of radio to transform the local into the international. Then, too, his program illustrated how global radio could also deal with topics from the deeply serious to the wild and wacky—from a consideration of current conditions in Siberia to questions about cleavage on an Oktoberfest poster girl.

getting a new program on the air: from guns to kids

Do you have an idea for your own program? Are you a good talker with an interesting subject others want to hear about? Today, even with a specialized subject for a select audience, it's relatively easy to get your program on the air—even in this age of networked and global radio. There are still niches for specialty network shows and local community shows. So if you've got an outgoing personality and some persistence, you, too, can do it.

To find out how, I spoke to Tom Gresham, a writer about guns for sporting magazines, who got his own program about guns— *Gun Talk*—on over 50 stations within four months. And to illustrate how even kids can do it these days, I spoke to Evan Roberts, now 12, who started his program on Long Island near New York City, when he was 10.

launching a network show

Gresham got the idea for his *Gun Talk* show while attending a firearms industry show in Las Vegas in January 1995. He was a writer of recreational stories—subjects like fishing and camping— and happened to stop by the booth of a man in the business who he had known for years. The man, aware that Gresham had done some work on TV and had written several books, asked "Have you ever thought about getting into radio?" That started the ball rolling, as Gresham explained:

> It turned out he was involved with a radio network himself, as a principal of the Talk America Radio Network, and he explained how it would work. I just needed a few sponsors to finance the cost of doing the program. So the next day, I went out on the show floor with only a general idea of what I wanted to do—a one-hour show talking about the recreational use of guns—and I talked to a few companies that I knew. Within an hour I had five national sponsors. So I went back to the man who suggested the idea and said, "Hey, I've got some people that would like to sponsor the show," and at

once he said, "Well, you've got more than you need for a one-hour show. You can go for two hours." So that's how it started.

How was Gresham able to get sponsors so quickly? A key reason is he had a 20-year track record in working with people in the business, such as manufacturers of guns and ammunition, since he had been the Arms and Ammo Editor for *Sports Afield* magazine, a national magazine, for about 6 years. Plus he had cohosted a show on ESPN, the cable sports channel, called *Shooting Sports America*. So he was able to approach the advertising director or president of the company on a first-name basis, describing what was then just a rough idea. As Gresham noted:

> I just said, "Here's an idea." And several said, "It sounds wonderful. Count us in. We want to be part of it." I had no rates. I had no idea what the show would be. I had no idea what it would cost them. I had no sample tapes, proposal, or anything—just an idea from a 20-minute conversation. I said I thought we might start out with about 20 stations. And within an hour, I had five national sponsors.

Another key factor in getting the quick support was that Gresham proposed offering a message that the gun manufacturers and distributors wanted to get out, since they believed they had been poorly represented in the mainstream media that were largely promoting a gun control message. So there was a natural fit between the content of his proposed program and what prospective sponsors wanted to say.

After the firearms show, Gresham began putting together his program. Basically, he arranged for a Comrex hookup, which is the standard method still used by most talk show hosts today, although many now use the more technically advanced high-speed ISDN hookups. All he needed was three regular phone lines, using this older method. Gresham described how the setup worked:

> I do my show by remote from Louisiana where I live, and I'm hooked up over telephone lines to Boston, where the studio is. While I'm doing the show live in Louisiana, the producer is in Boston handling the board and the calls coming in, and

they mix everything together as this happens live. Then, they
shoot up the program to three satellites which broadcast it, so
the stations airing the show can pick it up for instant or later
replay.

Initially, the program started on the 20 stations that take all of
Talk America's programming—mostly small stations that depend
on outside programming. But then it was up to Gresham to line up
other radio stations to carry the show. Finding them quickly
turned into a full-time job, though Gresham was only doing a two-
hour weekly show. The hard part was finding the stations to
increase coverage and then working out continuing sponsorship
arrangements based on increased coverage. How did Gresham do
it? He explained:

Though Talk America has a few stations to get a program
started, they don't really market it themselves. They are more
like a carrier … So I had to go out and find other stations. To
do so, I immediately bought a directory of all the radio stations in the country—the *M Street [Radio] Directory*[2]—which
is absolutely essential for anybody in the business. Then I
began calling.

I started cold-calling talk format stations, asked for the
person in charge of programming—the station manager,
owner, or program director. Once I found someone who's
interested, I said, "Okay, I'll send you a package." Then I put
together a complete promotion package with tapes and sent
that. By doing that over the course of four months, I'm now
up to about 56 affiliates.

His package, sent in a simple Duo-tang folder, included a
copy of an article about himself and the show from a newspaper in
a Florida city where the show aired, a bio, a Xeroxed photo of
himself, and an ad from *Talkers* magazine about the show. Plus, he
included a flier with information about the show's content, when
it was available on the satellite, and a program clock indicating
when the local station could its own commercials—about 1–2
minutes every 15 minutes during the program. And finally, he
included a tape of a full 2-hour show, just as it went on the air.

So Gresham was not only the host, but also the producer and
advertising manager of his own show. As he commented:

> I basically do everything. I own the show, and I don't have a producer I work with, so I do everything a producer does and more. I do the ad sales, I do the affiliate relations, I line up the guests. Talk America provides someone to run the board and put the show out on satellite, but I do everything else.

And now that the show was a success, besides trying to get even more affiliates, Gresham's next big task has been lining up advertisers to continue to support the show—though now the cost is somewhat more, since there are more stations. And this income is what Gresham will eventually use to pay himself a salary—the difference between what he gets in advertising and what he has to pay Talk America for carrying the show. Gresham explained his improvisational yet step-by-step approach to turning the show into a viable business:

> Now I'm going back to the original advertisers to make sure I'm on their schedules for 1996 when they set their budgets, as well as approaching new advertisers. As for setting advertising rates, like just about everything I've been doing, I make it up as I go along … Essentially, I started off with what I thought might be a good figure, since I didn't have many stations. "How about $150 for a 60-second spot each week?," I asked … So for a 13-week quarter, the cost was about $2000 for an advertiser, which is not a lot of money for a major company—about $8000 for a year. Then, since I had 10 minutes of advertising available to me for each hour, while the local station has 10 minutes in return for getting the show for free and airing my commercials, that works out to about $1500 a week or about $80,000 a year for the ad budget, though, of course, a great percentage of that goes to Talk America. So there's not a lot of money to work with to start.
>
> But now I'm looking at $2\frac{1}{2}$or almost 3 times the affiliates I had when I started. And I have much better affiliates. Much larger stations. Many are even 50,000-watt stations. And I'm in many good markets. So now I have to figure out what I'm going to charge next year, which will be more than I started, though I haven't decided yet.

The process sounded so easy that I called Talk America to find out what might be involved if I wanted to start my own show. If I was ready, I discovered, I could be on the air in a matter of weeks.

Almost anyone can. I called the head of Talk America, John Crohan,[3] and he told me my cost would be $200–300 an hour, depending on the time slot. I would then have 5 minutes of time to sell, and the Talk America network would have 1 minute for itself. In fact, there were even two time slots immediately available on the first network, meaning I would start with the same 20 or so affiliates Gresham did. All I would need was approximately $3500 in Comrex switching equipment—or an arrangement with someone in my area who had this—and I was in business. Or should I want to go on Talk America's second network, I could do a more leisurely, less expensive taped show and just send it in.

As for sponsors, that might be relatively easy to arrange, too—especially for a niche show where I could approach companies who might be interested in the show's particular audience. For example, Gresham told me:

> There's one show on Talk America that's basically an insurance show. And the host gets money from insurance companies. If you have a pet show, you might go to Hartz or Purina. And if you are already known in the business, you can probably just call people in the industry and say you're planning the show and quickly get a sponsor.

And if you aren't known? Well, it might take a little longer, be a little harder, but even that's very possible, as 12-year-old Evan Roberts's story illustrates. But before we meet Evan, I wanted to know a little about Gresham's show—the format and how he promoted it.

Gresham briefly explained the format, a common one for interview shows with guests. He started off with a brief monologue, then introduced his guest, who was typically someone in the field, such as the director of a sports shooting organization, the head of a firearms company, or someone in law enforcement talking about using guns for self-defense, since the program was designed to promote responsible, safe ownership. As for publicizing the show, besides contacting stations and seeking more affiliates, Gresham used a number of common techniques. As he explained:

One thing I do to get listeners is I send out press releases to magazines in the field, such as the dozens of gun magazines. Also, I have sent releases to some newspapers in markets where I know the show is running. And I have used one of the big on-line commercial services, CompuServe, to post announcements about the program to reach gun owners, and this has led some to call their local station to indicate they are interested. Then, after they tell me who they called, I follow up with a call to the station, and send further information ... So that approach has paved the way for several affiliates for me.

In turn, this targeted marketing to an audience with a high interest in the subject and no other competing show helped make the show a success. Along with lots of hard work and long hours. It's a formula others with an idea for a program might follow, too.

creating a local show: even kids can do it

Even young kids can put together their own show these days, as I found in talking to Evan Roberts of Valley Stream, New York, and his mother Janice. Now 12, Evan started hosting his own radio talk show for kids when he was 10.[4]

And he got his start when he was 6! It all began when Evan, who loved sports, decided that he wanted to have a career in broadcasting, and he began doing it at home. He started announcing all sorts of things—like his mother was now cooking dinner or his sister was washing her hair.

Then at 9 he got his first break. Evan explained how a song his mother wrote for him opened the door, after he experienced several frustrating years of being turned down by sports announcers because he was too young.

> I first got interested in sports because my dad was a big Mets fan, and when he was listening, he would tell me what was going on. He wouldn't just say it to me or tell me to listen to the news. Instead he would broadcast it to me like an announcer does, saying something like, "The Mets are trailing 2

to 1, and now the batter's coming up … and the ball is going into right field, and now the Mets take the lead."

When he did that, I would ask him lots of questions about radio, and then I began broadcasting the plays back to him. Eventually, I started going to a lot of games, and while I was there, I would broadcast them to my dad…. Then, after my dad told me about the tristate-area sports station, I started imitating the announcers, writing them, calling them up, trying to get on their programs to tell them what I thought. But they would always hang up on me because I'm underage. They would say, "How old are you?" and I would say, "I'm 21," and they would say: "You're not 21. Get outta here." And then they'd hang up on me.

Then, when I was 6, my mom, knowing how much I loved baseball and how much I loved to announce it, wrote a song for me. She had written many songs before as a song-writer for commercials, and this was called "Baseball." It goes something like this:

I wake up in the morning and I want to play.
I want the weather to be perfect, so that I can play.
Oh please, just get me on the diamond, each and every day.
Then ask me what I feel like … Baseball.

Well, my mom was working on a TV show called *Dynamets* that was a show for kids about the Mets, in which the kids would interview players and they would broadcast their interviews. My mom kept suggesting that the Mets organization should use this song on the show. Finally, they said it could be the theme song, and my mom asked: "Do you need a 9-year-old as an announcer?" And they let me announce. I got the chance to interview players too. I got to broadcast an inning and a half at the Mets game on TV.

A year later, at 10, Evan got his first radio show. The TV program had been so exciting that he kept telling his mother he wanted to be a sportscaster, so finally as Evan told me:

She suggested, "Okay, why don't you write the station?," and with her help I did. I wrote to WFAN on Long Island, and they invited me to come on the air on their morning show. Then I wrote to WGBB, in Babylon, New York, to get a real job, having my own regular show. The way I did it is I got a sponsor. I sent the station a tape of the TV broadcast I did, and they said I could be on if I got a sponsor. So I sat down and wrote letters to different companies and corporations saying I was 10 and wanted to do my own show.

A month later, he had a sponsor—a local dentist—and his own show—a sports show for kids called *Kids Sports Talk*. Soon after it started he was ready to expand—doing a show for kids on all different topics. By finding still another sponsor, Evan was ready for the next step. As he explained:

> I realized the show was only for sports fans. But there aren't that many sports fans around the world. So I decided to make it a show that all kids would listen to, and even adults, not just people into sports. So I wrote a lot of letters to different possible sponsors, picking out companies with products I thought kids would love. And one of them was Berzerkis, which is a fun indoor theme park for the whole family.

And so the show became *Going Bzircus*, described in a press release Evan's mother sent me as a "totally off-the-wall anything goes half hour of fun" for kids, which features "celebrity guests, wacky news, new product reviews, and everything else of interest to kids." Or as Evan describes it:

> It's a really wacky, wacky show. Anything goes. A lot of kids get to call up and voice their opinion about anything going on in the world. And we also have wacky news, like in the crazy tabloids … And we talk about it and make jokes about it … Also, during the week, I go on America Online, which is one of the sponsors now, and I gather up a lot of cool stuff that is new on America Online—and I talk about it. And anyone who calls in can give their opinion and talk about that too.

What kind of wacky, cool stuff? Evan gave some examples:

> Oh, we have a "What am I eating?" contest. That's where I take something, give a lot of hints about it, and eat it over the air … For example, I've eaten a lot of weird stuff like Chocolate Butterfingers, cereal, Lucky Charms, pretzels, a lot of junk food … The kinds of stories we talk about are like the one about this guy whose tongue was very long. It went down to his stomach. And then there was a story about a two-headed snake that was in the San Diego Zoo and one head ate the other.

As we talked, it reminded me of my elementary school and camp days. Although Evan indicated he occasionally had a few adult callers, largely the callers, like the listeners, were kids from about 4 to 15, particularly since the topics were geared to kids— especially the "weird stuff," as Evan put it.

Now for the next step, Evan was looking into taking the program national, just as his sponsor was planning to expand to other U.S. locations. Plus there were the inevitable TV appearances since he was one of the youngest—if not the youngest— radio host: *Sally Jessy Raphael*, *Live with Regis & Kathie Lee*, *A Current Affair* (since canceled), *America's Talking*, and others. Fortunately, as Evan's mother later told me, his teachers were very cooperative with his show business activities, such as giving him extra work when he missed a few days of school now and then.

Still, despite the hoopla, both Evan and his mother made it clear that school is the top priority: "He has to do well or this whole thing stops," Janice said. "Later his goal is to be a full-time radio sportscaster. But for now he's still a full-time kid."

As fascinating and unique as Evan's story is, it illustrates how just about anyone can get a radio show. Whether you start nationally with a network show like Tom Gresham or contact your local community station and line up local sponsors like Evan, if you have an idea for a program that people will want to listen to, you, too, can be on the radio.

notes

1. Interview with Mark Davis, July 1995.
2. The *M Street Radio Directory* is published by the M Street Corporation, 304 Park Avenue South, 7th Floor, New York, NY 10010. (212) 473-4668. The cost is around $45.
3. Their phone number is 617-828-4546.
4. Interview with Evan Roberts, July 22, 1995.

part two

talk tv

chapter eight

the beginnings of talk tv

While talk radio came of age in the 1930s and 1940s, talk TV got its start a generation later in the 1950s. Still, its roots go back to the experiments of the technology buffs in the 1920s—much like the computer revolution started in the garages of the 1970s. Those who saw the future early, like David Sarnoff, RCA, and NBC, took the lead in developing the first talk TV programs, like Ed Sullivan's *Talk of the Town*—later the *Ed Sullivan Show*, a talk and variety show that pioneered the way to today.

the beginnings of tv in the 1920s and 1930s

Though TV didn't take off until the 1950s, many of the same pioneers were involved in the early days of both radio and TV. When the technology for TV was developed enough, they plunged into television, too.

Take the way Westinghouse got in on the ground floor of both and started the first fledgling TV network in 1926. It started with a Westinghouse researcher near Pittsburgh, Frank Conrad. He had been supervising the manufacturing of receivers and transmitters for the U.S. government during World War I, and then worked on electrical switches.[1] On the side, he experimented with broadcasting radio signals in his garage and was part of a small network of broadcast amateurs who shared ideas and techniques. Among other things, he played phonograph concerts, using a Victrola and wireless telephone hookup.

When one of his supervisors, Harry P. Davis, a Westinghouse V.P., saw his regular concerts featured in a local paper, Davis had the idea for broadcasting the upcoming November election returns, with a stronger Westinghouse transmitter. After this proved popular, Westinghouse began a daily schedule, which grew from an hour each evening to several hours featuring all sorts of performances, including local bands, church services, prizefights, theaters, even political speeches. Soon Westinghouse had a growing network of stations from Massachusetts to Chicago.[1]

This growth led to Westinghouse being invited to join another growing alliance, led by RCA, which had gotten its start in international telegraph communications, after it acquired the American Marconi company in 1919. In 1922, David Sarnoff, who would later become a big name in TV, had just become RCA's president, after successfully developing the first commercial radio music boxes, and shortly after he became president, Sarnoff invited Westinghouse to join the RCA alliance, which also included GE and, until 1924, AT&T.* The plan was for GE and Westinghouse to make the receivers and parts, while RCA would market them.[1]

These early agreements by these big companies marked the beginning of dividing up the radio and then the TV universe, and keeping the amateurs out. There were many such amateurs, all over the country, putting together and selling sets, and besides expanding broadcast opportunities for themselves, the alliance sought to drive out these amateurs by appealing to Congress for legislation and regulation. Eventually these early efforts to stifle competition helped to turn TV into a highly concentrated industry, with the rise of a few powerhouse producers. Initially they dominated radio and then turned their competitive instincts on TV.

Soon after AT&T was out, in 1926 the big three—RCA, GE, and Westinghouse—joined together to create NBC, the first of the big networks that would later move into TV—owned 50% by

---

*Although AT&T was initially to sell transmitters, by 1924 it was pushed out of the alliance, since the other partners were afraid of its potential to dominate, as AT&T was trying to claim patent rights for some early TV technology (see Barnouw, *Tube of Plenty: The Evolution of American Television*, New York, Oxford University Press, 1990).

RCA, 30% by GE, and 20% by Westinghouse.[1] In 1927 and 1928, the big rush to commercial network radio began, and many popular shows, which were characterized by a down-to-earth, plain-folks approach, were subsequently transferred to TV. These shows, like *Amos 'n' Andy*, *The Goldbergs*, and *Real Folks*, featured ordinary Americans from typically working-class and ethnic groups, and in the late 1940s and early 1950s, many started migrating to TV. While there were no TV talk shows yet, these early series helped create the personalities who would become part of the first wave of TV talk, which featured short celebrity interviews, along with performances on variety shows like Ed Sullivan's *Talk of the Town*.

The rise of NBC and other networks also helped create the traditional relationship between the sponsor and program, in that the sponsor had control over what went on the air. This occurred because most network programs were produced by ad agencies, and after the network sold a period of time, the sponsor came to regard the program as that company's show. This sense of sponsor ownership was less important on radio, because the airwaves were much less expensive, and because in the 1950s the network structure broke down with the rush to TV and the rise of local radio. As a result, on radio, the trend was to have multiple and local sponsors with little control over programming, since one advertiser could easily be replaced by another. But on TV, from the beginning, the sponsors strongly influenced what went on the air, contributing to the blander, family tone that came to characterize most TV.[1]

Government regulation was quick to control TV, too, since the regulatory structure was already in place from the early regulation of radio, which began in 1927, when Congress passed the Radio Act and created a Federal Radio Commission to grant licenses. Though the networks could only license the airwaves for a limited term, eventually this meant they had unlimited use except for the rare loss of license for cause. Though the Act didn't specifically mention television, its definition of "radio" was broad enough to include television, since it defined radio as basically "any ... message, signal ... picture, or communication ... transferred by electrical energy ... without the aid of any wire."[2]

And so the stage was set for the beginnings of TV, when it

burst on the scene in the mid-1950s, after an early experimental period from 1927 to the end of World War II. It quickly drained talent and money from radio, as the networks put their money into this new medium.

experimenting with the new medium

The birth of TV as a fledgling commercial medium was marked by the introduction of the first magazine on TV in New York in 1927—*Television*. It occurred in the same year that the movies turned to talk when *The Jazz Singer*, produced by Warner Brothers, premiered.[1] This was also the year that the CBS network was born, initially called the Columbia Phonograph Broadcasting System. Meanwhile, the first experimental sets, with tiny screens about 4 × 3 inches in size, were starting to broadcast experimental programs, the first being the melodrama *The Queen's Messenger* in 1928 in Schenectady, New York, where GE was headquartered.

In 1929, the beginnings of the Depression posed a threat. But when the Columbia Phonograph Broadcasting System struggled on the verge of bankruptcy, it was saved when William S. Paley, a cigar tycoon who had recently taken over the company, sold Paramount 49% of the company for $5 million in Paramount stock,[1] forging an early link between Hollywood and TV. Later, Paley became one of the dominating figures running TV, much like Sarnoff got his start in the 1920s. Meanwhile, RCA, which was still a major industry player under Sarnoff, who became its president in 1930, continued to expand into related fields, most notably movie theaters and music.[1]

Though the Department of Justice tried to break up this growing media oligarchy with an antitrust suit against RCA, GE, Westinghouse, and AT&T (an early counterpart of the recent antitrust threats against Microsoft today), the suit eventually resulted in a settlement that ended some of the overlapping ownerships. Instead, after some reshuffling, the big networks reemerged a little slimmed down, but as strong as ever. NBC became a wholly owned subsidiary of RCA, with the right to manage the stations owned by GE and Westinghouse, while David Sarnoff ended up on top of RCA and soon became one of the big wunderkinder of the TV age.[1]

Ironically, the Depression contributed to the growth of TV, as well as radio, since it meant a decline in both theater and film audiences. Increasingly, home audiences grew, and the intense loyalty many felt to radio helped unify the nation around such things as President Roosevelt's "Fireside Chats" and the popular comedians and daytime serials. In turn, the big money contributed by the sponsors of these programs helped fund the launch of TV.[1]

Success, though, brought more regulation for both TV and radio. That's because then, as now, many people protested the growing commercialization of TV, with all sorts of things for sale, including questionable products like patent medicines and goat-gland rejuvenation transplants.[1] Thus, soon after taking office, Roosevelt established the Federal Communications Commission (FCC) to regulate broadcasting, as well as the telephone. Meanwhile, some members of Congress sought to redistribute channels as part of the Communications Act of 1934. Though their amendment lost, in fighting against it, the major networks began to provide unsold time to community groups, educators, and religious leaders, though not required by the Act. This sparked the growth of numerous public service programs, which were the first real talk programs on TV, such as the *University of Chicago Round Table* and the New York-based *America's Town Meeting of the Air*, both launched with network time on NBC.[1] These were essentially debate and discussion programs dealing with current issues and political topics, much like *Crossfire* and *The News Hour with Jim Lehrer* today.

the rise of the three networks and eclipse of tv during the war

Though TV probably would have gotten off the ground 10–15 years earlier, it got eclipsed by World War II. In the meantime, behind the scenes, tremendous battles were taking place in the courts and marketplace over who would control this new industry, before the big three networks created by the large corporations that already controlled radio eventually emerged triumphant. So, as cinema–TV professor Lynn Spigel at the University of Southern California points out, "the social agenda for television was largely defined by the corporate mind of the radio interests."[3]

The battles are a fascinating look at a kind of Jurassic Park survival-of-the-fittest battle, in which David Sarnoff of RCA and William C. Paley of CBS were like *Tyrannosaurus rex*, striking down any smaller prey who got in their way.

One of the few lucky ones was Philo T. Farnsworth, from a Mormon farm family in Idaho, who gained the support of a professional fundraiser from California, George Everson, who met him when Farnsworth was working on a community chest drive in Salt Lake City, and liked his ideas for an electronic television system. With Everson's support, he worked quietly in a small apartment in L.A. and later in San Francisco on his system; and in 1930, he obtained the first patent on an electronic TV, beating out RCA, which had its own researcher working on the project. Though RCA at first tried to buy him out for a low price, eventually it settled, giving a small outsider a rare victory.[1]

But RCA did manage to hold back the development of FM radio in the mid-1930s, after another inventor, Edwin H. Armstrong, got several patents for an FM system he developed. That's because Sarnoff saw FM as a threat to the emergence of television, since RCA was using the profits from the AM stations it controlled to fund TV development. So Sarnoff wanted FM out of the picture and fought Armstrong's efforts to gain FCC approval for FM airspace in 1934–1936. Though Armstrong eventually did get an FCC license and set up his first FM tower in 1938 in Philadelphia, for all practical purposes, Sarnoff had derailed these initial efforts to launch FM radio, clearing the field for TV to go public.[1]

Supposedly, this public launch was going to start with the 1939 World's Fair in New York City, where RCA had a widely publicized exhibit in a building shaped like a radio tube in a section of the fair called "The Land of Tomorrow."[3] But the launch never got off the ground as planned, despite a few preliminary TV events. For example, shortly before the fair opened, the stars of *Amos 'n' Andy* did a test broadcast in blackface, and after it opened on April 30th, Franklin D. Roosevelt spoke, becoming the first U.S. President to appear on TV. Also, the fair displayed the early RCA sets with 5- and 9-inch picture tubes. And over the next few months, a few programs were broadcast each day, including plays, comedians, singers, puppets, studio kitchen demonstrations, local field pickups from a baseball game or fashion show, and some on-the-street interviews. Even struggling CBS managed to have 23 small stations telecasting programs around the U.S. by 1940.[1]

But suddenly, the boom collapsed, in part because of growing war clouds and most immediately because the FCC pulled the plug. It did so because it had granted only a limited authorization for commercial operations, since there were as yet no national TV technical standards, and it wanted to discourage marketing sets to the public until these standards could be resolved. So TV went back to experimental status.[1]

Though this fight over standards ended in May, 1941, when the FCC accepted the NTSC (National Television System Committee) standards created by the Radio Manufacturers Association and gave TV the go ahead again, it was too late. The pressures of war had shifted public interest elsewhere. As a result, TV schedules were reduced to almost nothing—from about 15 hours a week to 4 hours, and soon most stations left the air. Only six remained with very limited programming. And there was almost no audience, since only about 10,000 sets had been sold, and new sets were dropped from the market.[1] It would be another decade before TV came back into public view.

In the meantime, though, scientists continued to work on technical improvements. For example, the scientists at RCA developed a more sensitive camera tube, so studio lighting didn't have to be so bright, and at both RCA and CBS, scientists experimented with color. Meanwhile, the battle for dominance by the big networks continued, while the FCC helped to influence the results, since after extensive legal battling, it ordered RCA, which had become so overwhelmingly dominant, to let go of one of its two networks. The result was the birth of ABC in 1943, turning network competition into a three-way rivalry, on more nearly equal terms.[1] Though NBC, with RCA's backing, was still the most powerful of the three, all were strong and ready to shape the relaunching of TV after the war. And talk—particularly celebrity talk—was among the first of the formats to be launched.

the turn to tv after the war

The end of the war changed everything. Suddenly, the economy was booming again, and TV manufacturers began to promote their receivers to a newly eager consumer market that had built up large savings, after a long period of wartime shortages and rationing. Beginning in 1946, a new generation of TVs with improved technology hit the market. Among the first out were black-and-white offerings by DuMont and RCA.[4] Initially, there wasn't much to watch, because few TV studios were producing anything after a period when virtually no one was watching. But over the next few years, as consumers flocked to buy the new sets, the networks quickly caught up with production, and soon the time for broadcasting programs expanded.

I remember those days marketing the birth, or perhaps more accurately the rebirth, of TV. I was about 4 or 5 years old, and had grown up listening to the radio serials, sitting during the day with my grandmother in a darkened room with the shades drawn. We listened to shows like *Helen Trent* ("Can a woman find happiness in a small town after 35?"), *The Shadow*, *The Jack Benny Show*, and other classics. I remember resisting this new medium, because I liked creating pictures in my head, rather than seeing the then very plain studio sets that lacked the exciting magic I experienced with my own pictures. But soon I, too, felt the growing excitement as TV fever swept the country.

I saw the changes across the street in a small radio store in Flushing, next to a dry cleaning store where my mother went several times a week. When the first TV set appeared in the window, it was a small dark brown wooden box with a 12-inch screen, and whenever I passed by, I saw a flickering test pattern that looked like a Maltese cross. Several times, I stood at the window for several minutes with other neighborhood kids just staring, waiting for something to happen. Then, after some time, when nothing changed, we drifted away and went home.

Then, about six months later, when my parents got one of these new inventions, there were a few programs in the early evenings, and we sat around watching. At first, my parents had to entice me away from the radio, since I kept protesting I liked the radio dramas so much better. But after a few months, I joined them more and more in the living room to watch. And now there was more to watch, too, as the number of programs on the big three networks kept expanding.

Meanwhile, the number of sets in the nation increased apace— from a penetration rate of 0.02% in 1946 to 9% in 1950, and 65% by 1955, which is when TV finally came to most of America. Until then, TV viewership was fairly spotty, since initially most of the stations were in the Northeast, as were most TV sets, largely because the industry was still wrangling over who could own stations where, resulting in an FCC freeze on allocating stations from 1948 to 1952.[4]

Concurrently, as TV spread, the influence of the corporate-owned networks and the domestic mood of the country after the war contributed to the gentle, noncontroversial family orientation of postwar TV. The first talk TV fit right into this mold. As TV historian Spigel observes, the theme of the period was "domesticity"—the quiet single-family dwelling in the suburbs was the postwar American dream. That's because, for the growing middle class

> During and after the war, the marriage rate rose to record heights…. The baby boom, which began during the war and lasted through 1964 … created a revitalization of the nuclear family as a basic social construct … [and] a new model for living—the prefabricated suburban tract home.[5]

the beginnings of commercial tv

It took about a decade for TV to fully break into the mainstream. In the meantime, the changes after the war prepared the way for the growth of TV by stripping radio of most of its drama, comedy, and talk programming, transforming it into the largely music radio of the 1950s. A major reason for this occurrence was that the big networks behind radio pulled funds from radio profits to finance the fledgling TV networks. And soon many successful radio programs began to migrate to TV, wooed by the competing networks. CBS, for example, enticed many top NBC radio comedians such as Jack Benny, Burns and Allen, and Amos and Andy to TV by offering them a chance to own their own shows and reap advantageous tax gains as a result.[1]

New programs were soon under development, too, some of them news-type shows adopted from radio. For example, in 1945 and 1946, NBC and CBS, the two largest networks, set up a television news service, which included a news-talk interview program that had been on radio for a long time—*Meet the Press*.[1]

Some of the new entertainment shows also included some talk through informal interviews with audience members or guests. As a child, I was on some of these shows, such as *Howdy Doody*, launched in 1947. When I was 5 or 6, I was a member of its preschooler and kindergarten audience called the "Peanut Gallery," and I recall a few ad hoc questions and responses by some kids mixed in with the antics of Howdy Doody, Clarabelle, and Uncle Bob.

Many of these early game and audience contest shows had short bits of repartee between the hosts and audience members or guests, and as these bits became extended on some shows, they turned into variety and talk shows. Again, I was an early guest on one such show, *Your Pet Parade*, in about 1948 or 1949, when I was 6 or 7. I appeared with my turtles, who did "tricks" like climbing out of a slipper and "jumping rope"—the latter involving my holding a piece of string in front of one turtle, and after he walked over it, I flipped it in front of him again several times. Meanwhile, the camera zoomed in for turtle close-ups, and afterwards, the host briefly asked me a few questions about how I "discovered these talented turtles and got them to do tricks." Several other kids with talented pets, such as a boy with a cocker spaniel, who won the blue bike first prize, were on too.

This early combination of a little talk with other formats—news, entertainment, kids shows, contests, and game shows—

continued to dominate as TV developed, because as a visual medium, TV liked to show action, not just talk. Though debate, discussion, and interview programs were well suited to radio, they were less so on TV, because it wasn't so interesting to see just talking heads in a conversation or meeting. From the beginning, TV wanted pictures of people doing things.

The content and style of TV talk was also influenced by the spirit of conservatism that swept the nation in the late 1940s, resulting in a concern with keeping everything comfortable and safe. It was an attitude that went hand in hand with the postwar trend to domesticity and suburbanization. For this was a time when the McCarthy hearings and Hollywood blacklisting were just beginning, and now that TV was an up-and-coming medium, it too was affected by these concerns.

This crackdown began in 1947 when the FCC started getting memos from J. Edgar Hoover, Federal Bureau of Investigations director, that potential licensees for TV stations might be members of the Communist Party or at least movement sympathizers. As a result, some parties didn't get a license, such as one group in California. And soon the crackdown began in earnest, spreading from the film world to broadcasting. A group of top Hollywood film executives agreed to drop writers "unfriendly" to the House committee's investigations, creating the blacklist, at the end of 1947, and soon afterwards, broadcasting executives and sponsors began receiving lists of questionable writers, artists, and organizations to avoid. Though Harry S. Truman tried to reverse the tide when he became President, arguing for a freer broadcast industry, the push in Congress supported the witchhunt.[1] Thus, television was formed in an atmosphere of fear, which guaranteed that all programming, including talk, would be safely conservative, too. As Barnouw notes

> These were ... the formative years for television. Its program patterns, business practices, and institutions were being shaped. Evolving from a radio industry born under military influence and reared by big business, it now entered an adolescence traumatized by phobias. It would learn caution, and cowardice.[6]

In turn, many who followed this formula for success scored

big, encouraging others to do the same as more money flowed into the industry and TV became increasingly powerful and began to push down participation in other entertainment industries. For example, between 1948 and 1952, when there were about 100 stations licensed by the FCC, mostly in the Northeast, movie attendance dropped 20–40% in cities with TV stations; attendance at sporting events declined; there was a drop in restaurant and nightclub patronage; jukebox receipts were down; and people read fewer books—both library attendance and book store sales were down. Radio listening dropped, too. The comparison between the TV and non-TV cities was so stark it was clear that TV was the wave of the future.[1] So more and more big money went into it. All America was getting wired—much like everyone is wiring into the info age today.

It was in this context that the first big variety shows that featured celebrity talk were born. Given the paranoia about communism sweeping the nation, the hosts kept their guests and comedy patter safe, too. The two biggest variety shows launched in 1948 were the *Texaco Star Theater* with Milton Berle (later known as the *Milton Berle Show*) and *The Toast of the Town* with Ed Sullivan, later called the *Ed Sullivan Show*.[1] Much like Jay Leno and David Letterman, Sullivan used big-name celebrities to draw in audiences. He sought the biggest names, and being a New York *Daily News* columnist helped get them since he could also give performers a plug in his column.

Sullivan also quickly fell into line in offering safe programs after one controversial incident when he booked dancer Paul Draper for an appearance in January, 1950. Unfortunately, Draper had been accused in a letter-writing campaign of being a procommunist traitor, and the program's sponsor, the Ford Motor Company, initially tried to pull out, though Draper appeared after a protest campaign by columnists and newspaper writers and the threat of a lawsuit by Draper. But after that, Sullivan backed down on any controversial guests, and if in doubt about an artist, he checked with one of the editors of *Counterattack*, which published lists of subversives, for guidance. In fact, by the middle of 1950, *Counterattack* had compiled a complete list of artists to avoid, called *Red Channels: The Report of Communist Influence in Radio and Television*. It listed about 150 people, mostly writers, directors, and performers, who had been prominent in radio and were now becoming active in television. These were some of the major creative people at the time, including some names still well known today, such as Leonard Bernstein, Ruth Gordon, Dashiell Hammett, Lillian Hellman, Lena Horne, Burl Ives, Gypsy Rose Lee, Dorothy Parker, Edward G. Robinson, and Orson Welles. For all practical purposes, they and others identified as politically suspect during these years were off the air.[1] They couldn't even be interviewed on air to give their side of the story as they might today, such as on top news or interview shows like *Larry King*. Instead, a code of silence pervaded most of the entertainment industry, including the news and variety shows, and any guests they might invite to appear.

the 1950s deluge: the rush to commercial tv

Despite the Red cloud hanging over the industry, by 1953 the rush was on, spurred by the end of the last technical hurdle. This occurred when the FCC removed its four-year freeze, in effect from 1948–1952, on the creation of new stations because of problems with standards. At once new stations raced to be on the air. However, the fear of accusations of communism—related to political activities or to anything considered controversial and detrimental to American culture—strongly influenced what or who got on the air. It created the conservative tradition that still hangs over some programming today.

This fear meant it was hard to have any thoughtful or controversial talk shows, since the topic seemed too threatening. And some of the most articulate people were muzzled by the blacklist and couldn't get jobs for years. So instead, there was a plethora of programs considered "safe," such as the tough-on-crime and family comedy shows. In the crime category, one of the most popular shows was Ralph Bellamy's *Man Against Crime*, which premiered in 1949 (and its sponsor was Camel cigarettes, so not only the cops, but also smoking looked good). Another show, introduced in 1951, was *Dragnet* with Jack Webb. Meanwhile, on the comedy front, *I Love Lucy* with Lucille Ball and Desi Arnaz debuted the same year and soon became a huge success. These were all comfortable, predictable shows that adhered to the era's formula of supporting the establishment and family values.[1]

Meanwhile, bland, comfortable talk TV took two main forms. One was the news talk format, which reported on current events; the other was the variety talk show. One type of news talk program that helped change the way political elections occur is the campaign broadcast. The first presidential election featured on TV was 1952's, and it helped make Ike—General Eisenhower—the first TV-age president. Before then, presidential candidates stumped the nation, and with the advent of radio, they spoke to the public through radio broadcasts. But now, though only about 15 million people watched TV and many more still listened to radio, the campaigners considered these viewers among the most aware or influential members of the public. So now all the major networks got sponsors and broadcast the conventions and election returns.[1] The good response—and Ike's election—guaranteed that future candidates would shape their campaigns around the more visual, short-sound-bite appeal of TV—characteristics quickly recognized in these first days of national TV.

Perhaps he would have lost anyway, but Ike's opponent, Adlai Stevenson was a disaster on TV, since he tried to continue his erudite, intellectual approach based on careful analysis. As a result, whatever his message, he tended to bore and turn off many viewers. By contrast, Eisenhower, with the support of an ad agency, Batten, Barton, Durstine & Osborn, ran the first media candidacy. He worked with scriptwriters who helped him fashion a short inspirational speech and 20-second question-and-answer spots. Plus, he cultivated the pageantry of entering and exiting his speeches like a hero.[1]

And then came the famous Nixon Checker's speech that secured Nixon a place on the ticket. The Republican leaders had been pressuring Eisenhower to dump him because of rumors of campaign fund-raising improprieties. But instead Nixon, backed by the Republican National Committee, used the talk format—a kind of 1950s' infomercial—to appeal to the nation in a half-hour chat that was broadcast over 64 TV stations, as well as on several hundred radio stations. His tearful appeal that he hadn't spent one cent of the questioned $18,000 for personal use and that he wouldn't return the cute little cocker spaniel he got as a gift because his 6-year-old daughter Tricia loved it so much, even if it meant the election, worked so well, he stayed on the ticket.[1] Like Ike, Nixon proved a master at using the new TV talk format to inspire and persuade, and the deluge of support for both showed the power of this new medium—and how to use it most effectively.

It was a lesson quickly learned by others, and it translated into the emotional, sound-bite politicking on TV that characterizes national campaigning today. Ironically, in the Kennedy–Nixon debates of 1960, Nixon seemed to forget the lesson he learned in 1952 about the power of the TV image. So he lost the debate in part because he looked gray and pasty, while Kennedy looked and sounded so young and vibrant. Since then, politicians and campaign strategists have been much more conscious of these lessons for using TV-image making dating back to 1952.

Some roots were also laid for more serious TV talk when some frequencies were set aside for nonprofit, educational use in 1952, after a campaign by the first FCC woman commissioner, Frieda B. Hennock, who was appointed by Harry Truman in 1948. Mainly to get rid of her pressure, the FCC decided to set aside channels for 242 educational stations across the nation on the VHF and UHF bands, and later the number of stations grew. No funding was provided at the time, however.[1] While many predicted that educators would fail to use the channels and industry would take them back, this didn't happen. Instead, though strapped for funds, then as now, these channels became one of the major forums for talk TV. Freed from the commercial pressures that pushed most TV to become visual and action oriented and disdain talk, these stations could feature more serious talk for a smaller audience.

Meanwhile, despite the pressure on programming to go commercial, there were a few pockets of more serious talk on commercial TV in the early days, when successful radio programs were moved over to TV, such as *Information Please*, a question-and-answer show, and *See It Now*, a dramatized documentary of history by Edward R. Murrow and Fred W. Friendly, previously aired as *Hear It Now* on radio.[1]

More generally, though, commercial talk TV went in the direction of the chatty variety show that turned into the *Letterman*, *Leno*, and early morning talk shows of today. The basic pattern for these shows was set on *Today*, hosted by Dave Garroway. It featured a combination of newscast and variety show with performers and guests who spent a brief time chatting with the host. But most notably, *Today* was known for the presence of a baby chimp, J. Fred Muggs. Before Muggs, the show had been floundering without a sponsor and much of an audience. However, after a staffer saw Muggs waiting for an elevator for an appearance on another show and thought he might make an amusing addition, Muggs became a show regular. And soon his presence helped set the level for what was especially popular on talk TV—lighthearted, celebrity-driven chatter, as Muggs became a sought- after star. It was wild—a kind of combination of Howard Stern and Kato Kaelin today. As TV historian Erik Barnouw describes it:

> Women proposed to him; advertisers fought for the right to use his photo in their supermarket flyers; Chambers of Commerces sought his good offices; actresses posed with him; officers of newly commissioned naval vessels demanded that he christen them.[7]

Muggs even was a featured guest at an "I Am an American Day rally," and he was given a room in a restricted hotel in Florida. It might have been closed to blacks in those days, but not to chimps. It was the beginning of a new age of TV talk show celebrity—and the first big star was a chimp!

talk tv in the 1950s

In 1953 and through the 1950s, TV came of age. The big three national networks spread over the nation, and big sponsors backed the increasingly powerful network programs. Big stars flocked to become part of the expanding schedules. Millions of people joined the rush to get wired.

Talk was just a small part of this rush, since most new programming featured more visual formats, like drama, documentary, dance, and opera. The political climate also discouraged dialogue and debate, as illustrated by the pressure put on some of the serious dramatic shows that were briefly launched in 1953 through 1955 as part of several anthology series, such as the *Kraft Television Theater*, *U.S. Steel Hour*, *Motorola Playhouse*, *Playhouse 90*, and *Omnibus*. These programs attracted top American writers and actors, but some were soon under attack when the sponsors began to come down on shows like Paddy Chayefsky's *Marty*, broadcast in 1953 on the *Goodyear Television Playhouse*.[1]

The problem with this show and others like it is that they dealt seriously with real life problems and showed ordinary people dealing with everyday issues of work, kids, and marriage. But the advertisers hated these shows because they made the romanticized world the advertisers were selling look phony. Also, while advertisers promoted quick solutions, like "Just take this new pill …," "Try this new shampoo…," "You'll love this great floor wax …," these dramas featured people struggling with difficulties at home and work.[1] And the last thing advertisers wanted was for people to think about the economic problems underlying these everyday issues, since the question of what to do about them had political overtones. And any political association made sponsors nervous, since in those days anything political raised the specter of being accused of Communist sympathies.

Thus, by 1954, and even more so in 1955, the sponsors and their agencies were increasingly interfering in the content of these programs, such as demanding script changes or refusing to green light programs they found objectionable.[1] As a result, by 1955, this serious realistic programming rapidly went into a decline—a trend that contributed to the stations having little interest in other serious programming, including more serious talk TV. Instead, the trend was toward the safe, predictable, upbeat series, typically featuring ordinary families—like *Father Knows Best* or *My Three*

Sons—that were usually happy and squabbled only over minor issues, much like the 1969–1974 hit, *The Brady Bunch.*

Similarly, the news shows of the early 1950s stayed on fairly safe ground, avoiding anything controversial, including questioning the McCarthyism of the period. Instead the news programs focused on covering largely staged PR-style events, like beauty contests, campaign speeches, and building dedications, and doing features on the more dramatic events of the day like fires, floods, and faraway wars. So, while the TV camera opened up vast new possibilities for "see it now" news coverage, it also pushed out dialogue and debate, making serious talk shows less likely.[1]

This shift to more visual and promotional staged events in turn meant more power for the event planners in government and business, who were involved in the behind-the-scenes staging of these events.[1] So, increasingly, these 1950s' counterparts to today's spin doctors and media and political consultants helped to determine what became news—and what Americans might talk about.

The fate of several of the more serious programs from the early 1950s illustrates this. For example, in 1953, when *See It Now*, hosted by Ed Murrow, did a story about Air Force Lieutenant Milo Radulovich, unjustly accused of being a Communist, CBS refused to advertise the program. So Murrow and his producer Fred Friendly put up the money for a *New York Times* advertisement, $1500, themselves. Then, in 1955 when Murrow did an interview with Dr. J. Robert Oppenheimer, one of the creators of the atom bomb, who had recently lost his Atomic Energy Commission security clearance because he had been accused of disloyalty to the U.S., Murrow and Friendly had to pay for advertising time again.[1]

By contrast, a more airbrushed celebrity-style spin-off of *See It Now*—*Person to Person*—launched in 1953, had much better luck. This program was a kind of forerunner to Robin Leach's *Lifestyles of the Rich and Famous* approach to TV interviews, and the idea for it began when Murrow and his camera crew went to visit celebrities on two *See It Now* programs. He asked questions as the camera trailed along on a tour of the house. On *Person to Person* Murrow continued the same format, which immediately became popular, because according to TV historian Erik Barnouw: "The series was seldom controversial; it had a *Vogue* and *House Beautiful* appeal, along with a voyeuristic element—larger than *See It Now*."[8]

This distinction made clear the direction in which TV talk was headed: light, upbeat, and celebrity driven, a trend with us today.

other directions: from big money to little money tv

By the mid-1950s, another type of talk TV was developing, namely, the big money audience participation show, which got viewers involved. Later this spun off into all sorts of game shows, and it was variously combined with variety and popular interview shows. But in the mid-1950s, the big hit was the quiz show. At the time, a series of small-scale quiz programs had already been running for several years. They offered small awards—about $50 or $64 in cash, or merchandise donated by manufacturers in return for a plug. But what brought these quiz shows to the top was the new program *The $64,000 Question*, which infused these shows with big money—and the attention that accompanied this.[1]

While much of the show was a quiz—with the contestants secured in a glass isolation booth while they answered questions—there were elements of talk in the informal personal exchanges of the host with the contestants. Through these brief personal glimpses, the host personalized them for the audience and encouraged audience identification. In fact, this personalizing process worked so well that it led to management intervention in the form of coaching some popular contestants by slipping them answers or clues, making it harder for the other, less popular contestants to compete.

As the success of *The $64,000 Question* precipitated dozens of imitators within a few months—such as *The Big Surprise*, *The $64,000 Challenge*, *Nothing But the Truth*, and *Twenty One*[1]—the behind-the-scenes manipulation to influence contestant popularity led to scandals. As is well known, the interviews with Charles Van Doren, then an English instructor at Columbia University, turned him into a media celebrity, which included big stories and covers on *Time* and other mass magazines. Then, it all collapsed, when one of Van Doren's rivals, Herbert Stempel, angry that he had been shunted aside for not being as crowd-pleasing, blew the whistle. He exposed the secret that Van Doren had been coached on the questions, leading to Congressional hearings on the integrity of these shows—a story portrayed in Robert Redford's 1994 film *Quiz Show*. In the end, the shows cleaned up and continued, evolving into a variety of forms, including the less intellectual game shows and no-talent shows in which viewers were invited to come on the show provided they were willing to make fools of themselves. As they did, they had a chance to briefly speak to the host and capture their few minutes of fame.

By contrast, the future of more serious talk TV didn't look so bright when in the fall of 1955, *See It Now* was canceled and its time period sold to Liggett & Myers, one of the big tobacco companies. It was big corporate sponsors like Liggett & Myers who contributed to keeping things bland, because they typically bought a big time block, giving them strong influence, if not control, over the program running during that time.[1]

Gradually, though, beginning in the mid-1950s, these big sponsors began to have less control, since there was now a push toward using a "magazine concept," under which the network was in charge of the content, and the advertisers bought insertions or time slots for advertising during the program. This change was initiated by Sylvester L. ("Pat") Weaver, soon after he became NBC president in 1953[1]; and soon this magazine approach was used on the popular *Today* show hosted by Dave Garroway. And later *Tonight*—hosted initially by Steve Allen, and subsequently by Jack Paar, Johnny Carson, and now Jay Leno—used this approach. But even though the sponsors had less direct control, the TV programs still felt their power, since the sponsors could pull their ads if they objected to the content enough—so there was still pressure to keep the shows bland and popular.

For example, on *Person to Person*, Ed Murrow mostly visited with the most popular, noncontroversial people of the day, like

Liberace, Eddie Fisher, Debbie Reynolds, Jayne Mansfield, Lawrence Welk, and a sprinkling of nonentertainment figures like Dr. George Gallup, Billy Graham, and the Duke and Duchess of Windsor. But he stayed away from guests like Martin Luther King, spearheading the recently growing civil rights movement.[1]

The notion of "family" TV also contributed to this blandness. The popular media and public opinion regarded television as something to bring the family together—a theme emphasized in the popular magazines of the day. TV was promoted as a kind of "household cement" to support the longing for a return to family values in postwar America after the disruptions of war. As Lynn Spigel writes in her study of TV:

> Television itself became *the* central figure in images of the American home; it became the cultural symbol par excellence of family life…. Television, it was said, would bring the family ever closer, an expression which … was continually repeated in a wide range of popular media—not only women's magazines, but also general magazines, men's magazines, and on the airwaves.[9]

Thus, in this desire for domesticity and safe, comfortable TV, talk, beside being a small part of variety, quiz, and game shows, was largely on the fringes. Instead, mid-1950s' TV filled up with theatrical specials like *Peter Pan*, which had been a Broadway success; dramatic and fantasy series like *Disneyland*; and dozens of Westerns, like *Wyatt Earp* and *Gunsmoke*. Plus, many Hollywood feature films now turned up on TV, on series like the *Million Dollar Movie*.[1]

In turn, the growing popularity and big money now in TV helped turn it into this action-packed variety land. In 5 years it had gone from a little more than 100 stations with 10,000 viewers in 1952 to over 500 stations. And now about 85% of all homes in America—about 40 million homes—were wired up, with the average viewer watching about 5 hours of TV a day. Assuming an average of 2 or 3 viewers per home, about 80 to 120 million viewers were now watching daily. And now that TV had become a billion dollar industry, the money for programming followed what was popular—what was visual, dramatic, funny, lighthearted, and upbeat, an approach that fit in with the conservative tenor of the age led by Ike in the White House.[1]

Thus, there wasn't much place for serious discussion and talk—at least not on commercial TV. By contrast, the one place left for talk was on the margins on noncommercial and educational TV. For the most part, this type of TV limped along without much funding, although there were a few bright spots. One was started by the Ford Foundation in 1952, when it created a $1.35 million grant to establish the National Education Television program production center, and it provided additional grants of $3 million or more from time to time to keep the network going.[1]

Also, in some cities, there was some success at raising local funding. One success was at KQED in San Francisco which was started in 1954 on Channel 9 and is still going today. At first KQED managed just one hour of broadcasting a day and was about to be dropped in 1955, when the program staff started an on-air auction that brought in enough bids to keep the station going—and year after year, this auction kept the station alive.[1]

Another approach of some noncommercial stations was affiliating with a local educational institution—typically a school or board of education. For example, in Houston, the University of Houston built station KUHT in 1953 and used it to beam out lectures to students who now didn't have to attend class to hear lectures. Instead, they could see them at home, in the dorm, or in a viewing room at school[1]—a predecessor of many classrooms of the air that use noncommercial community or cable stations today.

These noncommercial and educational stations, however financed, thus became the home of most talk TV, since the commercial stations, supported by powerful advertisers, generally avoided dealing with current or controversial issues. About the only exception was during the lower-viewer "fringe" periods, typically on Sunday afternoons, sometimes dubbed the "cultural ghetto."

But even then a program that took on too hot a topic could run into problems, such as when one 1957 NBC discussion program hosted by Tex McCrary invited a researcher on tobacco to share his views. Ironically, in light of the recent crackdown on the tobacco industry for concealing information from the public, his research findings were on just what the industry didn't want known, namely, the link between smoking and lung cancer. But the to-bacco industry lobbied hard to make sure he didn't get on the air, and refused to have anyone appear to present the other side of the story. So the invitation to the researcher was soon canceled and the program never aired.[1]

Just about the only time commercial TV did devote prime-time coverage to serious talk was during the elections, and then the lessons of Stevenson's disastrous 1952 campaign made it clear the best strategy was keeping any talk short and simple. Accord-ingly, during the 1956 elections, the Republicans used only brief 5-minute political appeals at the end of popular programs to avoid disrupting the schedule for these programs. And Stevenson, who was running again, kept to 5-minute spot ads as well. This year was also the first time that both conventions were aired on TV, and one popular feature was the commentary of NBC newsmen Chet Huntley and David Brinkley, who later became regular news an-chors. Then, when Eisenhower and Nixon won by a landslide, this contributed to continuing the upbeat, don't rock the boat ap-proach on prime time that discouraged any serious talk. Popular entertainment was in, not serious news or talk.[1]

And so the shape of TV and the role of talk in it was set in the 1950s—a legacy that continues today. Despite the wave of social concern that sparked a new interest in current events and issues in the 1960s, once that wave of protest and upheaval died down in the 1970s, TV largely went back to entertainment and action as usual, and talk was mostly back on the fringes again.

notes

1. Erik Barnouw, *Tube of Plenty: The Evolution of American Televi-sion*, New York: Oxford University Press, 1990.
2. Barnouw, p. 60.
3. Lynn Spigel, *Make Room for TV: Television and the Family Ideal in Postwar America*, Chicago: The University of Chicago Press, 1992, p. 30.

4. Spigel, *Make Room for TV*.

5. Spigel, pp. 32–33.

6. Barnouw, p. 112.

7. Barnouw, pp. 147–148.

8. Barnouw, p. 178.

9. Spigel, p. 39.

chapter nine

the rise of talk tv

Just as talk and other TV in the 1950s mirrored the spirit of domesticity and family togetherness that characterized the times, so did talk TV reflect the spirit of the age in the following decades. That's why in the 1960s, it soon became intertwined with the news and deeply political, as the materialism and Communist paranoia of the 1950s gave way to questioning the foundations of American society in the 1960s and early 1970s. Then, as people began to turn inward in the 1970s and later sought success in the 1980s, talk TV followed along, too. In an age increasingly saturated by the visuals and slogans of a media culture, talk TV was the natural accompaniment—and it both reflected and helped to create the main characteristics of the age.

the power of talk tv in the 1960s

I was in my sophomore year at the University of Rochester when talk TV began to reflect this new seriousness. There were a few hints of what was coming in the late 1950s, as when Nikita Khrushchev appeared in 1957 on the CBS-TV series *Face the Nation*, answered questions from a panel of reporters about where the USSR was going, and thereafter became a frequent guest on American TV, including being the subject of several special features in 1959, such as *Khrushchev in America* and *Mr. Khrushchev Abroad*.[1]

Then in late 1959 and 1960, a new wave of serious documentary and political TV began rolling across the media screen. The first burst came when the quiz show scandals exploded into TV reports of legislative hearings on how the shows were manipulated to favor the most popular contestants. So instead of just being popular entertainment, the quiz shows turned into serious news, too. Meanwhile, other investigations began probing into an equivalent scandal on radio—the bribes ("payola") to the big disk jockeys—and these became the subject of a TV report as well.[1]

But besides grist for the TV news/talk mill, these TV and radio scandals led to the major networks' decision in 1959 to start a series of documentaries on serious subjects. It was a complete reversal from the trend to drop serious programming that had led CBS to drop Ed Murrow's *See It Now* program a few months before. Instead, it now looked like TV suddenly got a conscience in response to all of the government investigations—or at least, TV now sensed that the public was interested in weightier fare, and so began these documentaries. For example, CBS unfurled *CBS Reports*, produced by Fred W. Friendly, while NBC announced that its news division would have some special documentaries. Still, these documentaries were just a small part of prime-time programming—since after dropping the big prize quiz shows, the networks generally turned to telefilm series.[1]

Still, there was a big change in TV's expanded news and political coverage, which combined headline news with talk and commentary, blurring news talk boundaries. Increasingly, talk TV became a source of the news as well. For example, at the end of 1959, the White House announced on network TV that a big summit of the major powers—the U.S., Britain, France, and Russia—would be held in Paris in 1960, and afterwards President Eisenhower would do a goodwill tour of the Soviet Union, with the TV networks tagging along. It was the beginning of creating news for TV.[1]

Then came the Kennedy–Nixon Great Debates in the fall of 1960. It was my sophomore year at the University of Rochester, and I remember how a group of us sat around in the dorm lounge glued to the TV and discussed the debates for days afterwards. Who won? Who lost? It was like arguing the OJ trial today. And this time Nixon experienced his TV debacle because he forgot the message he knew so well when he gave his 1951 Checkers speech. As then, the message was inseparable from the image—and unfortunately, this time, Nixon didn't look very good. Whereas he came across as a pasty-faced, washed-out has-been, Kennedy appeared as having the knowledge, confidence, glibness, and power of a young, dynamic president. Or as media historian Erik Barnouw describes it:

> The first debate was disastrous for Nixon. This had little do with what was said.... What television audiences noted chiefly was the air of confidence, the nimbleness of mind that exuded from the young Kennedy.... A Nixon glimpse showed him haggard; the lines on his faces seemed liked gashes and gave him a fearful look....

Among those who heard the first debate on radio, Nixon apparently held his own. Only on television had he seemed to lose.[2] After Kennedy won, his commitment to the new medium contributed to the growing use of TV to document world events, through expanded news, documentary, and interview show coverage—much like current political leaders such as President Clinton and House Speaker Gingrich are embracing the information highway today. Even before he won, Kennedy contributed to this trend by agreeing to have a camera crew, headed by Robert Drew of Time, Inc., follow him around through the campaign, starting with the Wisconsin primary. It was the first film to document the day-to-day details, and though it was rejected by the networks and only shown on a few stations owned by Time, when Kennedy saw it shortly after his election, he stated he wanted to have his presidency documented in a similar fashion.[1] In turn, his imprimatur furthered this growing renaissance of documentaries and other news/talk coverage during his administration, which continued into the Johnson years. It was, in effect, the use of TV to support democracy in America—a thrust renewed in the 1990s by President Clinton, who in many ways adopted Kennedy as a mentor.

Though Kennedy wasn't attracted to the fireside chat style of Roosevelt, in interviews he strongly expressed his support for documentaries, believing them a way to help keep citizens informed about government activities. So documentary producers felt they had a go-ahead from on-high, at a time when Kennedy challenged the nation to strive toward all sorts of dreams and possibilities.[1]

The result was a spurt of all sorts of socially conscious documentaries on news-talk programs, such as "Harvest of Shame" about the migrant workers on *CBS Reports* and "Yanki No!" about what was happening in Cuba on ABC's *Close-Up* series. And NBC contributed, too, such as on its *White Paper* series, in which it reported on the beginnings of the civil rights movement in "Sit-In" which combined newsfilm of black resistance to segregation in restaurants and department stores with interviews with participants. Meanwhile, Kennedy invited Drew's filmmaker team, which had filmed *Primary*, to document some day-to-day highlights of his own administration in a film that became *Adventures on the New Frontier*.[1] Was it a film; was it talk TV? In those days, the borders between different forms of news, documentary, and interviews were highly permeable, as news producers flocked to create new forms of talk TV in a more socially conscious age.

documenting the transformation in american culture

Though still a small part of TV generally, talk TV in its various forms served to document the upheavals in U.S. culture that characterized the 1960s. And perhaps it was fitting that it did, since in a short decade, TV had become the major way in which people got their news. From about 100 TV stations in America in 1952 when the freeze on TV stations was lifted, by 1962, there were stations all over the country and well over half the U.S. population got its news primarily from TV. But more than just news, television was now the way in which people understood and related to the world. It had, to quote Barnouw, for most people "become their window on the world. The view it offered seemed to be *the* world. They trusted its validity and completeness."[3]

Today, we may criticize the media spin and hype; TV's violence and excesses. But at the time, TV still had the magic of offering unlimited possibilities; the early backlash against TV as a "wasteland" was only just beginning. Instead, in the early 1960s when many people pushed for the vision of transforming society, TV was seen as a transformative tool that could help shape ideas as well as document what was happening.

It was also seen as a way to expose deception. For example, TV was there when the Bay of Pigs fiasco in Cuba unraveled in 1961. At first, TV documented the government line that the U.S. government had nothing to do with the attempted coup to overthrow Castro. But later, as various groups mobilized to show that the CIA was involved in arming and training Cuban exiles with the support of the Kennedy administration, TV news reports and interviews on news/talk programs documented the latest accusations and denials, and the reasons for the invasion's failure were widely discussed.[1] It was a little like an early version of CNN.

Similarly, TV was right there documenting America's first plunge into space in February, 1962 when Lieutenant Colonel John H. Glenn, Jr. went into orbit around the earth, and in July, 1962, TV launched its first communication satellite into space, Telestar I. It was the beginning of TV going global, since events could now be transmitted live from all parts of the world.[1] At the same time, TV began creating new media heroes, as over half the nation watched history being made.

Meanwhile, with the blessings of Kennedy and wide support in Congress, new legislation was passed to help support the technological transformation. This legislation was the Communications Satellite Act of 1962, which went into effect soon after the launch of Telestar I. This authorized a private corporation, called COMSAT—the Communications Satellite Corporation—to work with both private industry and foreign governments to set up a global system of satellites for international broadcasting. The new entity's board and stockholders included some of the major players in the communications field—AT&T, RCA, Western Union International, and the International Telephone and Telegraph Company—and it offered half its stock to the general public, too.[1]

Ten years earlier, TV sets had barely made it into 10,000 homes. But now TV had truly gone global, giving everyone a ringside seat on worldwide events.

Yet ironically, while TV had this great power to document and influence a transforming society, many were disturbed by the other side of TV some began to call a "vast wasteland." It was a split into two parallel developments in TV that continues today—and is reflected in the two styles of TV talk that have emerged as well.

This serious side of TV was the one that Kennedy and others viewed as vital to the democratic process. In a 1961 address to the National Association of Broadcasters, Kennedy spoke of these possibilities:

> The flow of ideas, the capacity to make informed choices, the ability to criticize, all the assumptions on which political democracy rests, depend largely upon communication. And you are the guardians of the most powerful and effective means of communication ever designed.[4]

But in contrast, at the same meeting, Newton Minow, a lawyer Kennedy had recently appointed to chair the Federal Communications Commission, spoke about the destructive power of TV to numb and dumb down society with the mindless shows and images of violence he felt were proliferating on the airwaves. Ironically, his words might be expressed by many today—as if little has changed, except now many talk shows would be added to his critique. As Minow commented, after praising good television:

> But when television is bad, nothing is worse. I invite you to … keep your eyes glued to that set [from when it goes on] until the station signs off. I can assure you that you will observe a vast wasteland. You will see a procession of game shows, violence, audience participation shows, formula comedies about totally unbelievable families, blood and thunder, mayhem, violence, sadism, murder, western badmen, western good men, private eyes, gangsters, more violence, and cartoons. And endlessly, commercials—many screaming, cajoling, and offending.[5]

Now, over 30 years later, some say almost the same thing of

TV. In fact, back then, there was even a crackdown on violence, much like today, led by Senator Thomas J. Dodd of Connecticut, who went after the TV crime shows for their excessive violence, though he backed off about a year later—apparently because he gained financial support from some members of the media industry for an increasingly lavish life-style.[1]

Meanwhile, then as now, noncommercial TV was struggling, although in the 1960s the situation was even worse. There weren't any outlets in some of the major markets, such as New York, Los Angeles, and Washington, DC, although some steps were taken to improve the prospects for some noncommercial programs. For example, in 1961, a small production group, National Education Television, gained FCC approval for access to Channel 13 in New York for its noncommercial programming after some political bargaining. And in 1962, Minow convinced Congress to pass legislation requiring that new sets after January, 1963 be equipped with UHF as well as VHF channels, so they could broadcast additional channels, many of these expected to be noncommercial.[1]

Still, despite the wasteland accusations and the struggles of noncommercial TV, which became the strongest home of talk, mainstream TV news/talk had some major high points in chronicling the developments of the age. For example, with the support of network TV, in 1962, President Kennedy accused and then confronted the Soviets of planting missiles in Cuba. In a national hookup with all of the networks on October 22, he went on air to explain that he had photographic evidence from the CIA that missiles pointing at U.S. cities were in Cuba, and he demanded that Khrushchev withdraw them to restore peaceful relations between the two nations and avoid U.S. military action and a continued blockade to quarantine Cuba and keep out Soviet ships. Such parries and thrusts were already common in regular diplomacy, but what was unique was the use of TV to provide a platform for this statement, which gave Kennedy's threat even more force. Within two weeks, the Soviet Union began taking down its missiles, ending the blockade and Kennedy's threat to invade Cuba.[1]

It was a signal moment showing the power of news/talk TV to not only report events but also to influence them. It could be used as an advocate or a political tool for social change. In turn, this power of TV to influence and advocate helped set the stage for future TV demonstrations that helped to power the civil rights movement and Vietnam protests. Though much of TV might qualify as Minow's "wasteland," some TV was at the forefront of the social movements of the decade. In fact, TV often helped to build these movements and give them far more power than they would have had without the camera eye to spread their message to the world.

Many of these TV high points are well known, such as Martin Luther King's massive 1963 march on Washington and his searing "I have a dream" speech at the Lincoln Memorial to 200,000 people in Washington and millions around the globe. And in November, 1963, the image of a dying President in Dallas seared the soul of the nation, as did the dramatic shooting of the chief suspect Lee Harvey Oswald at Dallas police headquarters a few days later.[1] Within seconds, these images and sound bites flashed around the world, and besides reporting the news, the TV news crews helped the nation and the world share the emotions evoked by these incidents, from the exhilaration of King's dream speech to the grief over the King and Kennedy assassinations.

As such, TV often had a unifying and healing effect in times of uncertainty, upheaval, or tragedy, a role it has continued to play—acting as a kind of national focus of connection pulling everyone together. In fact, as TV historian Barnouw points out, nationally, many praised the TV industry widely, because they felt it not only informed but also "helped the nation pull together."[6]

But some had reservations that the dark side of TV outweighed the good in turning a tragedy into a national drama—a harbinger of the complaints of overzealous reporting and intrusiveness that would be expressed in reaction to the crime and gore sagas like the Simpson and Susan Smith sagas today. For example, after the Kennedy assassination, the American Civil Liberties Union accused the Dallas police of turning their procedures into something of a "theatrical production for the benefit of the television cameras." Moreover, they not only accused the officials in Dallas of "succumbing to television," but they "blamed television for creating the atmosphere and pressures to which the officials had succumbed."[6]

So from the very beginning, the structure and power of TV made it able to be both the very best and the very worst use of the communication medium possible. Mostly, though, during the 1960s, the social activists wanted the cameras with them documenting their activities, and they played to and used the cameras to help promote their agenda. After taking over the presidency, Lyndon Johnson continued this activist tradition.

changing america in the 1960s

Since I was attending U.C. Berkeley from 1961 to 1963 and moved to San Francisco in 1967 when the hippie transformation was starting, I was right in the thick of the changes. Often after seeing these events during the day, I would see them again on the evening news or on interview and talk shows. Though we now take all this coverage and talk for granted, at the time, this was very new, and all of this TV attention contributed to the idealism many felt about the promise of a new age of peace and brotherhood, brought about with the help of a newly media conscious younger generation. Though the protests were inspired by a great deal of anger over injustice, there was a feeling of hope for liberation and a new, better world. And what was unique was for the first time this social transformation was being documented and propelled along with the assistance of national TV.

Kennedy had set much of this TV coverage in motion with his strong support for this new medium. And now Johnson embraced it, too. As a result, the big news of the day—most notably the growing civil rights drama, the growing concern over Vietnam, and the spreading peace movement—turned into dramatic televised theater and talk events writ large, as well as news.

By 1966 and 1967, there was an outpouring of documentaries on these subjects, particularly on the heightening crisis in Vietnam that was convulsing the nation. Then in 1968, when Johnson was up for election and the dissension over the war erupted into riots and demonstrations on college campuses and in city ghettos, the TV news and talk shows featured this too, just as they did the tumultuous Democratic National Convention in Chicago that was the scene of protests in the streets.[1] Eventually, all of this turmoil contributed to Johnson's decision to step down, preparing the way for Nixon's rise to power—which subsequently turned into a battle with the press and talk TV.

Meanwhile, as this more serious side of TV news/talk coverage gained force, recording the social movements of the age for both commercial and noncommercial TV, the rest of TV as usual continued. Though some might consider it a "wasteland" as Minow had dubbed it, for others it was more popular than ever. Though the media spotlight was on the people who were demonstrating, marching, and protesting by the middle of the decade, most Americans were still living fairly ordinary lives going to work and raising their families. So they continued to look to TV as a source of relaxation and entertainment, even a "psychological refuge" or "fortress"[7] which presented a reassuring picture of the world, filled with images of success, the good comfortable life, and attractive stars.

Thus, to appeal to this broad mass audience, the growing concern with international and political events inspired some more escapist, entertainment fare. These included a wave of shows debuting in the mid- to late 1960s dealing with spies, foreign invaders, or beings from outer space, such as *The Man from U.N.C.L.E.*, *I Spy*, *Mission:Impossible*, and *Star Trek*, or comedy-fantasies like *I Dream of Jeannie*, *Nanny and the Professor*, and *Bewitched*.[1] The expenses—about $80,000 to $300,000 for a 30- to 90-minute show*—were so high because ratings were the name of the game. Idealists and activists might be on the frontlines protesting and trying to reshape a more just, compassionate America. But for most of TV land, the push was behind largely entertainment driven, escapist fair, which included a new wave of entertainment-

---

*According to Barnouw, the 30-minute *Bewitched* and *Hogan's Heroes* now had budgets of $80,000 or more per episode, while the 60-minute programs *Bonanza*, *Mission: Impossible*, and *Star Trek* cost $180,000 or more each, and the 90-minute programs were close to $300,000 to produce.

oriented celebrity-driven talk shows, commonly on late at night or early in the morning.

This push to lighter, entertaining fare is because more than ever, TV had become bottom-line driven. As a result, the more serious news and talk shows like *CBS Reports*, unless they were covering some dramatic upheaval, were of less interest to the program decision-makers, because they were not getting the numbers other types of programming were drawing. Then, too, some new types of popular programs were especially big money-makers, like the National Football League games, first televised in 1964 and 1965, and the daytime soap opera serials, which became big successes when they were expanded to 30 minutes each in 1964, instead of the 15 minutes that had been the usual length for the soaps on radio.[1]

In turn, these new entertainment talk shows prepared the way for similar—and sometimes the same shows—today. For example, in 1962, Johnny Carson took over the *Tonight* show from Jack Paar, and created a highly popular formula that combined an opening monologue, light talk with celebrity guests, and entertainment. Meanwhile, in the early mornings, *Today* continued to provide an amusing mix of chatter and variety entertainment oriented toward the female viewer—who was at the time largely a homemaker who turned to TV to accompany her early morning work at home.[1] These shows featured a magazine-like combination of interviews along with performances by entertainer guests, news bits, presentations, and audience participation—sometimes with the host going into the audience. In fact, audience involvement was a key element in the longevity of these shows. It helped people identify with and feel part of these shows, even when a particular joke or performance fell flat.[8]

The mid- to late 1960s was also marked by a proliferation of the audience-participation variety and game shows, which prepared the way for the *Donahue*-style talk shows that gained popularity in the 1970s. For example, Art Linkletter, previously on radio, continued to host his *House Party Show*, earlier called *People Are Funny*, directed toward a largely female audience during the day. Typically, the show began with a pan of audience members talking to each other as at a "house party," and then invited comments, questions, or advice from the audience. As an example, in one show, Linkletter invited a three-year-old girl to show off the techniques she learned from a dancing instructor, offered advice on how children can be taught though they have short attention spans, and invited several audience members to tell him the "silliest things they ever did."[9]

Some shows, first launched in the late 1950s or early 1960s, took this audience participation format even further, like *Stand Up and Be Counted!* Viewers were invited to send in letters describing their problems, and if chosen as a contestant, they related their story to the studio audience of about 200 people, who the host invited to share their advice. In shades of Donahue and future hosts who would roam through the audience, the host then passed the microphone around to audience members in the front row. Then, all audience members voted on what the person should do by "standing up and being counted." Home viewers were invited to write in with their advice as well, with a prize offered for the best advice. Typically, problems were presented in a simple, easy-to-vote way; for example, should a woman who had spent her life caring for her aging parents use her inheritance for travel for fun or invest in her brother's business and hope for a comfortable retirement?[8] The advice was usually to take the chancier road to gain more happiness—a reflection of the growing individualism and desire for freedom and self-expression characterizing the age.

Confrontation also became a form of entertainment in the late 1950s and 1960s—paralleling a growing combativeness in society. For example, some insult humorists, now gaining in popularity, such as Mort Sahl and Don Rickles got their own shows or became guests on other shows like *Tonight*. (And some have continued to appear today, like Don Rickles, on a recent *Letterman* show.)

The confrontative approach even became characteristic of some late-night interview shows, such as two programs hosted by Mike Wallace—*Nightbeat* and *The Mike Wallace Interview*. As talk show historian Wayne Munson describes it, this approach often resembled a cross-examination or grilling, such as a 1957 confrontation with Hugh Hefner over his decision to quit *Esquire* and launch *Playboy*. Wallace critically questioned Hefner about his character in founding such a magazine, considered risque for the times. In the 1960s, this confrontative tone continued, became even more intense, and set the stage for the still more combative talk shows that followed. As Munson relates, "Wallace's questions strove for a sensationalized intimacy.... Journalistic interview became a dramatic showdown."[10]

Soon other such shows followed—some using a host–guest confrontation format, like *Open End*, which later became the *David Susskind Show*, syndicated from 1960 to 1986. Among its first guests was the controversial Nikita Khrushchev in 1960. Another show in this format was the political program *Firing Line*, hosted by William F. Buckley, Jr., which began in 1966 and was syndicated through the mid-1990s. In the 1960s, in keeping with the spirit of the times, the show used a more aggressive debate format, in which a conservative Buckley encountered a more liberal or radical guest (such as the Black Panther Eldridge Cleaver), and a panel of questioners and moderator posted questions that were debated back and forth. Later, in the more conciliatory 1970s, the program switched to a more low-key format, in which Buckley and the guests engaged in a "more civil exploratory exchange of ideas," as Munson describes it.[11]

This was also a time when there were a number of political talk shows, generally in the smaller audience time slots like Sunday afternoons and late nights, such as *Town Meeting of the World*, an occasional CBS Sunday afternoon special in the mid-1960s. In · *Town Meeting*, several debaters on opposite sides of the Atlantic shared their views, and often the discussion concerned the latest turmoil in society, such as one 1965 program devoted to discussing whether the U.S. should honor its commitment in Vietnam.[8]

But perhaps the most combative of these shows—and the most widely syndicated, reaching about 85 markets at its peak— was *The Joe Pyne Show*. Pyne, formerly a radio host, was like the Howard Stern of his day, and the show thrived on outrage. At one time a Marine and a strident ultraconservative, Pyne invited guests on his show with a view to demean and insult them. And amazingly, they appeared and took his abuse, just as they still appear for abuse on the insult shows of today, for their 15 minutes of fame, as Andy Warhol would say. For example, in an especially notorious 1965 exchange that helped establish Pyne's reputation nationally, a black guest suggested that a race war was in the offing in light of the Watts riots. Pyne responded: "Let 'em come! I'm ready for 'em," and pulled out a gun to show he was.[12] Shades of G. Gordon Liddy advising listeners on how to be ready to gun down FBI agents if they barge into your house uninvited today. Many of these combative talk shows also pushed the limits of what could be talked about sexually. So now once-private behavior or tabooed words became aired nationally—another way of pushing the limits of what was publicly acceptable, much like the protestors were trying to change these limits in politics.[8]

Then, in the late 1960s, some of the daytime interactive and celebrity variety talk shows began, such as *Donahue*, launched in Dayton, Ohio, in 1967.[8] But these shows really came into their own in the 1970s, when the spirit of the age—and the attitude of the hosts—turned more sensitive and caring, not just confrontational.

In short, TV in the 1960s, including talk TV, was characterized by a kind of split consciousness that paralleled developments in society. On the one hand, there was a success-oriented America captured on most of TV, including the early morning and late night celebrity talk shows. But on the other hand, there was an angry, questioning and protesting America that was gaining increasing attention from the more serious news programs, specials, and combative talk-shows.[1]

Meanwhile, another development that would have a tremendous influence on talk TV today was just getting started in the 1960s, namely, cable TV, originally referred to as community antenna television (CATV). The technology for transmitting TV signals via cable was first developed with the birth of TV and was initially set up for radio back in the 1920s—primarily designed to connect homes unable to get regular signals, such as in isolated rural areas. Starting in 1964, entrepreneurs began to see the potential for putting programs on this system on a pay-per-view or subscription basis. There were already about 1000 of these systems around the country, and the entrepreneurs felt that instead of just receiving waves from other TV stations, these systems could become a source of original programming. Slowly, these entrepreneurs began to seek the necessary approvals, which sometimes involved engaging in political battles to fend off objections. For example, in California in 1964, a big campaign against "pay" TV kept TV free for a time.[1] But eventually the pressure to open up cable TV for original and pay broadcasting paved the way for many of the syndicated talk programs of today.

on into the 1970s and early 1980s: a time of transition and consolidation

By the end of the 1960s and into the 1970s and early 1980s, the basic trends from the 1960s continued. On the one hand, news and talk TV continued to document the big events of the age—like the 1968 shooting of Martin Luther King, Richard Nixon's election campaign, the first manned Apollo launch in 1969, and the Watergate scandal and hearings in 1972 through 1974. Since the precedent for covering such events in various ways—from straight news to theater, discussion, and debate—had been established, much talk TV became the most common way a majority of Americans got their news and understood daily events. People read less; they looked at newspapers less. Instead, TV news/talk increasingly showed them what was going on in America, though it tended to play up the turmoil, since it was more dramatic and because many journalists were sympathetic to these attempts to change America.

Concurrently, much entertainment-driven programming continued, including celebrity talk. However, now a new strain infused these popular programs. Beginning in 1969, there was more concern with relevance in all sorts of programs—from dramas and comedies to the talk shows, which were still mostly aired in the morning and late at night. As a result, both the content and look of programs in the 1970s became more reality based. Not only did the drama and comedy shows increasingly feature characters from black and other ethnic groups, but so did newscasts, special events, and panel discussion shows. At the same time, the hippie look associated with the flower children and protesters of the late 1960s began to go mainstream, and increasingly, performers, commentators, and talk show hosts and guests began to adopt this more casual look. Social problems and issues also began to hit prime time in shows like *All in the Family* (debuting in 1971), which featured a bigoted working-class Archie as a foil for attacking prejudice. In turn, these shows became a topic of conversation in the news and on talk shows.[1]

Another big change was the increasing prominence of women in nontraditional roles in telecasts and on news/talk programs. For example, some now became newscast correspondents, once an almost exclusively male preserve, and they weren't just limited to doing fashion or household news. Instead, now they were out there reporting all over—from the courthouse and Congress to the inner-city slum and factory.[1]

This was also the decade in which the popular daytime talk shows, primarily appealing to women, came into their own. Some had started in the late 1960s, and now they really flourished. Perhaps a key reason is that after a decade of upheaval and challenges to the establishment, the 1970s was characterized by a more inward, reflective turn. For some, this occurred because people became so frustrated at trying to change society that they gave up and looked closer to home for what they could change— themselves. Then, too, a new watchword of the age was "change" or "improve" yourself first; only then can you change things around you. In response, all sorts of workshops and therapies sprang up, especially in California, and people flocked to various programs and individual gurus for personal change or growth.

The new shows reflected this self-help attitude. Many shows still featured celebrities, led by big-name hosts like David Frost, Merv Griffin, Mike Douglas, and Dinah Shore. But now besides the mix of "controversy, confrontation, audience participation, and product promotion" that characterized these shows, the hosts encouraged more in-depth sharing of personal experience. Also, there was more interest in providing useful information that viewers could apply at home.[13] In effect, the popular therapy and self-help movements of the day were translated into a subject for popular TV shows. And just like women were especially prominent in these movements, so they were the main audience for this fare on TV.

Phil Donahue, in particular, led the way in creating the model for this new daytime women-oriented talk show as the sensitive, caring host. Through the 1970s his popularity grew, until by 1979, *Donahue* was *the* show to be on. What made it work so well, according to TV talk historian Munson, is that Donahue presented himself as:

> … the feminized, sensitive male who admits his insecurity ("folks, you've got to help me out") and "cares." He has a "boyish charm" and seems "nonthreatening" even while his show has been perceived as an explosive hybrid—"part psychodrama, part street theater, part group therapy … something live, spontaneous, rawly emotional, and *real*."[13]

It was, according to Munson, Phil Donahue's "nonthreatening, caring affect combined with a passionate intensity" that helped counterbalance the shock of many of his topics. As a result, he appealed to his largely female audience and was considered safe by the broadcast industry and his sponsors.[13] He also added to the show's popularity with his technique of roving through the audience and encouraging questions and feedback, thereby creating a bond with his audience that helped create the intense involvement everyone felt.

Then, seeing the popularity of this format, other shows began jumping on the bandwagon in the 1970s. And many continued into the 1980s—such as the *Sally Jessy Raphael Show* and local equivalents, like *AM/LA*, *AM/New York*, and *AM/San Francisco*.

Television news and talk even played a major role in helping to elect Jimmy Carter in 1976. When he decided to run, Carter was an outsider, having been a governor from Georgia and a peanut farmer. But he broke through by winning a few early primaries from local campaigning. Then the TV bandwagon began promoting him as a front-runner. At once, he was not only all over the news, as TV cameras covered his campaign stops, but he began talking informally and personably on talk programs to the nation.

It was powerful combination, for once TV had opened the door, his folksy down-to-earth approach was captivating. After a decade of turmoil, scandals in the Whitehouse, the growing menace of drugs, and other developments that provoked fear and anxiety, Carter's informal style and cheery optimism seemed so reassuring. In turn, TV news and talk helped spread that image across a tired, anxious nation. Then, when Carter won, TV was there to reinforce this warm and friendly image—from filming his inaugural walk to broadcasting his fireside chats in office. As Barnouw notes of Carter's symbolic walk:

> Jimmy Carter and his wife Rosalyn forsook the limousine inaugural drive down Pennsylvania Avenue to walk the final miles, smiling and hatless—a master touch of television symbolism, that seemed to announce the end of the imperial presidency.[14]

the beginnings of a backlash

Yet, in reaction to the growing power of TV, there were the stirrings of a backlash. Newton Minow had first alluded to this danger of TV as a "wasteland" back in 1961. But now in the late 1970s and early 1980s, the reaction against it grew, in part because the broadcasting industry had passed a number of milestones, generating some reflection. For example, in 1976 and 1977, NBC and CBS celebrated their 50th birthdays—dating back to their origins with the birth of radio. Also, in 1976, the Museum of Broadcasting was launched in New York, and the telephone itself was 100 years old.[1]

But as popular and powerful as TV had become, the big criticism was that it was so influential and as a result was undermining all sorts of American institutions, instead of living up to its early promise to inform, uplift, and inspire. Such an attack would be lobbed later at the talk shows of the 1990s; but now the target was TV generally. Critics began to complain that children were spending too much time on TV, with the result that their parents, teachers, and other authority figures in the community were losing influence. Critics expressed the fear that TV was contributing to the dumbing down of America, leading to a declining interest in reading, since TV viewing was so simple. Viewers had no need to learn anything—just watch. As a result, a growing concern was that we were in danger of becoming a nation of zoned-out "couch potatoes"—a cry that became especially shrill after Jerry Mander published his book *Four Arguments for the Elimination of Television in 1978*. Since then Mander is, in fact, still fighting, though now much of this argument has shifted toward accusing talk TV in particular of contributing to the dumbing of America—not just TV generally.

In turn, one reason for these developments is that TV was increasingly bottom line-oriented, as program directors seeking to attract sponsors, went after the most popular demographics for advertisers, as reflected in the Nielsen ratings. At one time, these ratings only described the size of the viewing public. But in the 1970s, demographics became a way to break down this audience into segments, and then, as now, the advertisers were attracted to younger viewers, who were more eager, impressionable buyers.[1]

As a result, much programming was geared to this primarily under-50s market. And soon programmers segmented this demographic further into male and female audiences and targeted programming, with the accompanying ads from sponsors, to these groups. For example, they developed action-oriented programs and sports shows for males, who might be interested in cars and sporting goods, whereas they pitched much of daytime TV, such as the afternoon soaps, to women in the cities, who were the big buyers of mass marketed products in supermarkets and drugstores— like makeup, food, and snacks.

Meanwhile, the growing critique of TV was fueled by the parlous state of non-commercial or public TV, which was regarded to be TV's "Great White Hope"—the source of all that was good, informative, educational, and uplifting on TV, such as offered by the more serious talk shows like *The News Hour with Jim Lehrer* and serious documentaries like *Nova* and *National Geographic* features.[1] But with all of the funding appeals on public TV stations to get matching funds for federal support, it was obvious public TV was struggling. Though it was increasingly able to get corporate funding for noncontroversial cultural topics, like shows about nature, now a major staple of public TV, it became more and more difficult to put on the more controversial issues-oriented shows. There were some. But more and more funding went to programs that were comfortable and safe—a trend that continues today. It was much the same as the problem faced on public radio, perennially short of funds, too.

the world of the mid-1970s and 1980s

Thus, by the mid-1970s and into the 1980s, TV had largely fallen into a split pattern. One type was a bottom line-driven commercial TV targeted to hit the most favorable demographic groups; the other was a struggling noncommercial public TV that had most of the educational and serious TV talk, but little of the audience.

For the mainstream audience, commercial TV had become segmented by day-parts and demographic groups into several types of entertainment and escapist-oriented programming. The most popular programs included occasional special movies, family sitcoms, simple action-driven dramas, and afternoon soaps; and characters were typically larger than life, many with superhuman powers, because the demographic data seemed to favor these. For example, some shows that debuted in the mid-1970s and thrived with these "super" characters included *The Six Million Dollar Man* (launched in 1973), *The Bionic Woman* (1976), *Charlie's Angels* (1976), and *Starsky & Hutch* (1975).[1] As Barnouw describes this phenomenon:

> Man and his products could repair all the deficiencies of nature.... Television supermen and superwomen did not fail: day after day they overcame mysterious enemies and saved themselves as well as the universe from disaster.[15]

At the same time, the most popular talk shows were celebrity driven or much like interactive game shows, in that they featured audience participation and hosts who encouraged people to share personal topics. The programs weren't as revelatory as today, but they were moving in that direction.

Meanwhile, there was a growing dance between the push to sex and violence in these shows—packaged as romance and domestic conflict in the shows primarily for women, as lust and aggression in the shows primarily for men—and the opposing forces of morality and decency. It's an opposing tension much like that today. For example, in the mid-1970s, in response to the threat of Congressional regulation, pressed by Senator John Pastore who chaired the Senate Communications Subcommittee and FCC Chairman Richard E. Wiley, the National Association of Broadcasters created a "family viewing" or "Family Time" period from 7 to 9 p.m. Eastern time. Supposedly, tamer programming would be concentrated then, while other time slots could have more "adult-oriented fare." But then, much like today, free speech advocates protested, such as the Writers Guild of America which sued, opposing the restrictions on First Amendment grounds. Finally, in 1976, the support of industry writers and producers convinced Federal District Judge Warren J. Ferguson to decide that it was up to the networks to voluntarily decide individually if they wanted to adopt such a policy, though the NAB or FCC couldn't require it by law. Still, whether or not such limitations for family viewing were required, much of mainstream commercial TV did adopt a policy of playing it safe, while titillating the audience with violence and intimations of sex and sexy talk.[15]

the new wave of talk in the 1980s

In the 1980s, this trend toward openness and revelation, combined with increasing doses of sex and violence continued in all sorts of shows, including talk. As today, these shows seemed to increasingly push against the edge. The desire was to be even more "real," "more honest," "more cutting edge." For some shows, like the *Morton Downey, Jr.* show in the tradition of Joe Pyne, the revelations came through stare and scream-down confrontations with the guests and demeaning insults by the host. In others, revelations resulted from the host drawing out the guest to make heart-to-heart confessions, often revealed for the first time on national TV—the approach of the *Donahue-* and *Sally Jessy Raphael*-type shows.

In a decade that so honored success, the bottom line pressure to increase ratings and build audiences was more important than ever. So these shows often featured especially tantalizing and controversial topics during the May and November sweeps when the major biannual ratings were scored.

doing the tv talk show circuit

I was on a series of these shows in the mid-1980s, because I had written a book called *Erotic Power*[16] about people exploring what was considered an unusual life-style: playing with erotic dominance and submission (D & S). Starting in October and November 1985, I was on *AM/San Francisco*, CNN, *Hour Magazine*, *Sally Jessy Raphael*, *AM/New York* and *LA*, and *Donahue*.

My experience was much like being on many popular talk shows today. The show was divided into short segments of about 5–7 minutes interspersed with commercial breaks, and commonly I was on for two or three segments. While several of the shows used the more straightforward host–guest interview format (CNN and *Hour Magazine*), others were more interactive, like most popular shows today: the hosts led off with a few questions, and then invited audience members and sometimes national callers to ask questions and make brief comments. Then, like a coach or pep team leader, the host was all over the audience revving up enthusiasm, and then like a conductor, he selected particular participants to orchestrate the tone and direction of the show.

In turn, the audience members and callers seemed much in tune with the attitude of the host, perhaps because the program attracted people with similar views and values. For example, when I was in San Francisco on the *AM* show, with a few representative members of the local D&S community, the comments from callers were largely tolerant, and some callers even shared their own personal experiments of D&S with their partner. But on *Sally Jessy Raphael*, the audience members who asked questions, like Sally Jessy Raphael, asked more psychological probing questions, such as "Why are you doing this?" And on *Donahue*, with a more conservative audience, the questioning was more adversarial, in part because the producer had lined up a group of fairly strange-looking people for the panel, rather than the more professional and business participants in this activity I had interviewed for my book.

the developments in talk in the 1980s

My own experience in the 1980s reflected the general trend to target these big-celebrity-driven talk shows to a younger audience of 18–49-year-olds, especially the female viewer, interested in more trendy and titillating subject matter. And through the 1980s the *Donahue* show was the leader—on 215 stations by 1980, and even more as the decade wore on. Sponsors liked these viewers because they were better consumers, so the topics were chosen accordingly—and the style of the show became faster-paced, snappier, with more audience participation, a forerunner to the Ricki Lake, MTV style of talk today.[8]

As these shows grew in popularity in the early 1980s and increasingly incorporated bits of daily news with talk, programming executives perceived a growing interest in information programming generally. Thus, more and more of these programs combined news, features, and talk, presented in an entertaining way—and soon a new name was applied to this programming mixing documentary information and entertainment, namely, "reality" programs. Among the most popular were *Real People* and *That's Incredible!*[8]—a kind of 1980s' forerunner to programs like *Hard Copy*, *Inside Edition*, *American Journal*, and others of today.

Two key factors contributing to the growth of these shows

were economics and technology. Economically, they were much less expensive than the dramatic shows, which required scripting, paid actors, and rehearsal time. Instead, the talk shows just required one or two hosts who could quickly respond to the day's guest list, along with a booker or producer (or staff of bookers and producers as these shows grew) to line up the guests—an average cost of about $25,000–50,000 per half hour. Such shows could quickly be put together and taped for national distribution in a day or two; or even broadcast live to permit call-ins and taped for later replay,[8] such as the *Donahue* show I was on. At the same time, the growing use of satellites, cable stations, and syndication organizations made it increasingly feasible to launch these shows and sell them to stations, whether or not the networks were interested.

During the 1980s, the typical guests for these audience participation shows were a mix of celebrities, ordinary people drawn into the headlines of the day, and experts knowledgeable about a topic (many on book tours with a book to plug like myself). In turn, to support these shows, as well as like talk programs on radio, an increasing number of reference materials, like directories with guest bios, appeared. Typically, these were paid for by the prospective guest—some of which I was in myself. For example, one such directory, started in 1984 and now in its 12th edition, is *The Yearbook of Experts, Authorities and Spokespersons*, which began with 48 pages and 68 listings—and grew to 912 pages and 1540 listings in 1994.[17] Another, published three times a month, is the *Radio–TV Interview Report*, started in 1986. These guides are sent to show producers and bookers in the hopes they might find an appropriate guest, generally an expert on some subject, to be on the show.

But while these guides provided a resource for many of the more serious guest experts, the trend through the 1980s was for the shows to increasingly look for the unusual, the bizarre, the real person with a problem. Why the fascination? Perhaps it was a reflection of a society increasingly coming apart at the seams, a result of growing breakdowns in the family, in educational institutions, in the criminal justice system, and in the inner cities—and more and more people felt alienated and had problems in relationships. But for whatever the reason, increasingly the audience, and therefore the show producers, were interested not just in ordinary people with run-of-the-mill difficulties, but people encountering especially difficult or unusual problems or having unusual life-styles, backgrounds, or relationships. It was the beginning of tabloid TV—a trend that has mushroomed in the 1990s.

An early precursor was *PM Magazine*, which began in the mid-1970s. Then in 1981, *Entertainment Tonight* was launched, which bounced around on different networks for its first few years. Its initial focus was on celebrities, especially those in the news and/or in trouble. But more and more documentaries and interviews with everyday people in the headlines or in trouble were added—a formula featured in *A Current Affair* and *Inside Edition*, both of which began in the late 1980s and soon became very popular (at one point among the top ten syndicated shows[8]), though *A Current Affair* was canceled at the end of 1995—perhaps a victim of the backlash against these shows.

The mid-1980s also marked the rise of a number of the prime-time news and documentary shows, many of which are still on—or were on until recently—such as *20/20*, *60 Minutes*, *48 Hours*, *Saturday Night with Connie Chung* (later becoming *Eye to Eye* until Chung was dropped by CBS in 1995), and *Prime Time Live*.[8] Such shows try hard to distinguish themselves from the more sensational tabloids—and when I wrote to the producers for interviews, indicating I was writing a book on talk shows, they wrote back claiming they weren't talk shows; rather they were documentary or news shows.

Though I would certainly consider interview and news talk programs a form of talk, perhaps a reason these shows sought to distinguish themselves is because talk shows today have gotten the lightweight reputation of the late-night and afternoon chat and variety shows. However, it has become harder and harder to draw clear lines, in that these shows mix a variety of talk elements in varying combinations—news, documentary, interviews, commentary, panels, discussion, film clips, and so on. Just about the only thing the documentary hosts don't do is rove through the audience and have on-the-spot audience questions and call-ins (although Ted Koppel made a brief exception when he was interviewing Phil Donahue about his recent decision to retire after 29 years and went around the audience to select a few guests).

In any event, through the 1980s and into the 1990s, the tone of these talk shows has become increasingly confrontational, gossipy, scandal oriented, shrill, fast paced, and strongly confessional. It's as if people are seeking support and absolution on national TV for their increasingly disjointed, alienated, and dysfunctional lives. Or alternatively, people are eager to see others attacked and browbeaten, making the viewers feel better because they see that others have problems, too—especially the fallen celebrity in trouble.

For example, from 1987 to 1989, Morton Downey, Jr. launched his late-night insult-the-host show, using an image of a big mouth as a logo, which at its peak aired on about 70 stations. Much like his predecessor Joe Pyne on radio and later on TV, Downey sought to appeal to his audience's feelings of anger—in contrast to the more feminized, confessional type of talk shows then proliferating during the day like *Donahue*, *Oprah*, *Sally Jessy Raphael*, and *Geraldo*. He did so by adopting the "rude" political talk show format so popular on radio for TV. He sought to encourage angry, loud, aggressive audience participation, seeking to appeal especially to males, with the result that he was often yelling and screaming at his guests. And if he didn't like what someone said, he would yell at them: "Zip it!"

For a time, his show was quite effective, as well as controversial, and he attracted a mostly male audience from Manhattan and the surrounding boroughs to provide an active cheering section, who sometimes sounded like guys giving a Bronx cheer at a baseball game. To some extent, he did try to deal with some serious relevant current issues, such as drugs and homelessness. But his strident tone tended to trivialize and polarize these issues, turning the discussion of the topic into something of a prizefight in a sports arena, rather than a serious political debate or town meeting. Eventually his mix of sports, political debate, and a participatory talk show with him moving around the audience and sometimes calling on guest experts proved too volatile a mix. There were just too many angry hostile explosions, and finally his assaultive, loudmouth style offended enough people that his show was canceled after two years.

By contrast, the mix of titillation, scandal, emotional confrontation, and confession, typified by *Geraldo*, *Oprah*, and *Sally Jessy Raphael*, proved much more long-lasting and spawned another generation of these programs in the 1990s. Many—like *Rolonda*, *Ricki*, and *Vicki!* (canceled in 1994)—had one-name hosts that underlined the intimacy of the host–guest–audience–viewer relationship on these programs.

In the tradition of *Donahue*, these shows thrived on unpredictability, even chaos, with the host acting as a kind of group facilitator, cheerleader, religious confessor, and sometimes reporter, all rolled into one. While celebrities sometimes appeared, the staple of these programs became the audience member or invited guest with special problems, unusual experiences, or an expertise in some area of interest. Then, once the on-air lights went on, virtually anything could happen. In fact, the hosts encouraged this possibility to keep the viewers tuning in to find out what. But there was little concern with how the participants felt about the experience after the show was over, at least until a murder of one participant after a confrontation of two men on *Jenny Jones* in 1995 triggered some industry soul-searching. But afterwards, it seems like it was back to business as usual, since when I watched about three dozen of these shows in the fall of 1995, as will be described in Chapter 11, it didn't seem like much had changed.

As a year or two earlier, the participants and guests were commonly treated much like a programming commodity. The producers' concern was getting them to appear on the show and make it exciting for the viewers, thus keeping ratings up. Then, after the show was over, the participants and guests could, like everyone else, go home. It's an approach I saw firsthand when I was a guest on the now-syndicated *Jerry Springer* show, when it was first starting in Cleveland in 1992. I had recently published a book *Resolving Conflict* on the techniques for doing that, and I was invited to be the expert for a program on "Families that Fight." The producers had lined up three couples or families to be on the show, and they planned to have three segments of about 15 minutes each between commercials for the guests to air their gripes. After each group had shared their woes, I would give some instant advice on what everyone should do.

Unfortunately, the best laid plans soon unraveled, as I discovered after I arrived. I found the producers desperately conferring back and forth to decide what to do. Apparently, one fighting couple consisted of a husband and wife who argued every day; and on this day, after a big blowup, the husband decided he didn't want to go on the program and he walked out when the limo came to pick him up. All efforts to placate him had so far failed. Meanwhile, a second problem was that some local groups had been invited, but the producers discovered they didn't have enough people to fill the audience. Plus those who had come were largely middle-aged or over. So the producers were in a panic about this too small and too old audience. Unfortunately, at this late hour, there didn't seem to be enough time both to find more people for the audience and to get another feuding couple.

Ultimately, they decided to give two segments to one of the families with the most difficult problem (a dispute that had led the two sides of the family to stop talking to each other). Then, that decision made, several producers set out to corral an audience by stopping people walking by on the street. Somehow by the time of the show, they had managed to pull enough of an audience together, and with the camera crew instructed to shoot tightly to make the audience look fuller than it was, we were ready to go.

The program began with the members of the two "feuding families" sharing their problem and reasons. Then, I gave some advice, although it was hard for me to see how two minutes of suggestions could resolve problems that had been festering for years and involved many complex issues. But as I had been coached, I broke in from time to time over the uproar with a few 30-second sound bites of advice. Finally the last on-air light went off and the credits rolled.

Afterwards, we were all escorted back to the green room and given instructions on where to find the taxis to take us to the airport. Then, with a quick goodbye to everyone, the hosts and producers were out the door. The show was over, and they were on their way home. As for the guests, the man and woman in one feuding couple were still yelling at each other, and the two sides of the feuding family were seated glaring at each other on opposite sides of the room. They hadn't seen each other for several years until brought together for this show, and it was apparent that after the show they would not be seeing each other again. As we waited for taxis in front of the building, when I asked one woman if she had gotten any ideas from the program to help her overcome the conflict, she launched into an angry tirade against the other side of the family—just what I urged family members not to do on the show. And so, after a brief time on syndicated TV, the guests were on their own again.

Only later, after the *Jenny Jones* incident, would hosts and producers become increasingly concerned about whether their guests, who had just been involved in an intensely emotional or confrontative experience on TV, might perhaps need some de-briefing or follow-up to deal with their experience. But for now, they were generally considered just another part of the info-entertainment ratings game. At least I got the chance to plug my book.

notes

1. Erik Barnouw, *Tube of Plenty: The Evolution of American Television*, New York: Oxford University Press, 1990.
2. Barnouw, pp. 273–274.
3. Barnouw, p. 339.
4. Barnouw, p. 299.
5. Barnouw, p. 300.
6. Barnouw, p. 337.
7. Barnouw, p. 403.
8. Wayne Munson, *All Talk: The Talkshow in Media Culture*, Philadelphia: Temple University Press, 1993.
9. Munson, p. 53.
10. Munson, p. 58.
11. Munson, p. 59.

12. Munson, p. 60.

13. Munson, p. 61.

14. Barnouw, pp. 464–465.

15. Barnouw, p. 473.

16. Gini Graham Scott, *Erotic Power*, New York: Citadel Press, 1983.

17. *The Yearbook of Experts, Authorities and Spokespersons*, published by Broadcast Interview Source, 2233 Wisconsin Avenue, N.W., Washington, DC 20007. (202) 333-4904.

chapter ten

making it big
barbara, oprah, ricki, and the late-night shift

just as radio has a few superstars, so too has TV talk developed its own, and most have popular biographies written about them. Since TV is so powerful and visible, it has even more and even bigger superstars. Also, unlike radio, where the audience, callers, and superstars are predominantly males, TV has a mix of big stars—primarily female hosts on the afternoon shows which appeal mainly to women, and male hosts on the late night shows with a more mixed audience. Today, the biggest stars of daytime TV include Oprah and Ricki—commonly called by their first names only, which promotes a feeling of intimacy with their audience. As for prime-time and late-night TV, among the biggest stars are Barbara Walters and David Letterman, and recently Jay Leno and Larry King (transferring his popularity on radio to TV) have joined the pantheon. These stars—talk TV's equivalent to Hollywood's A-list—are the ones who have the bios written about them (or now in the works in Leno's case), and they receive the most attention in the media, particularly in the tabloids.

And then there is the more everyday stardom of the many other hosts, who are variously rising and falling in the TV firmament, depending on the popularity of their shows—stars like Ted Koppel, Kathie Lee Gifford, Jenny Jones, Sally Jessy Raphael, Montel Williams, and others. Until recently, Phil Donahue would have certainly been on the A- or B-list, but after 29 years in the business, his show began losing markets and his syndication deal was cut back in 1995, so in January, 1996, he decided to retire from the talk show world.

Just as I asked about the radio superstars, how did these TV superstars break through? What made them so successful? To look at this, I've chosen the stories of four of the biggest stars, namely, Barbara Walters, Oprah Winfrey, Ricki Lake, and David Letterman. If the stories of Larry King and Howard Stern were not a part of the earlier discussion of the radio superstars, I would have included them here. And the only reason I haven't included Jay Leno, whose *Tonight Show* has recently topped David Letterman in the late-night rate wars, is that he only recently joined "the group" and his bio is just being written. So here I'll focus on the Big Four.

the big breakthrough: the story of barbara walters

Barbara Walters's breakthrough is quite amazing, since she made it at a time when women had not yet gained acceptance as talk show hosts or news anchors—beginning her ascent in the early 1960s. In addition, she had the handicap of a slight speech impediment, and initially had a fairly chilly shy personality that made her seem aloof and inaccessible—not generally traits one would associate with being a charismatic host.

But what made the difference for Walters is her strong goal-centered outlook. Once she decided what she wanted, she threw herself into achieving that goal through hard work, determination, aggressiveness, and persistence. In addition, she had some important personal connections arising from her family background, schooling, and social ties, helping to open doors for her to big-name celebrities. And she had a driving curiosity about people that helped her get these big names to open up to her, so she became known for her ability to get the interviews others couldn't.

in the beginning

In *Barbara Walters: An Unauthorized Biography*, author Jerry Oppenheimer describes her story.[1] Early on, Walters seemed an unlikely candidate for success, since she grew up very insecure and shy because of her family background. She was born in 1929 at the beginning of the Depression, and her life was full of extreme financial ups and downs, for her father was a vaudeville booking agent at a time when vaudeville was disappearing with the rise of the talkies. After he went into the nightclub business, there were periods of booms and busts. At times, he provided the family with an extremely lavish life-style; at others, they had to cut back as a result of financial reverses, including a bankruptcy when Walters was in her mid-20s and a chain of nightclubs he tried to start went bust.[1]

Still, Walters had certain advantages that helped to prepare the way for her later success, once she decided what she wanted. Despite the sporadic financial difficulties, her father sent her to some of the best private schools, including the Fieldston School in New York. And when she went to college at Sarah Lawrence, Walters began to make friends with powerful wealthy people. Also, in college, after briefly exploring becoming an actress, she focused on literature and writing, which helped prepare her for the writing jobs she got in television which led to on air opportunities.[1]

After she graduated in 1951, her family connections helped open doors and fueled her ambitions to become a TV star. After taking a secretarial course and getting a part-time job with an ad agency, where she did some copywriting, she was attracted by the glamour of the growing TV field and asked her father to help her get a job at a local station. His show business connections helped. He called an important industry contact, Theodore B. Cott, vice president and general manager of WNBT in New York, which was owned by NBC, and asked Cott if he could find anything for his daughter. He could and did. He sent her to the station's publicity, promotion, and advertising department, and in early 1952, Walters got her first TV job—writing press releases for various programs. It also helped that Cott was attracted to Walters, and they began seeing each other, which helped introduce Walters to key New York media people—some for whom she later worked or who helped her get other jobs, such as Tex McCrary and Jinx Falkenburg.[1]

the keys to success

Once on the job, Walters began to demonstrate her ability to get a story, though initially just a writer. For example, soon after she arrived at WNBT, there was a newspaper and cab strike in New York, and the publicity department where Walters worked helped gather news about it. Walters managed to set up an exclusive interview with a taxi association official and find a photo of him—an early coup that impressed station higher-ups.[1]

Walters's personal connections helped, too. Though she had little experience, Ted Cott, who she was still dating, arranged for her to act as the "producer" for a live 15-minute daily program for kids, called *Ask the Camera*. It was mostly a gofer job in which she and a helper selected letters from kids for the host to read and comment on, but Walters used this opportunity to get a brief story about herself as a producer in *TV Guide* in May, 1953, which described her as one of the "bright young people in responsible jobs" in television.[2]

Though she was out of a job by 1954 after the program was canceled, and spent the next couple of years as a married high-society woman going to a round of social activities, her WNBT experience helped when she got ready to go back to work. After a month of looking, she landed a job at CBS's *Morning Show*, a news and special events program, which was struggling to compete with the more popular *Today* show, hosted by then reigning superstar Dave Garroway. Walters's job was primarily to be a guest-getter, and she was good at getting on the phone and finding interesting guests.[1]

The job helped hone her talents and work toward becoming an on-air personality. As Oppenheimer describes it:

> Barbara had found a home in television.... She loved the excitement, the immediacy, the freneticism, the deadlines. It suited her personality.... She relished being an insider.... Interesting, powerful men—the type to whom she always was drawn—were paying attention to her. It was like joining a family where she felt loved and wanted.[3]

Thereafter, Walters's ability to thrive was helped by a combination of ability, hard work, getting publicity and recognition, and
allying herself with powerful people who could help her get high-
power interviews or advance her career in the competitive TV
news/talk world. Importantly, too, she created programs that
appealed to the target market she wanted to reach. And her timing
was ideal, because the mid-1960s and 1970s was a time when
women were becoming more vocal about equal rights and some
barriers to women were coming down. As a result, when the doors
began to open, Walters was right there to march through, and she
used her femininity in a soft, seductive way that was appealing, not frightening to the audience and the TV powers making
decisions.

For example, soon after she got her *Morning Show* job, Walters, who had a strong interest in fashion, proposed that the producers add fashion segments to the show, and after they agreed,
Walters produced the segments, and sometimes did the commentary. Female viewers loved these shows, which were inexpensive
to produce.[1]

At the same time, Walters used her social graces to make the
all-important celebrity and industry connections that helped her
to get the high-powered guests. And as she gained increased
recognition for doing this, she had more power to attract more and
bigger celebrities.[1]

Then, too, Walters early on showed an ability to get the interview or story that impressed producers and directors. For example, in 1956, after the crash of two ocean liners—the Swedish
Stockholm and Italian *Andrea Doria*, Walters and a producer brought
back a major scoop, which included bringing many survivors to
the studio for interviews.[1]

Also, her ability to make important connections led to opportunities later. For example, after the *Good Morning Show* folded in
1957 and Walters was out of the business working in PR for several
years, when she tried to get back into TV, a former CBS staffer,
Fred Freed, who knew her from their CBS days together, hired her
as a writer for the *Today* show. Getting onto *Today* was a major
coup, since it was the biggest morning show of the day. Though

Walters started as a lowly writer on a freelance basis paid slightly over Writer's Guild minimum scale—then about $300 a week—she used that opportunity to gain more exposure and craft a more polished professional persona. For instance, she began looking for stories she could do on camera herself to gain more public awareness, such as visit to Revlon's midtown Manhattan salon, where she personally demonstrated a total make-over, appearing with a towel around her head, her face covered with cosmetics, and her body wrapped in a big sheet.[1]

She also quickly mastered the art of office politics, getting to know everyone on the staff—from directors to camera operators to other writers—who might help her later.[1] And the luck factor contributed, too, since she joined *Today* at a time when it was undergoing major upheavals, as its host, Dave Garroway, was on his way out. So she was in on the ground floor, as *Today* shifted toward becoming more of an entertaining news/talk show than the variety/entertainment program it was under Garroway and chimp J. Fred Muggs. Then, too, she already knew the overhauled *Today* show's new producer Shad Northshield from her days at CBS, and he made Walters a full-time staff writer. He also supported some of her suggestions for stories that gave her on-air exposure, such as a story about bicycling in Central Park and another on a big Paris fashion show featuring the latest Dior and Maxime collections.[1]

breaking through the barriers

Then in 1962, Northshield assigned Walters her first big story—accompanying First Lady Jacqueline Kennedy on a 27-day goodwill visit to India and Pakistan. It was an international story filled with glamour and pageantry, opening doors to the Washington political scene, and Walters brought to it the gossipy "woman's touch" that became characteristic of many of her celebrity interviews, such as when she talked about what Jackie was wearing and how her hair looked. And by using her connections and some effective theatrics, Walters was able to score a personal interview, despite Jackie having promised an exclusive interview to her close friend Joan Braden, with the *Saturday Evening Post*. Walters had appealed to Jackie's social secretary Letitia (Tish) Baldridge, whom she had met when both were doing PR work, explaining that this was her big chance to break through and her career depended on getting the interview. Finally, after Baldridge presented her appeal, Jackie agreed to a brief interview.[1]

It was an incredibly important coup, which Walters used to create other opportunities, such as a *Good Housekeeping* article about Jackie's sister Lee Radziwill, whom she got to know better on the trip, resulting in her first byline in a national magazine.[1] And then she interviewed Jackie's close friend Joan Braden, who wrote the *Saturday Evening Post* article, on *Today*, talking about behind-the-scenes details of the tour. In turn, the show not only contributed to Walters's growing recognition and prestige, but her contact with Braden opened doors into the highest levels of Washington, including even Henry Kissinger.[1]

Then, a few months later, another breakthrough occurred, when another *Today* producer, Al Morgan, decided to make it more of an entertainment show to improve ratings, and the increased show business orientation was ideal for Walters because of her contacts and approach. Additionally, the show paired Walters from time to time with a new anchor, Hugh Downs, with whom Walters still works today on *20/20*. At first, Walters just did occasional on-air special reports, followed by a brief discussion with Hugh Downs. Then, at Downs's urging to management, Walters finally got her first contract as an on-air reporter, in part because she had an ability to work well with the film crews and tell a story well, and was willing to work long hours and do a good job. Plus, as Oppenheimer noted in his bio of Walters, she was good at office politics, or as he put it, Walters was "a brilliant corporate politician and gameswoman, with a talent for cultivating the right people."[4]

Then, when more doors opened, Walters was ready to step in, developing her own PR machine to further build her image with the American public. The next big break occurred in 1964 when the show's Today Girl interviewer slot as a kind of light-weight foil to

Hugh Downs opened up after actress Maureen O'Sullivan was dismissed for not being a strong enough interviewer. Walters, who had worked behind the scenes, writing most of the copy and questions for O'Sullivan, lobbied hard for the job, with a little engineered help from the media, including an article about herself by a *New York Post* TV columnist, stating that she was "being groomed for a more prominent role on the 'Today' show" after the O'Sullivan departure. Some even believe she phoned in the tip for the article herself.[5]

Then when she got the job, she put together a business management and PR team to turn her from a TV journalist into a star. Her first business agent, Ray Katz, negotiated a substantial salary increase—from a few hundred a week as a writer to about $800 weekly as a reporter. Also, he set up interviews and speaking engagements and hired her first personal publicist, the PR firm of Arthur Jacobs and John Springer, and the firm helped her get personal items in columns, feature stories, and other types of press attention. The goal was to get her name more widely known among the general public, not just *Today* viewers, and to the NBC brass. Then, presumably, this greater name recognition would help her move up the media ladder.[1]

As the strategy worked, it helped propel her to superstardom. In 1965, her first year as an on-camera personality, major features began appearing about her rapid rise from writer to on-air personality in the newspapers and mass magazines of the day, including *TV Guide* and *Life*. After this media attention triggered a small backlash from Hugh Downs and NBC executives, who felt the focus on Walters was eclipsing Downs, the show's main anchor, Walters turned off her PR machine. But by then the PR already had succeeded and her name was becoming well known, leading to further opportunities, including guesting on Johnny Carson's *Tonight* show.[1]

In turn, her increased prominence led to more high-visibility projects, status, and power. For example, soon after Gloria Steinem wrote about being a Playboy Bunny, launching her own career, Walters went to bunny school herself and talked about life as a bunny with Hugh Downs on *Today*. She also began doing more big celebrity interviews that became her specialty—with noted interviewees like Mrs. Rose Kennedy, Truman Capote, Princess Grace of Monaco, the First Ladies Mrs. Johnson and Mamie Eisenhower.[1]

Then, too, Walters's ability to move up the ladder was helped by good timing, since big opportunities were now starting to open up for women in broadcasting and she was there, ready to step in, with the help of her contacts, hard work, and media savvy, and do a high-quality professional job—a masterful combination of skill, personality, and luck. And later, her superstardom helped provide a lesson for those who followed on what to do to achieve stardom, too.

becoming a superstar

What turned Walters' growing visibility and power into superstardom? One key was her ability to develop ties with whoever was in power, opening doors to getting additional high-profile exclusives, which became Walters's niche in news talk over the next few years. Then, in the 1970s, she parlayed that specialty into the first million dollar contract for a journalist-turned-superstar.

In the late 1960s, when the country was convulsed with protests and debates over social issues, Walters likewise turned more serious in her interviews, such as interviewing Dean Rusk in 1969, after he resigned as Nixon's Secretary of State, which led to a front-page *New York Times* story, gaining Washington credentials, and bigger and bigger assignments—including covering Prince Charles's investiture as Prince of Wales in 1969. Adding to her growing reputation, Walters came out with her best-seller book in 1970—*How to Talk With Practically Anybody About Practically Anything*.[1] Today, just about anybody in the media gaining visibility gets a book deal, but at the time, her book was something of a first for a TV talk personality—and a model for future talk show hosts.

Though Walters's fast rise began to evoke criticism from some critics who still regarded her as a lightweight, her popularity still soared, and with the help of agent Lee Stevens, she negotiated a nonexclusive contract with NBC. So besides *Today*, she could do specials and news programs—among them a show called *For Women Only* (later called *Not for Women Only*) launched in 1971, which was the forerunner of the popular women-oriented shows like *Donahue* and *Oprah* in the 1980s. Some topics even sound like those of today, such as "Is the Family Dying?," though Walters did high-profile celebrity interviews, too. And the print media helped affirm her star quality, as when *Newsweek* did a 1974 cover story announcing: "Barbara Walters—Star of the Morning."[6]

Soon she became officially the cohost of *Today*, and after a couple more years of high-profile coups with world leaders, including Fidel Castro of Cuba and the then Shah of Iran, she got her million dollar contract with ABC. At the time, ABC was last in the race for network news ratings, and ABC saw hiring Walters as a way to enhance its own reputation. Plus it saw publicity value in making her the first female anchor, as well as being an interviewer.[1]

So the million dollar deal was struck—half paid by the news side, and half by the entertainment side for which Walters would do her glitzy celebrity talk specials. The news side, though, soon came in for criticism, since many journalists remained critical of her as a journalist, seeing her more as a personality, rather than a reporter. In fact, soon after her deal was announced the critics and comedians went to work. For example, the late comedian Gilda Radner of *Saturday Night Live* did a spoof of Walters being interviewed about her new million dollar job, in which she exaggerated Walters's muddy speech and slight lisp, resulting in Walters's new nickname "Baba Wawa" that made many viewers take her less seriously.[1]

But for all the furor and criticism about whether she was "worth a million," Walters thrived, and her deal prepared the way for other celebrity "journalists," many whom were more like entertainers than reporters. This development unnerved many traditional media journalists, like Walter Cronkite, who said he felt "the sickening sensation that we were all going under, that all our efforts to hold television news aloof from show business had failed."[7] Instead, as Washington columnist Charles Seib observed, it was a time when "the line between the news business and show business was erased forever."[8] And soon, other high-visibility reporters began to demand higher salaries and become stars, too.

Ironically, one of the early critics was Connie Chung, then working as a Washington correspondent for CBS. She remarked that Walters was just "an interviewer, a talk-show hostess," who "does specials, not reporting," whereas Chung and other journalists "actually cover stories and then go back and report them."[7] The irony is that about 20 years later, in the 1990s, Chung herself would become just "an interviewer and talk-show hostess," who encountered her own donnybrook after her infamous interview with Newt Gingrich's mother.

In any event, though there was a war of egos for a while between Walters and her coanchor Harry Reasoner on the *Evening News* after her debut in October, 1976, the specials helped save her. Besides having high-powered guests, like President-elect Jimmy Carter and his wife Rosalyn, which helped her gain even more power and prestige, her intimate, impertinent, gossipy questions in the interviews made them especially popular.[1]

In turn, the appeal of such questions to the audience contributed to the tabloidization of interview shows today. For example, one of her questions to Carter that was especially controversial was: "Do you sleep in a double bed or twin beds?" But again, Walters weathered the storm, as the ratings shot up; and her increasing power and prestige led to still more specials—50 by 1988—and to her new prime-time visibility as a contributor to *20/20* with Hugh Downs—starting in 1980. By 1985, she became the official cohost of the program, a spot she still holds today.

Her approach today is still to feature the high-profile celebrity subjects, though now the choice of these subjects reflects the tabloidizing of TV talk. Originally, Walters's big coups were getting world leaders, the superwealthy, and the movers and shakers in Washington and elsewhere to be on her show. But beginning in the 1980s, her celebrity roster changed as celebrity-hood increasingly became linked with crime and scandal. For example, in 1980, two of Walters's *20/20* interviews were with headmistress Jean Harris, who was convicted of murdering her lover, Herman Tarnower, the Scarsdale Diet doctor. And in the following years, other interview subjects included former Miss America Bess Myerson, who was acquitted in a big 1988 influence peddling case involving her boyfriend; Leona Helmsley, the hotel queen convicted of evading taxes in 1989; Donna Rice, whose Monkey Business boat photos with Gary Hart triggered the media storm that ended his presidential chances; and Fawn Hall, Oliver North's secretary, who was accused of helping him shred papers in the Iran Contra scandal.[1]

In turn, this shift to crime and scandal reflected the growing American appetite for sensationalism rather than serious commentary and discussion—and for seeing media superstars rather than more sober thoughtful leaders. And Walters's own success story illustrates this trend—both in the way she turned herself into a superstar and in the sort of subjects and stars featured on her show.

from poverty to prestige and power: the rise of oprah winfrey

Unlike Walters, who started out with a good education and powerful social and show biz connections, Oprah Winfrey had hardscrabble poverty beginnings. She could have easily ended up broke on the streets, not the highest paid woman on talk TV today. But like Walters, Winfrey had some important qualities going for her: one was a talent for speaking out and getting people to talk to her, and she had a focused dedication as to what she wanted to do, combined with lots of hard work to get there.

hard times beginnings

By now, through personal revelations on her show, tabloid accounts, and her bio, Winfrey's early struggles are well known. She was born in 1954 as the illegitimate daughter of a single mother who initially left her with her grandparents on a pig farm in Mississippi for the first six years of her life, where she grew up learning farm chores. She spent the next seven years mostly with her mother who was struggling to survive by working as a maid in Milwaukee, and had a brief stay with her more stable middle-class father and his new wife in Nashville. She returned to stay with them in Nashville for about eight years before she struck out on her own.[9]

Her years with her mother were ones of desperate struggle, along with abuse and experiences of rape and promiscuity. But when she finally moved in with her father, who owned a small grocery and barbershop, and his new wife, they had strict rules of conduct that led her to settle down and express her talents. As a result, in East Nashville High, she became active in drama classes and student politics. She even was elected student council president, running on a platform with great student appeal—"better food in the cafeteria and a live band at the school prom." Soon she was in demand for doing dramatic readings and speaking, such as from Margaret Walker's *Jubilee* story of a slave family at local church and civil groups—something she had first done when she lived with her grandmother and performed for church groups as a child.[9]

In 1970, at age 16, Winfrey developed her fierce determination to become someone, triggered by an invitation to give a recitation to a church in Los Angeles. While there, she took the Hollywood tour in which she passed by the handprints of stars at Grauman's Chinese Theater. When she returned home, according to biographer George Mair, she vowed to her father that "her handprints would someday be in the concrete courtyard" of the theater, too. From that point on, she was determined to "be somebody" and worked hard toward this goal.[10]

Among other things, while still in school, she entered beauty and popularity contests, acted in plays, and continued speaking to groups around town. She even won a number of contests, such as the Miss Fire Prevention Contest sponsored by radio station WVOL in 1971 (which she was the first black woman to win), and an Elks Club beauty contest, which gave her a four-year scholarship to Tennessee State. And she got her first broadcast job as a high school senior. She had gone to WVOL and persuaded one of the DJs to sponsor her in a local March of Dimes fund-raising walkathon and was back to collect the money. The DJ liked her voice and asked her to read some news copy off the Teletype, and after she did, he hired her as a part-time news reporter. She got $100 a week to do reports after school and on weekends, a substantial sum of money in those days.[9] Winfrey was on her way.

breaking into tv

The WVOL job led to her first TV job on WTVF—the CBS affiliate in Nashville—and she decided to drop out of Tennessee State University, feeling this was the opportunity she had gone to college to find. It also represented two firsts, as she was the first female and first black to become a newscaster in Nashville. She was only 19—and making $19,000 a year. Thus like Walters, Winfrey was early on accumulating a number of firsts in the industry, as well as focused on a career, rather than the social and political struggles of the day. Though it was a time when her peers were mounting campus demonstrations, biographer Mair notes that "Oprah was winning beauty contests and learning where to look when the red lights appeared on the camera." Or as Winfrey put it: "The other kids were all into black power. I wasn't a dashiki kind of woman."[11]

In time, her focus paid off, as she moved up from coanchoring the weekend news to becoming a weeknight coanchor in her three years at the station from 1973 to 1976; this at a time when Walters was breaking new ground for women in TV nationally with her million dollar ABC contract.[9]

Winfrey's WTVF job opened the doors to her next big move— to WJZ-TV in Baltimore for the next seven years. It soon became clear, however, that she wasn't a very good straight news reporter, because she brought too much compassion and emotion to her report. These qualities would later help transform her into a TV talk star. But at the time, these traits were considered liabilities.

For example, while covering a fatal house fire, she found it too hard to do the story, since the woman who survived the fire was grief-stricken at losing all of her seven children. Winfrey even urged her superiors not to broadcast the film, but they did, and as the tape ran, she cried along with the woman who lost her home. Then, too, instead of just reading the news copy straight, she ad-libbed using the more conversational style she had used successfully in Nashville. But the Baltimore station expected her to be slick and professional, so her own approach didn't fit well. However, with a six-year contract, she kept trying. She even, at the station's request, went to see a voice coach, who urged her to be tougher—to stop being so nice.[9]

Finally, in 1977, with a new station manager, Bill Carter, Winfrey got her first shot at talk TV which turned into a roaring success. Carter decided to try out Winfrey as a cohost on the new morning show *People Are Talking*, which was up against the syndicated *Donahue* show, then the top-rated talk show in the country. But despite the competition, Winfrey's freewheeling style and good chemistry with cohost Richard Sher made for an exciting show, which, tailored to the Baltimore market, soon trounced *Donahue* in Baltimore.[9]

The show was especially important for Winfrey, because it helped her develop and show off her unique style of listening with sincere interest and compassion, which helped her get close to audience members and viewers. As Mair points out:

> Commonly, broadcast interviewers ask a question and do not listen to the answers. They are either distracted by something else or thinking about the new question…. But Oprah listened closely to the guest and used the previous answer to delve deeper into the topic. That is her style to this day, and it works very well, for she communicates to the audience and the guest that she cares about what is going on in their lives.[12]

The *People Are Talking* show wasn't one that Winfrey could take national, because it was too focused on issues in Baltimore, where it thrived, and it helped Winfrey realize the synergy, energy, and emotion she could stir up with a live audience. Meanwhile, she kept working hard to perfect her approach to be the best talk show host she could be.[9]

Her style, though, was very different from Walters's cool, gossipy, probing style. Winfrey's compassionate, listening approach gave her a great appeal and power with the audience as "every woman's friend" or "an inquisitive neighbor" who wants to know and understands.[13] Whereas Walters was selling an inside look at celebrity, wealth, and power in America, Winfrey was appealing to the ordinary hard-working and often suffering person at the bottom and middle of American society.

moving on and going national

By the early 1980s, when Winfrey was ready to move on beyond Baltimore, she was clear about the kind of show she wanted to do and was good at. She wanted a bigger market with more prestige and more money, and after considering different cities, she decided to follow her *People Are Talking* producer to Chicago in January, 1984.[9]

At first, the station execs wanted her to do an *A.M. Chicago* format, featuring a mix of light talk, fashion notes, some tips on homemaking and cooking, and perhaps a guest. But after looking at local demographics, Winfrey concluded this was a basically white middle-class audience, and she felt she couldn't use that approach since she wasn't white, middle-class, a housewife, or much of a cook. Instead, what she felt a more workable format would focus on common interests in achieving personal fulfillment and good relationships with mates and children. And so she recast the program, using a frank "this is how things are" approach.[9]

The results were immediate. Within four weeks, the show went from last in its time slot to number one, and after three months, Winfrey had roundly beaten national star Donahue in the ratings—with about 250,000 to his 150,000 local viewers.[9] And thereafter, she began her rapid rise to the top of the national talk show heap.

What made her show so appealing was the close rapport she created by making herself seem one of the audience and by asking the personally revealing questions that audience members wanted to know. As biographer Mair notes:

Audiences related to Oprah because she was one of them and always came up with surprising questions or revelations. She startled everybody on her staff and in her audience by sympathizing with a child-abuse victim and revealing for the first time on the air that she had also been abused as a child. The reaction was electric.[14]

Although Donahue had started breaking this kind of ground by bringing in everyday guests who talked about personal and often controversial subjects, Winfrey took this even further. As she did interviews with ordinary people about real-life experiences, she turned her show into a kind of group-therapy session, in which people began to reveal the most personal and secret part of themselves. Though they might not have told anyone else, now they revealed these intimate self-glimpses on national TV. They talked about things like sex, incest, child abuse, prostitution, oppressive bosses, difficulties with diets, problems with self-esteem and low confidence.[9] It was fascinating and captivating to hear these stories—a kind of national catharsis for the participant as well as for many viewers who could share or sympathize with the particular problem or issue. In time, the show's success contributed to the trend to such programs today.

Meanwhile, Winfrey's business sense in packaging the program and taking advantage of other opportunities helped make her very rich—ultimately the richest woman in talk TV. One big opportunity came when one of the coproducers of *The Color Purple* visited Chicago in 1984, saw her show, and invited her to play "Sophia," a feisty woman who was abused by her husband and prison guards, because she was outspoken and forthright. When the film was released in December, 1985, its success and an Oscar nomination gave Winfrey even more national publicity, at a time when King World began to syndicate her show nationally. King World had gotten its start syndicating *Wheel of Fortune* and *Jeopardy*, and after seeing the rapid success of Winfrey's show, they invited her to be their third program—a deal that gave her 25% of the syndication proceeds. The show began nationally in September, 1986, on 138 stations, and grossed about $125 million—resulting in about $30 million after costs for Winfrey in 1986—and even more in the years ahead. By the following 1987–88 season, she was on close to 200 stations, with approximately 10 million viewers nationally. In 1988, Winfrey signed a five-year renewal with King World, and by 1993, not only was King World the top distributor of talk and game shows, but Winfrey's show had become its top show. In fact, she earned over $100–200 million from her show since it went into syndication in 1986.[9]

In turn, the show's popularity led to further national recognition through appearances on other shows, like David Letterman's, and it made her a kind of national imprimatur for the books and products of people who appeared on the show. Other talk shows, of course, do this, such as when an author comes to plug a book, an actor a film, or a manufacturer a product. But Winfrey was much better at doing this than other hosts because of the close rapport and trust she developed with her audience. For example, though diet and health author Callan Pinckney had trouble selling her book *Callanetics* and sold only a few thousand before appearing on the show, after a plug from Winfrey, book sales soared to over 300,000 within a few months, and Pinckney was invited onto other shows. Similarly, Winfrey's recommendation turned Marianne Williamson's book *A Return to Love* into a 1992 best-seller, selling over a million copies, and making Williamson a national celebrity.[9]

Through the mid-1990s, *Oprah* remained the top-rated TV talk program, and Winfrey was the TV host with the biggest earnings. For a time, in the late 1980s, she was in a close race with Donahue, who had been the reigning talk show king—he led in the morning, while Winfrey was tops in the afternoon, since the shows generally ran in different time slots.[9] But gradually, while Winfrey's numbers increased, Donahue's star began to fade, particularly after 1994, though now Winfrey has started to decline somewhat herself, as younger competitors, like Ricki Lake, have started to increase their own market share.

Ironically, perhaps a key reason for Winfrey's recent slow-down is her decision to take a higher road in the subjects covered, at a time when TV talk has become increasingly criticized for pandering to the worst instincts of the general public. The criticism has targeted these shows for featuring dysfunctional people and families having trouble coping, and for exploiting and humiliating them for public titillation, rather than seeking to inspire or help people feel better, which was the thrust of Winfrey's show when it began. Given this general lowering of talk show standards, since 1995, Winfrey refocused her show to pave a more inspiring, spiritual path and moved away from the more exploitive tabloid approach of many of the shows. But though her ratings dipped, Winfrey recently renewed her contract to continue her show for at least 2 more years (according to an April 9, 1996, phone call to the Research Department at the Oprah Winfrey Show).

In any case, Winfrey has been and still is a major force in shaping the many TV talk shows of today—particularly the morning and afternoon shows designed to appeal to women. Though her initial approach was directed toward inspiring self-help and therapy, her intimate confessional style and the types of topics covered helped pave the way for the tabloid style of much of talk today.

reaching out to new markets: the rise of ricki lake

While Walters and Winfrey may have risen to the top of talk by having a clear firm goal and determinedly working for it, Ricki Lake gained her success more by chance resulting from a management marketing decision—to reach out to a new untapped talk show market, namely, women from 18 to 34. By the early 1990s, when the number of new talk shows exploded, this was one group that was not really served, since the women watching daytime shows were generally older, and the late-night viewers were a mixed group. So when producers decided to do such a show and went looking for an actress to step into the host role they envisioned, Lake turned up at the right time. And within months her fast-paced irreverent show for this market became a super success. It was the number one favorite among 18- to 34-year-old viewers, and a major challenger for *Oprah*'s number one spot.

How did it happen? Where did Ricki Lake come from?

Though she had a warm, effusive, outgoing personality and natural gift for performing from an early age, her background is not one that would immediately spell talk show success.

beginnings

Being part of the increasingly visible "Generation X" helped her reach out to this market. Lake was born in 1968 and grew up in Hastings-on-the-Hudson, New York, a suburban town north of New York City. In contrast to Walters's high-society upbringing and Winfrey's impoverished beginnings, her background was middle-class ordinary. Her father ran his own pharmacy, while her mother took care of the house. But while her parents had typical middle-class dreams of college and an ordinary 9-to-5 job for her, from an early age, Lake was attracted to a show business career as an actress, and she showed a strong determination to do whatever she could to get that.[15]

From the beginning, Lake showed an ability for performing. By 5, she was able to play the piano and read sheet music, and she soon began putting on performances for her family. For example, according to biographer Robert Waldron, she "entertained her family by grabbing a candlestick, planting her feet in the middle of the living room and belting out songs."[16] She loved pleasing others by putting on a show, and at age 5 she announced her decision to become an actress. Initially, since she loved the programs she saw on TV, her goal was to be a TV star, such as an actress in a series like *The Brady Bunch*, then popular in reruns.[15]

By 13, she even gained her first entry into acting, when she answered some ads for auditions in *Backstage* and *Show Business*, and got featured singing roles in two low-budget off-Broadway reviews—*The Early Show* and *Youngsters*. Afterwards, though her parents remained dubious, she persuaded them to let her attend the Professional Children's School in New York instead of her local high school. While there she worked hard to develop her acting abilities and gain additional exposure. This included performing in some small cabarets in the New York area, appearing in a few commercials, and getting bit parts on some TV series.[15] Meanwhile, in school, she was very popular with classmates because of her outgoing, friendly personality, which would later help her break into talk TV.

The other major early development that influenced Lake's career was her weight. Beginning in her senior year, her weight began climbing—eventually up to 200–250 pounds—which led her initially into offbeat character roles—including her first big break in *Hairspray*. These roles followed a brief stay at Ithaca College. She was restless there, and her parents finally agreed she could try to make it in show business for six months—if not, she would go back to college. Then she landed her first movie part in *Hairspray*—and from there, there was no going back.[15]

getting started in the movies

Hairspray was a low-budget off-the-wall film by John Waters, who specialized in films with offbeat characters. The film was a send-up of suburban women with teased beehive hair, featuring the cross-dressing character actor Divine as the mother. And Waters wanted an overweight teenager to play her daughter Tracy. The part was perfect for Lake, and after a successful screen test, Waters cast her for the part. *Hairspray* became a cult hit after its release in February, 1988, and made Lake into a kind of underground star. Lake found that people now approached her on the street with praise for her performance, and sometimes came up to her in restaurants for her autograph.[15]

Soon Lake landed a few other small character roles—including bit parts in *Working Girl*, *Cookie*, and *Last Exit to Brooklyn*, playing variously a bridesmaid, gangster's friend, and pregnant teen. Then she got the lead in a TV movie, *Babycakes*, playing an attractive overweight woman trying to find love.[15] The role, was like a metaphor for her own life at the time.

Soon thereafter, she headed for Hollywood to increase her

chances of landing roles in films. Though her first effort at being a lead in a new pilot, *Starting Now*, bombed, by 1989, she had a second film with John Waters lined up—*Cry Baby*. It was a send-up of the juvenile delinquent films of the 1950s, in which she played a "good girl from the right side of the tracks" who falls in love with the bad guy, played by Johnny Depp. But after *Cry Baby* struggled with only a limited release, Lake had trouble finding movie roles, switched agents, and turned her attention back to TV. The result was a role as a semiregular on the new drama series *China Beach*, and for a time she appeared frequently on TV talk shows promoting the series. But after the show was renewed for the next season, Lake's character was dropped, and she found it even harder to get jobs. It took her a year to line up a small part in a low-budget film, *Where the Day Takes You*, playing a runaway teenager, but after that, nothing.[15]

So by 1991, Lake was struggling to survive financially. Meanwhile her weight was ballooning, making it even more difficult to find roles, as well as hurting her health. Though she was only in her early 20s, she found it hard to walk up a flight of stairs or do any physical activities. The final blow came when she lost out on a role she really wanted in *Dogfight*—the part of an unattractive, insecure waitress, invited to a party by the lead character on a bet to bring the most unappealing girl he can, who later falls in love with her. Lake thought the part fit her perfectly, and when she lost it, she decided it was time to change—and she began her crash diet, leading to the new svelte Ricki Lake, who suddenly became potential talk show host material.[15]

Her weight loss itself helped to attract the attention that would make her a talk show star, because as she slimmed down toward a normal weight—losing about 120 pounds in the process—she became news. Magazine editors contacted her, asking her to write articles about how she lost the weight. She began discussing her weight loss with the media, too. Concurrently, a few new acting roles opened up—among them the lead in a horror movie, *Skinner*, in which she played a glamorous character with love scenes for the first time.[15]

becoming a talk show host

Her big break came in 1992 when two network producers—Garth Ancier, who had helped launch the Fox Broadcasting Network, and Gail Steinberg, who had won an Emmy for producing *Donahue*, decided to create a new type of TV talk show to appeal to women 18–34.[15] It was a different approach than Walters and Winfrey had used in creating their shows to match their unique personalities. Instead, Ancier and Steinberg used a market-driven approach, researching the talk market to see what kind of show might be needed. Then they looked for a person to match the kind of host they determined would be good for the show.

To decide the kind of show to produce, they reviewed the TV shows then on the market, including top performers like *Oprah Winfrey*; *Donahue*, the longest running talk show on TV; *Geraldo*, known for its controversy; and *Sally Jessy Raphael*. Then, having found a void in the market, they began their nationwide search for the right person, deciding they needed someone in this 18–34 age group with "enough life experience to have a worldview," plus a certain charm and spark to create a lively show. Lake's name soon came up. One producer, Stuart Krasnow, who had helped book Lake for *Late Night with David Letterman*, remembered her as having the qualities Ancier and Steinberg were looking for, and after Ancier located Lake in L.A. through a friend, he met with her and invited her to host their pilot. Ironically, Lake just thought of the pilot as a source of a quick $5000, having done a sitcom pilot that went nowhere three years earlier. But since she was struggling just to survive at the time, she welcomed the money.[16]

Then, the pilot hit paydirt. Lake had an easy comfortable style with the audience, successfully ad-libbed her own probing questions beyond the prepared questions she was given, and quickly got audience members sharing their own opinions. Soon Ancier and Steinberg arranged for a distribution deal with Columbia Tristar Television Distribution, which quickly had the show set to air by the spring of 1992 in 85 markets, including 25 of the top 30 cities—about 30% of the U.S. They projected having 85% of the U.S. market by the show's premier in the early fall.[16]

Meanwhile, as the distributors lined up cities for syndication, marketing *Ricki* as a relationships-oriented show to attract young-adult viewers, Lake helped build interest by doing the media-talk show circuit—an example of how talk shows promote each other. This included a spot on *Late Night with David Letterman*—where an earlier spot had helped her land the role in the first place; and she visited with two other talk show hosts—Jerry Springer and Oprah Winfrey—when she was in Chicago promoting her new show. As she watched behind the scenes, she got some ideas for her own show, especially from watching Winfrey. In particular, she planned to use Winfrey's approach in dealing with relationship issues, though she wanted to make her own show "hipper" and "faster." For example, instead of having a typical 6 guests in an hour, she would have 12.[16]

Over the summer, before her show started, Lake managed to appear in three new films, including *Serial Mom*, a wacky satire on serial killers and suburban mothers directed by John Waters which later came out in 1994. Then in the fall of 1992, her show debuted. At the time, there were 17 talk shows on the air, including two new shows, which started off with great promise since they were in development longer and had gotten spots on more power-ful VHF stations—*The Bertice Berry Show* and *The Les Brown Show*. But while these soon faded, Lake quickly captured her desired audience with her fast-paced show and good choice of appealing topics. Her first September 13th show, for example, began on an upbeat romantic note with several women talking about the topic "I'm Getting Married, but I Haven't Met My Husband Yet." Then, the next day, Lake had a group of women talking about how "I Love to Steal Other Women's Men." The first reviews were highly positive, and by November, the ratings showed a big jump from her September launch—up 10% in New York alone.[16]

What helped Lake's show break through whereas others didn't make it? To some extent, she drew on some of the same elements Walters and Winfrey used to get to the top—doing some-thing unique and different; and being the first to identify and reach out to a new market (in her case, 18- to 34-year-old women interested in men and relationships). Plus keeping the show upbeat, fast-paced, lively, and always changing contributed to its appeal. Among some of the ways she achieved this mix, according to biographer Robert Waldron, was having a new group of guests every segment, surprise entrances by guests through different doors, a set that looked like a cozy and hip New York loft, a young 20-something ethnically diverse audience, lots of upbeat music throughout the show, and man-on-the-street interviews on the day's topic at the beginning of each segment.[16] In short, she cultivated a lively, freewheeling atmosphere and topics that appealed to the Gen X generation.

Additionally, Lake used techniques that helped keep emotions high, present conflict and confrontation, and keep everyone guessing, since the unexpected was likely to happen. In some cases, too, she adapted popular formulas to her own program. For example, drawing on *People's Court* as a model, she featured a "relationship court" in one program where she had a "judge" listen to a young husband who accused his wife of nagging him and pass the sentence: learn to be friends with your wife. In another case, borrowing from *The Dating Game*, she had a group of mothers on the show who had interviewed the women interested in dating their sons to decide who measured up. Plus Lake often used surprise as a tactic by confronting guests with people they didn't expect to meet or with unexpected information, though the guests were warned in advance to expect possible surprises.[16] This particular tactic would later come under strong fire when Jenny Jones used it to introduce one guest to his secret admirer and the guest later shot and killed him, but Lake's producers did provide a therapist to talk with guests who needed someone to talk to after the show to feel better about whatever happened.

In Lake's view, the show was not supposed to be exploitive or take advantage of people. But then, that's an issue that has been subject to much debate, particularly when some confrontations are highly charged, such as when Lake had one pregnant guest who told her boyfriend on the show that it wasn't his baby, or when a man told his overweight girlfriend to lose weight or their relationship was over. Sometimes, such encounters led to near brawls, such as when three parties involved in a romantic triangle— a married woman, her husband, and his ex-girlfriend who wanted him back—began a screaming match which soon escalated.[16]

In any case, the idea of the show was to present the "conflicts of real people" and people with "problems her audience could identify with," since Lake and her producers felt this is what her audience wanted to watch, and they did. Perhaps one reason is that watching helped people feel better. They saw others suffering from some difficulty, and they could either identify with the people in trouble or feel lucky these problems weren't happening to them.[16]

Thus, for various reasons, the show's format worked, and as in similar relationships and problems shows, people were willing to reveal all sorts of intimate details about themselves. In many cases, they felt better for having someone to talk to, for getting the support of the audience and viewers, or for helping others avoid the same difficulties. And Lake tried to help them reach some kind of "agreement or resolution," so they gained something for themselves from their appearance on the show, while their revelations contributed to the show's strong appeal to viewers.[16]

Was such an appeal exploitive? Did the show take advantage of people having problems? That debate would come to envelope Lake's show, like other similar talk shows, as more and more of them appeared over the next few years. But for now, Lake was riding high as her ratings zoomed higher and higher in her first season—up to 4.0 by January—representing nearly 1 million TV households. She even got three Emmy nominations, including for "best talk show" and "best talk show host," though ultimately Oprah Winfrey won as the best host.[16]

The following 1993–94 season, the ratings went even higher, with 42 new stations and 95% of the country covered. In many markets, her show moved into better time slots—such as from late night to late afternoon, which was a much better time for appealing to the young adult and teenage market, just back from school or work. By November her show was even more popular than *Oprah* in the targeted 18–34 age group. And by December, she had become the second highest-rated talk show in the nation, inspiring other talk shows like *Jenny Jones* and *Montel Williams* to adapt their own formats to feature more relationships programming, since Lake was so successful at doing this.[16]

In turn, this success meant that the licensing fees for the show went up—to two or three times the original fees, depending on market, although this increase didn't result in the same kind of earnings for Lake as for Winfrey. That's because Winfrey was a co-owner of her show and gained a percentage, whereas Lake's show was owned by the producers and Lake just got a salary and a seven year contract. Still, Lake's earnings did go up, and the show's success opened up more possibilities for other film and TV work, which was really her goal, not just hosting a talk show.[16]

Success also meant becoming the brunt of a growing tide of criticism against the talk shows for airing the nation's dirty laundry. Additionally, many critics, such as Jeff Jarvis of *TV Guide*, jumped on her for bringing this approach to a new younger generation. Lake and her producers argued back that they tried to have the people who shared their stories work things out and come to some "resolution."[16] But could they really resolve anything in the 5 to 10 minutes allotted to the rapidly changing panoply of guests? I couldn't do much in the few brief segments I was on *Jerry Springer* to help the two fighting families I encountered on that show, and after the program, the distance between the family combatants was as big or bigger than ever. So how can one achieve resolution in fewer minutes with an even greater number of troubled guests?

Another problem that Lake's show, like other similar shows, began to attract was the hoaxer with a phony story. For example, on one 1993 show, one of Lake's guests claimed to have AIDS, and spoke about having unprotected sex with as many people as she could before she died to take as many people as she could with her. But a few days later it turned out that she had made up her story in order to be seen on national television, and she felt the more sensational her story, the greater her chance of being invited back. In another case, two battling roommates really weren't— they just wanted their chance to be on the air.[16]

Though Lake's producers tried to counter such hoaxes by requiring the perpetrators to pay back airfare and expenses and sign a release stating that their story was true and they understood legal action would be taken if not,[16] the growing number of incidents on Lake's show and others like it reflected a basic problem with these shows—the eager willingness of people to appear and reveal and demean themselves on national TV.

Yet, despite the criticism and hoaxes, which perhaps even resulted in more viewers from the publicity, Lake's success contributed to the growth of still more personal demolition derbies on TV, the growing reaction against them, and to Lake's own career. She found another opportunity to appear in films, such as the 1996 romantic comedy *Mrs. Winterbourne*, opposite Shirley MacLaine, so that she was no longer considered an overweight character actress. She also became a newsmaker as well, such as when she got arrested in 1994 just before her appearance on the *Late Show with David Letterman* for marching in a PETA (People for the Ethical Treatment of Animals) demonstration. She and about a dozen other people, including her husband, had marched into the showroom of designer Karl Lagerfeld and began posting antifur stickers on the walls, furniture, shoes, and clothing, to protest that "Fur is murder!" When Lake was arrested and charged with criminal mischief and third-degree burglary, a felony in New York, that was considered big news. And later, like most big celebrities accused of a first offense, she got off by paying a fine of about $15,000, with funds contributed by supporters in Hollywood—Robert Altman and Miramax films.[16]

As of this writing, while her ratings are down a little and her show is being toned down a little in response to the strident attacks of critics and a new wave of clean up the worst of tabloid TV by the industry, her show is still flying high toward the top of the ratings. Where? Check the latest industry ratings to find out.

combining comedy and talk: the success of david letterman

Today, after a few missteps—notably a poor performance hosting the 1995 Oscars, bad publicity, and the difficulties of

CBS—Letterman's spot at the top may be shaky. As of this writing, Leno has recently been winning the late-night ratings game more and more frequently. But until mid-1995, Letterman dominated in the late-night comedy category and has influenced the shape of other late-night shows as well; hence, I have still included him among the big four—though perhaps writing this six months from now I might have included Leno instead. It depends on what happens in phase two of the Late-Night Wars.

Letterman's early bio shows some of the same early signs of future success as with Walters, Winfrey, and Lake. He, too, showed the same early charisma and drive that would later shape his TV talk persona. And he, too, showed the same commitment and hard work, combined with luck, that translated into getting ahead.

beginnings

As a kid, Letterman showed the same goofy prankster personality he would bring to his late-night shows. Like Lake, he had a fairly ordinary suburban upbringing. He was born in 1947 in Indianapolis, where his parents owned a house in the Broad Ripple section, basically an area of small tract homes built after World War II. His father owned a flower shop, while his mother devoted herself, like many women in those days, to raising the kids.[17]

Early on, Letterman evidenced his humorous outlook on life, with some of this influenced by his grandfather on his mother's side. For example, when he was a young boy, as his biographer Bill Adler describes it, his grandfather took him out "hunting watermelons" and explained it was necessary to "sneak up on the watermelons" to catch them. So the two of them would go tiptoeing through the watermelon patch, grab a watermelon, and run quickly away to escape with their catch.[18]

It was a comic approach to life that Letterman continued to draw on, as he began devising all sorts of pranks, and had the good fortune to be around adults who generally found what he did amusing or looked the other way. Then, as he grew up, Letterman continued to pull pranks, since he was otherwise not very popular or adept socially, particularly with girls, as a teenager. So being funny was his way to gain attention—and over the years, Letterman expanded on and embellished his prankster repertoire until he found a way he could express this and actually get paid for it—first on radio and then on TV.

For example, one of Letterman's early pranks, described by biographer Adler, involved building a tree house with another boy. The two would sit in the tree house and use a mirror to shine the sun into the eyes of approaching motorists, causing a few near collisions. Eventually, when they were discovered, the punishment was relatively minor—and scarcely enough to keep Letterman from devising future pranks—the boys could only use the tree house on overcast and rainy days.[17] Meanwhile Letterman continued his pranking elsewhere.

A few other examples. At an eighth grade graduation dance, to mock the festivities, he wore a madras sport coat, Bermuda shorts, and funny knee socks. In high school, while working at a local supermarket, he announced a phony raffle in which the winner would get an automobile; on another occasion he announced a phony mah-jongg tournament; sometimes to liven things up he announced there was a fire drill over the store intercom; and one time he stuffed an open corn flakes box with corn husks and tassels. But the easygoing store owner found Letterman's pranks amusing, so he was never fired for any of these pranks.[17]

Meanwhile, while still in high school, Letterman realized what he wanted to do. Though he had found his other classes a struggle, it was easy for him to get good grades in speech class. Then, he remembered how as a kid he had played at being on TV or radio, mimicking some of the hosts of the day such as Arthur Godfrey and Garry Moore. He also recognized that he had a talent for making people laugh. Suddenly he knew what he wanted to do, and determined to go to college to study broadcasting.[17]

getting started in radio and tv

Having decided to go into broadcasting, he went to Ball State University in Muncie, Indiana, to do just that, and in 1967 he got his first job in the field at the college radio station, WBST. His job was to announce the upcoming pieces to be played on the mostly classical music station. But soon he was bored doing straight announcing, so one day he tried out his humorous approach after introducing the next selection as Claude Debussy's *Clair de Lune*. In a joking tone, he added the words: "You know the de Lune sisters. There was Clair, there was Mabel." Unfortunately, the station manager didn't like the joke and fired him. It was about the first time Letterman was seriously penalized for his humor.[19]

But he quickly bounced back. He found another radio slot on a pirate student radio station run out of a broom closet at the men's dorm. Not so big as the college station, but more fun. After he graduated, he got a job as a substitute announcer at a local radio station, WERK. His job was to spin records and read the news, and this time, he did play it straight, since now he had just gotten married, was out in the real world, and needed a steady job. But he was still waiting for an opportunity to surface where he could let his offbeat sense of humor out.[17]

Finally, Letterman's chance came a few years later when he got a job at a local TV station, WLWI. His role couldn't have been more routine. He was supposed to host the late-night movie, interview local kids involved in 4-H activities for the Saturday afternoon show, and report the weather as the substitute weekend weatherman. But soon he was adding in humor where he could. For example, he began calling the late-night movie program *Freeze-Dried Movies*, and improvised jokes along with reporting the weather, such as the time when he gave the temperature readings for Muncie (42) and Anderson (44), and quipped: "A close game, that one." He sometimes made up weird disasters occurring in places that didn't exist.[20]

But after several years of this, he realized he was getting nowhere. It was time to move on. In 1974, he tried a brief fling as a radio call-in host, but soon found that this wasn't for him either, since he didn't "care about politics" or "about the world economy." So he decided to head for L.A. in 1975.[21]

The first couple of years there didn't result in any immediate openings into big-time TV. But starting in 1975, Letterman made some connections through the Comedy Store, a popular L.A. comedy club for stand-up comics, where he first met Jay Leno, who was then just starting his struggle to succeed, too. Like most starting comics, Letterman spent several weeks appearing in try-outs, seemed promising, and so the Comedy Store hired him to become one of the regulars—which meant he actually got paid for telling jokes. Soon afterwards, Jimmie Walker, a local comic featured in the sitcom called *Good Times*, hired him to write 15 jokes a week for $150.[17]

Then, in 1977, Letterman picked up his first agent, Jack Rollins, who was with the prestigious firm of Rollins, Joffe, Morra, and Brezner. Soon Rollins got Letterman a small part on *Mary*, a short-lived CBS variety series starring Mary Tyler Moore, which only lasted a few weeks in the fall of 1978. He didn't like the part, particularly since he had to dress up as a clown and he felt very stupid about what he was doing.[17] But at least it was a beginning.

In 1978 the first tentative breaks started coming. Though he didn't feel comfortable on *Mary*, it did bring him some notice from the top late-night show, *The Tonight Show*. And in November of 1978, soon after the Moore show died, he had his first appearance as a guest with Johnny Carson on *The Tonight Show*. This opened up other opportunities, among them being a panelist on *The Gong Show*, appearing as a celebrity contestant on *The $20,000 Pyramid*, hosted by Dick Clark, and appearing on *The Liar's Club* as a celebrity.[17]

All of this visibility helped. Finally, in 1979, Letterman got his first network break through a two-year contract with NBC, though it took about two years to get the right formula. The first effort was a project that never got off the ground, tentatively called *Leave It to Dave*, in which Letterman was supposed to sit on a throne in a set with Egyptian pyramids and guests sitting on pillows. He hated the idea anyway, and the next attempt was an offer from NBC exec Fred Silverman to do a morning show to be broadcast from New York. Unfortunately, though, one of the top producers, Bob Stewart, had previously produced game shows, and there was a great deal of tension over what the show would be about. As a result, the two top producers resigned a few days before the show was about to debut in June, 1980. So that show didn't fly either. After three months, in September, the show was canceled, and Letterman returned to L.A.[17]

breaking through

Finally, in 1981, after some scheduling changes, which involved reducing Johnny Carson's hit *Tonight Show* from 90 to 60 minutes, and after some misfires in filling the spot with light show business chatter and new comics, NBC decided to give the time slot after Carson to Letterman. In part, the opportunity occurred because Carson supported Letterman after Dave had guested a number of times on the show. So in February, 1982, *Late Night with David Letterman* premiered in the 12:30–1:30 a.m. slot. And now late at night, Letterman's wacky brand of humor found its audience.[17]

The show was something of a parody of TV, in which spoofs of everything were fair game. Letterman dressed in his low-key informal nerdy style, wearing jeans and a jacket, and the show became a perfect vehicle for his offbeat pranks, where the unexpected became the expected. For example, on one of Letterman's walking tours of the set and nearby environs—which became a show staple—as he walked into the control room, the show's staff were dressed up like Bavarian peasants, chugging drinks and singing bawdy songs. Then, when he peeked into the green room, it was very green, since it was filled with flowering shrubs, plants, and trees.[17]

Letterman also began his frequent parodies of New York—a city easy to parody for its rough-talking cabdrivers, rude waitresses, brusque pedestrians, and the attitude common to New Yorkers that if something terrible can happen it probably will. And soon he added features that became staples of the *Late Night* show, such as his "Stupid Pet Tricks," loopy interviews with a mix of celebrity guests, starting off with comic Bill Murray, and ridiculous activities by Dave or his guests. For example, on one occasion Letterman announced that he wanted to know what it felt like to be a potato chip dipped in onion dip. So his staff covered him with hundreds of potato chips and "dipped" him into a large vat of dip. Other features included a rambling introductory monologue with a mix of jokes and commentary on names and events in the news.[17]

Meanwhile, the critics weighed in with largely favorable reports, observing that his zany antics seemed to fit perfectly with this late-night hour, such as a *Variety* critic who observed:

> With his casual, unpredictable sense of humor, Letterman is an amusing man. His low-key, slightly off-kilter way of looking at things seems well-suited to a late-night time slot.[22]

The results were soon noticeable, as the show began to catch on and acquire a cultlike following with an eclectic late night crowd, described by Letterman's biographer Bill Adler as a mix of "college kids, insomniac adults, sophisticates of all ages, 'in' people, and a handful of movers and shakers." In September, 1985, Letterman added his "Top Ten List," and, though he initially planned to do this for just a few weeks, the List quickly became a big feature—an ideal format for briefly commenting on the current issues and names of the day.[23]

By mid-1986, after Letterman had been doing the show for three years, he had become a star, which *People* magazine duly observed by giving him his first celebrity cover in July, 1986. In turn, this added celebrity led to still other opportunities and perks of celebrity, such as a 1988 deal with Walt Disney's Studios to be in a future movie, and a 1990 book featuring a selection of the show's Top Ten Lists.[17]

Yet, on the downside, there were now the occasional lawsuits from people who didn't appreciate Letterman's style of humor, such as when Letterman parodied Martha Raye's dental powder commercial by suggesting she was pushing condoms and she sued for defamation. As is common in show-business suits, they were settled out of court by the NBC legal department. Meanwhile, also on the downside, Letterman acquired his own celebrity stalker, Margaret M. Ray, a mentally unbalanced woman, who showed up uninvited at his home in New Canaan, Connecticut, from time to time between 1988 and 1991. Once she was even found driving his stolen car, and she ran up some tabs in his name claiming to be Mrs. David Letterman (though he is unmarried). On one *A Current Affair* show, she announced she was in love with him. But eventually, after she served a few months of jail time for camping out on Letterman's tennis court, she faded away from his life.[17]

All of these events contributed to Letterman's growing celebrity persona, which continued to be the somewhat dweebish, boyish kidder, who was ready to joke about everything. It influenced the nature of talk on the program as well—nothing ever too heavy or serious. This approach was a perfect fit between Letterman's personality and the style of the show; and the show was a source of personal release for him, too. On it he found a personal acceptance and power, a kind of pleasurable rush he once compared to being injected with a "huge dose of morphine" and another time to getting an "emotional" charge, perhaps a little like sex.[24] As for viewers, perhaps they found the show so compelling because in identifying with Letterman as the host, they felt the same kind of release in stepping into his wacky, off-center, unpredictable, crazy world of late-night TV. Just like Letterman, they could escape from a more mundane reality for a while in this *Late Night* world as seen by Letterman.

Thus, for various reasons, the show turned Letterman into the "king" of late-night TV, and when Johnny Carson stepped down from *The Tonight Show* in May, 1992, the ensuing battle over the succession with Jay Leno turned Letterman into an even bigger star.[25] Though Leno ultimately won the initial battle in the succession wars and took over *Tonight* with a $6 million contract for three years, starting in September, 1992, Letterman's fight to get that slot ultimately led him to leave NBC for a new show on CBS, which further brightened his star-power. That occurred because his new show not only benefited from all of the publicity and earlier time slot, but turned him into a $14 million man with a six-year CBS contract. And in a talk-TV and Hollywood world where money translates into worth, this meant that for now at least, Letterman was considered a bigger star than Leno—and in the first years of the rivalry his ratings showed it. The Letterman–Leno clash had been a defining battle for dominance of the late-night arena, a little like lions or gorillas might battle to be the alpha male, and initially Letterman won, becoming "king of the hill."

Now, his star may be fading, as ratings decline, related in part to CBS's general decline as a network, to some of Letterman's own bloopers, such as a disastrous performance emceeing the Oscars in 1995, and a feeling by many viewers that his "shtick" has become stale. As a result, as of this writing, increasingly Leno is winning the ratings battle, and he has been given his own increased contract for five years at NBC, which, according to popular media estimates, is $15 million, topping Letterman. Meanwhile, Letterman himself has been toying with the idea of returning to L.A.—though it's not clear if that possibility is more a way of recovering from the recent bruising his show has taken or as a way of reviving the show with new life leading to improved ratings. In any case, whatever the outcome of the current phase of the Late Night Wars, for a time, Letterman was definitely king.

summing up

Looking back over the meteoric rise of these four TV superstars, it would seem that they all shared some of the same elements that contributed to their stardom. They all had a special personal charisma, a uniqueness that set them apart. They also were typically the first, best, or most attention-getting in whatever they were doing. Plus they had a strong, entertaining show, supported by strong marketing and promotion. Then, too, they were characterized by a mix of hard work, persistence, expertise in maneuvering through competitive industry politics, and lucky breaks.

Finally, they were good team players. In radio, one could be more of a loner in creating a show, finding a good producer and backing, and marketing and promoting it directly to the public. But in TV, one had to be more of a team player to be chosen to host a show by a top brass that looked closely at the ratings, as well as at how well the host played the game.

notes

1. Jerry Oppenheimer, *Barbara Walters: An Unauthorized Biography*, New York: St. Martin's Paperbacks, 1990.
2. Oppenheimer, p. 92.
3. Oppenheimer, p. 115.
4. Oppenheimer, p. 200.
5. Oppenheimer, p. 223.
6. Oppenheimer, p. 297.
7. Oppenheimer, p. 354.
8. Oppenheimer, p. 355.
9. George Mair, *Opray Winfrey: The Real Story*, New York: Birch Lane Press, 1994.
10. Mair, p. 30.
11. Mair, pp. 35–36
12. Mair, p. 48
13. Mair, p. 52.
14. Mair, p. 81.
15. Robert Waldron, *Ricki!*, New York: Boulevard Books, 1995.
16. Waldron, p. 11.
17. Bill Adler, *The Letterman Wit*, New York: Carroll & Graf, 1994.
18. Adler, p. 10.
19. Adler, p. 23.
20. Adler, p. 34.
21. Adler, p. 36.
22. Adler, p. 51.
23. Adler, p. 57.
24. Adler, p. 127.
25. Bill Carter, *The Late Night Shift*, New York: Hyperion, 1994.

chapter eleven

look who's talking
from entertainment to information on talk shows today

oday one can watch talk shows around the clock, because there are so many of them. Besides about three dozen nationally syndicated shows on the networks and major cable stations, like CNN, CNBC, or E!, there are many local or regional shows in each market. They range from entertainment-oriented shows that mix talk with games and variety programming to more information-oriented shows with commentaries and discussions on current events.

Given the rising criticism against many talk shows, many documentary and magazine programs describe themselves as "not talk shows"—at least when I sent letters requesting interviews with talk show hosts or producers (they wrote back saying, "We're not a talk show—we're a [news ... documentary ... magazine show]." But I consider them a form of talk. Publishers and list brokers who market lists of different types of programs generally group them there, too.

In any event, I devoted three days to seeing most of the major talk shows, and after watching from 7:00 a.m. to 2:00 a.m., I saw about 30 different programs, ranging from the very good to the "terrible and trashy" as they say. Here's an overview of the different types of programs I saw and what they say about ourselves.

the different types of shows

One problem with much criticism of popular talk shows as tabloidizing American culture with dysfunctional guests airing personal problems is the critics are primarily targeting the relationship shows. But there are many others—and some self-help shows try to take a serious, if necessarily brief, look at some major social and personal issues, and do help in thinking about what to do about these problems. Accordingly, it's important to distinguish these many types of shows which appeal to different types of audiences at different times of the day.

To some degree, the types of shows mirror the wide variety of shows attracting different audiences in radio. But because of the much higher costs involved in a TV show, there are far fewer shows. Unlike radio, an individual or small group, unless heavily funded, can't normally put together a show and quickly find a home for it on one of many local stations or syndication services. Instead, because of high production costs, including the need for exciting graphics, location, remote guests, and action shots to keep audiences interested, the TV "talk" shows have become very much show business too, becoming less information driven in the process—another source of criticism.

In any event, among this panorama of shows from the more information oriented to the more show biz type, there are four major types of shows: news/information shows; variety/comedy/interview shows; relationship, self-help, psychology, and everyday living shows; and specialty talk shows for special niche audiences. More specifically, these four types of shows are:

the news/information shows

These include:

□ The morning news/magazine shows, like *Today*, *CBS This Morning* (currently under revamping), and *Good Morning America*

- ☐ The news discussion and analysis shows, which range from commercial network shows like *Nightline* to the more serious discussion-type shows on public and cable stations, like *Charlie Rose* and *Equal Time*, with Mary Matalin and Dee Dee Myers
- ☐ The news discussion, guest interview, and call-in shows, like *Larry King Live* and *Geraldo Rivera*
- ☐ The prime-time documentary/magazine shows, like *48 Hours, 60 Minutes, Prime Time*, and *Dateline* which really don't see themselves as "talk shows"
- ☐ The tabloid news and interview shows, like *Inside Edition, Hard Copy, American Journal, A Current Affair* (recently canceled), which don't describe themselves as "talk shows" either

the variety/comedy/interview shows

These include:

- ☐ The late-night comedy interview entertainment shows, such as Leno's *Tonight Show* and Letterman's *Late Show*, and several even later shows with a similar format, such as Conan O'Brien's *Late Night*, Greg Kinnear's *Later*, and Tom Snyder's *Late Late Show*
- ☐ The opinion interview entertainment shows, from the more serious *Charles Grodin* show to the unpredictable *Howard Stern*
- ☐ The early morning what's happening interview and entertainment shows, like *Regis & Kathie Lee*, *George & Alana* (recently canceled), and *Mike & Maty*

the relationship, self-help, psychology and everyday living shows

These include:

- ☐ The personal problems and dysfunctional relationships as entertainment shows, which has the largest number of shows today, including *Ricki, Jenny Jones*, and *Jerry Springer*, and several more. A number of these are now in trouble and have recently been canceled, such as *Carnie, Danny!*, and *Mark Walberg*.

☐ The more serious personal problem and self-help psychology shows, like *Montel Williams, Leeza, Rolonda,* and *Real Personal*

☐ The more serious relationships and everyday living shows, like *Oprah, Maury Povich,* and *Gordon Elliott*

the specialty talk shows for special audiences

These include:

☐ The money and business advice shows
☐ The religious and spiritual inspiration, opinion, and interview shows
☐ The other specialty shows, dealing with sports, pets, and other topics

In short, talk shows come in all varieties, with most of the criticism directed at two major categories: the tabloid-type shows with their sensational take on news and feature stories (which generally don't consider themselves talk shows); and the personal problems as entertainment shows, which feature individuals with problems confronting one another in a few short segments. The problem with this criticism is it often lumps all talk shows together, using complaints about certain types of shows to tarnish talk shows generally. But this isn't fair, especially since some of the shows are now cleaning up their act, and some of the more exploitive shows are in trouble and may be taken off the air because of low ratings, in part related to the recent popular reaction against trash TV. The different types of talk shows should be considered separately, which is what I want to do here.

the news/information shows

Many news/information shows represent the best of what talk shows can be. The early morning news/magazine programs (from about 7 to 9 a.m.) provide a kind of unifying national snapshot of what's going on in the world, featuring short clips of international, national, and local news combined with quick guest interviews and upbeat commentary. The later news discussion, interview, and analysis shows, most from early to late evening, provide a kind of a democratic forum to help people understand events and get a sense of general public opinion about them (and sometimes call in with their own views). Despite some criticism about their choice of issues (such as an overconcentration on O.J. Simpson and sensation crime news) and their failure to pay more attention to more serious matters, like problems with the U.S. economy and the war in Bosnia, the topics chosen reflect current popular interests. Also, this national TV forum provides a national gathering place to monitor public opinion.

True, the tabloid shows have helped to create a cast of tarnished celebrities like Joey Buttafuco, Tonya Harding, and John Bobbitt, along with a culture that honors fallen heroes, that has helped to undermine traditional values and the value of more serious achievements. But in their sensational way, these shows have also, at times, provided a valuable public service by calling attention to social wrongs, such as scams against the public, evoking a justified outrage that sometimes leads to correcting the problem. Then, too, they sometimes make great escapist afternoon or late-night entertainment.

the morning news/magazine shows

At one time, the daily newspapers used to create a unified national awareness and consensus of opinion, and to some extent, the news services like AP and UPI and papers like *USA Today* still do by providing a basic pool of information shared by all. But now that newspapers have declined, so that less than half of the population reads a daily newspaper and most people get their news from TV, the morning shows provide TV's equivalent to the daily paper. But they are still primarily talk shows, rather than news shows, because they mix brief bits of news with features and interviews with celebrities and recent newsmakers. Also, instead of hosting the show in a news setting, the anchors appear in a more casual setting, like the kitchen and living room set of Katie Couric and Bryant Gumbel on *Today* or the studio type setting of Charles Gibson and Joan Lunden on *Good Morning America*. In turn, this setting gives a homey or more informal feel to the show, which helps audience members identify with the hosts. It's as if the hosts, like viewers, are just getting up to the day themselves. Then, they provide viewers with a quick look at what's going on around the nation and world with brief reports from news reporters. And for seasoning, there are the interviews and presentations with guests in the studio or on remote. These morning shows also use a male–female cohost format to appeal to a mixed audience, with the woman doing the more female-oriented features like cooking demonstrations, and the man covering more male-oriented features like new activity toys.

For example, on the day I watched—Wednesday, October 25th—each show featured pretty much the same news. Even the timing for commercial breaks and cutaways for local news, weather, and traffic (at 7:25, 7:55, 8:25, and 8:55 a.m.) was largely the same. The main difference was in the hosts and features between news segments.

All of the shows began with the hosts offering a few chatty words of welcome followed by a plug for upcoming highlights, such as special guests to expect, and on *Today*, Couric spoke tantalizingly about how viewers would learn the secret of making great-tasting sticky buns. Then, after introductions, cut to the news desk and learn the major news stories of the day—in this case budget talks in Congress, a big train and bus crash in Chicago, and the growth of a human ear on the back of a mouse. But what most distinguished the shows, between these news cutaways, was the special interviews and features that helped viewers decide which show to watch.

For example, on *Today*, the featured interviews included an interview with their Washington anchor on whether Powell would run, an interview with photographer Harry Benson about the Beatles, an interview with the children of Anne Morrow Lindberg, now 98, about how her bookkeeper had ripped her off, and a chef's demonstration on making sticky buns.[1]

Meanwhile, on *CBS This Morning*, hosted by Harry Smith and Paula Zahn, the mix of interviews and features seemed a bit more serious, with a little more of a focus on Washington, including a remote interview with Stephen Ambrose, director of Citizens for Powell, on Powell's positions on key issues and whether he would run; an interview with Ralph Reed, executive director of the Christian Coalition, on the conservative's attitude toward power; an interview with health correspondent Howard Torman about a new study on the lack of health insurance in America, and a panel with Jesse Jackson and black civil rights leaders about where blacks in America are going now with audience questions.[2] (This show is currently being revamped.)

As for *Good Morning America*, its mix of interviews and features hosted by Charles Gibson and Joan Lunden had a little more emphasis on the pop culture side. For example, after a serious interview with Vice President Gore about his progress in cutting government expenses and regulations, there was an interview with the show's computer editor, Gina Smith, about what's on the World Wide Web; a report on how red has become a popular color for hair, featuring interviews with guys stating why they like red hair; and an interview with Mary Steenbergen, who grew up in Arkansas, about her new movie *Powder*, along with clips from her wedding to Ted Danson at the White House. The last few features included a discussion with money editor Tyler Matheson about the difficulties faced by the average individual today, a demonstration by Bob Domine of *Family Fun Magazine* of some recommended new toys; an interview with Eddie Murphy about his new film *Vampire in Brooklyn*, along with a film clip; and a report on an art contest by Crayola judged by kids.[3]

In short, with just a minute or two for feature segments, these news magazine shows provided a broad sampling of what was going on in the world for viewers with little time to do more than catch a brief glimpse. In turn, despite the general similarities in format and news coverage, each show had its own personality designed to attract different sorts of viewers. At the more informal, neighbors next door side of the spectrum was *Today* with upbeat and chatty Katie Couric and Bryant Gumbel who interviewed their guests in a kitchen or living room setting, and ended with a cooking demonstration, which Couric alluded to throughout the program. At the more serious extreme was *CBS This Morning* with the more serious hosts Harry Smith and Paula Zahn, who moved about in a state-of-the-art studio environment and featured more of a political/scientific mix of guests. And somewhere in the middle was the mix of *Good Morning America*, with more of a consumer orientation, in its discussions about cutting government, making it financially, new computer and hair color developments, and new toys, with a bit of politics, science, and culture thrown in. Such differences, in turn, help to shape the audience that's watching. While all of these morning shows are designed to appeal to a mixed audience, *Today* is skewed for more of a female audience with its lighter more informal take on the news; *CBS This Morning* for a more male audience with its heavier political, science, and sports slant; and *Good Morning America* is somewhere in the middle.

the news interview/discussion shows

These are the shows most media commentators consider TV talk at its best. Though there might be some disagreement about political orientations and positions, in general, these shows, high in information content, are viewed as promoting understanding and informed debate. Some of these shows were hijacked from covering the more serious issues of the day by the O.J. trial, such as *Nightline* and *Larry King Live*, which devoted several dozen programs to trial highlights and interviews with key players—provoking accusations they were joining the drift to tabloid talk. But apart from this diversion, most of these shows provide a valuable forum for better understanding current news and trends. They're a little like newspaper columnists and editorial writers reacting to the news of the day and getting a sampling of opinion from others.

And to keep it interesting visually, the most popular shows—

like *Nightline* and *Larry King Live*—include cutaways to show photos and video clips, feature brief interviews with participants and commentators, and often include call-ins to vary the pace and viewer feedback to learn what people are interested in and how they feel about current issues. Conversely, the less popular low-budget shows on public television or cable TV—like *Charlie Rose* and *Equal Time*—just feature people talking around a conference room or in a living room setting—which keeps both the budget and viewership down.

The shows at the pinnacle—*Nightline*, which sometimes beats out Leno and Letterman, and *Larry King Live*, which often rules in its time slot—have become major shapers and movers of public opinion. In turn, key public figures have sometimes used these shows to announce major news developments, turning them into something of exclusive national press conferences, subsequently picked up by the rest of the news media. For example, when Clinton decided to run for President, he announced it on *Larry King Live*, and later Ross Perot used the show to announce his own presidency on a new party and criticize the other major parties.

To stay up-to-the-minute, these shows use a relatively short time-line in booking guests. Often, the producers take a story that has just broken in the headline news that morning—and they have the newsmakers on the air as guests, generally via camera remote, that night. And frequently, the guest's comments are mixed with cuts from the story.

Apart from having high-profile newsworthy guests, these top shows are further compelling because of their slick professional format combining information with strong visuals. For example, *Nightline* typically starts, after a brief introduction from the host (usually Ted Koppel), with a 4- to 7-minute documentary news piece about the story, such as clips of recent developments in Bosnia. Then, after the host briefly announces who the usually two to three guests will be "when we come back," the guests are commonly windowed in close-up head shots, with screen title overlays. In questioning them, the host, usually Koppel, switches from one to the other, so each gets about the same amount of time, reflecting the show's middle-of-the-road or neutral position on most issues. Then, in this tightly controlled format, the guests are guided through questions, many previously prepared, to bring out the main points or sides of the issue in a normally 30-minute show (except for a few longer specials). In this short time period, any debate is limited. So the show generally just airs the main views to get people talking and thinking—and come to their own conclusions. It's an approach that contributes to the program's broad viewership across political differences, since the program doesn't generally take a stand.

Similarly, the *Larry King Live* format uses a mix of guests, callers, and video cutaways to keep the program lively. Typically, the program focuses on one, and occasionally two, top news stories—such as who is Colin Powell and is he running and the reaction to the verdict in the pop star Selena murder case—and generally has on three or four guests, panelists, or commentators. After King, or occasionally a stand-in host, kicks things off with a few key questions, the phone lines are opened for callers from all over the world. The format is much like King's radio show used to be, though with the guests featured in the studio or via video remote. King keeps the pace moving by keeping his questions short and prodding his callers if they go on too long. Also, his guests usually answer quickly or King cuts in with another question, or goes to another guest. King's generally middle-of-the-road neutral approach similarly contributes to his appeal to a broad audience.

Geraldo Rivera's show *Rivera Live*, syndicated on CNBC, uses the same sort of format: interviews with high-profile guests in the news, call-ins on some programs, video clips for background. But instead of focusing on a single topic, Rivera uses more of a magazine format. At one time Rivera got a reputation for confrontative programs, such as when two guests discussing racism began yelling at each other and one threw a chair, and another time when a neo-Nazi guest broke Rivera's nose. However, I found the sample program I watched one of the more serious, informative news-oriented programs I viewed and not sensationalistic or exploitive. (In fact, Rivera has since announced his intention to focus on more serious journalism.)

For example, the day I watched, the first guests were several participants or commentators in the Selena trial, discussing the strategies used and the likely outcome since the verdict was not yet in. Then, with the recent O.J. verdict still news and Nicole's diary recently headlined in *The National Enquirer*, the rest of the program focused on domestic violence, including clips from an interview with juror Brenda Moran who didn't think the domestic violence evidence relevant, followed by interviews with experts in the field who felt it was.[4] Though the guests had only a minute or two to present their views, given the medium's limitations and the general public's interest in getting news quickly in an information overload society, I think such programming provides a valuable service in keeping people informed about the range of views on an issue. Then, those who want to know more can turn to newspapers, magazines, or books, and those who don't have time, will at least have a brief overview of the issues.

As for the other programs in this genre, the more serious talking head shows like *Charlie Rose* and *Equal Time* don't have the same popular appeal, because they are more like radio discussion shows on TV, with the added attraction that one can see the hosts and guests. The goals of these programs are noble and they do present a more in-depth look at the issues. But few people are watching compared to the programs with more entertainment value, so they don't have much influence, like a professor or politician talking in a lecture hall with only a few listeners. That's unfortunate, because these shows are taking on some of the important issues of the day, which people should perhaps be thinking about more.

For example, when I watched *Charlie Rose*,[5] with about 20 minutes per guest, the first guest was Fox Butterfield, a *New York Times* reporter and author of *All God's Children*, discussing his book about a man in prison for life who began a life of crime as a juvenile. Why did he do it? How could he and others like him be stopped? Then, Susan Taylor, the Editor-in-Chief of *Essence*, a magazine mainly for black women, talked about black men in America, how the recent Million Man March gave black men more confidence, and the influence of women in power. Finally, economist Jeffrey Madrick, author of the *End of Affluence*, talked about the declining American economy and what to do about it. The *Equal Time* program I watched,[6] similarly dealt with current issues—in this case, the guest was the highest ranking woman in the State Department, Joane Spero, Undersecretary for Economic and Agricultural Affairs, talking about the difficulties of women gaining power in America today.

These programs thus featured a serious look at important issues and a concern with resolving current problems. But few are watching—and the format does not make for compelling TV, except for a small percentage of the population with the time and interest to watch. But then that's the basic difficulty of doing serious talk TV: it doesn't work very well on a visual medium in an age where living is fast-paced and people have short attention spans. Hence, the low viewership for such programs. As a result, even when these shows try to point up serious problems and suggest solutions, they generally have little effect, since few are watching. It's a central problem of our age and talk TV—important informational content generally translate into low viewership, because it doesn't play well on TV in a culture that wants its information quickly and dramatically in a multimedia age.

Even Rush Limbaugh, with the top-rated radio show, who deals with current political and social issues from a conservative viewpoint, hasn't been able to have the same success on TV. The basic problem is it's hard to deal in any depth with serious issues in a medium not well suited to this. For example, when I watched *Rush Limbaugh,*[7] he was talking about how the Democratic party was currently "unraveling," and he featured occasional photos or video clips of people like Jesse Jackson to show the Democrats looking foolish. There were also occasional cutaways to show his largely business and professional audience of well-dressed men and women in suits. But mostly, the show focused only on Limbaugh as he talked, sitting at a large desk with a potted plant behind him. And as engaging as Limbaugh might be for a radio listener, who is often listening while doing something else—driving a car, working at home, or gathered with a group in a "Rush Room"—the format doesn't seem so compelling on TV.

the variety/comedy/interview shows

For viewers, these variety/comedy/interview shows are a daily escape from the everyday, since they are filled with glamorous celebrities, offbeat stunts, glitzy settings, humorous exaggeration, and unexpected appearances and events. They are also characterized by a light style of talk that ranges from the frothy chatter of the early morning shows like *George & Alana* (to be canceled), *Regis & Kathie Lee*, and *Mike & Maty*, to the more satiric approach of the late-night comedy shows like the *Tonight Show* and *Late Show*, and the even later shows like *Late Night*, *Later*, and the *Late Late Show*. And there's the even more over-the-edge, often cynical humor of *Howard Stern*. The escapist release comes from the celebrity glamour, unpredictable events, and lighthearted humor.

Yet, underneath the humorous glitz, these shows also give us some insight into ourselves as a society, in that what we laugh about reflects both what is important to us and what worries us. Through laughter, we can feel better about these issues; so we can relax and feel better ourselves. This dynamic has always been true of much comedy—and it is very true of these shows today.

For example, take Leno's *Tonight Show* and Letterman's *Late Show*. Leno's monologue and Letterman's opening remarks highlight some of the big events of the day, but with a comedic spin that makes them seem strange, ridiculous, and so less threatening. A prime example, for instance, was Leno's continuing series of jokes about O.J. and the trial—which included everything from stand-up jokes comparing O.J. to John Wayne Bobbitt, to skits with the dancing Itos and screaming lawyers played by child actors. Funny, yes. But underneath the humor one can detect serious concerns about O.J.'s guilt or innocence, questions about Ito's competency on the bench, and real anger at the lawyers for making the trial into a long-drawn out sporting match rather than a search for truth and justice. Meanwhile, Letterman checked in himself with frequent jibes at the trial and O.J. Thus, while these shows may be funny, there's an underpinning of deep seriousness, too.

mornings: with the folks and celebrities next door

In the early morning shows, the basic setting for featuring light chat and humor is at home with a middle-aged couple for hosts who are like friendly neighbors, welcoming their audience of mostly women into their living room or kitchen. The shows are named after the first names of the hosts (with the male's name first), in keeping with the informal intimate approach, though the setting and style differ somewhat from show to show. For example, on the highest rated of these shows, Regis Philbin and Kathie Lee Gifford are the suburban folks next door, contributing to audience identification, while on the show with the lowest ratings, George and Alana are a glitzy Hollywood couple in a glamorous L.A. style ranch house with a pool beyond the glass door in the backyard. As for Mike and Maty, their setting and their ratings are somewhere in the middle.

Apart from the humorous chatter, these morning shows seemed to a great extent like infomercials, with guests promoting one product or another to viewers in the role of consumers. They were pitching things ranging from other TV shows and films to recently released records, books, and assorted products. For example, on *Regis & Kathie Lee*,[8] the opening discussion with Regis and Kathie Lee at the kitchen table focused around Kathie Lee's plans to get her husband Frank Gifford a new boat. Afterwards, Regis and Kathie Lee moved into the living room, and their guests came on, promoting one thing or another.

First up was Suzanne Somers, who briefly noted that her own talk show had been canceled after eight weeks, though she still had a weekly sitcom *Step by Step*—and now she was also promoting the Thighmaster and Buttmaster to improve thighs and buttocks. To illustrate, she set up a demonstration, in which she, Regis, and Kathie Lee put on the device—a kind of clamp—around their legs. Next up was Eric Braden, from a popular soap opera, *The Young and the Restless*, plugging an upcoming prime-time special for the show, who spoke about how he got into show business. Finally, there was pop songwriter and singer Brian McKnight plugging his latest album.

Similarly, *George & Alana* was a mix of chatter, humor, and product promotion against a more glitzy Hollywood backdrop. Unfortunately, this time their first guest, Roger Clinton (President Clinton's brother and wannabe singer), who was coming in a motorcade, was late. So they spent a little extra time worrying about where he was, talking about their upcoming guests, and describing how people could write in for recipes from previous shows. But finally, Clinton arrived in a mock celebrity motorcade— a battered taxicab led by three bicyclists—and after he briefly greeted singer James Brown, who had just "dropped by" with his wife and was in the Green Room, Clinton spoke about his new CD and how he got started as a singer at 16 with his first band. Then to humanize him further, George invited a staffer to bring out Clinton's 17-month-old son, who George held briefly, and the segment closed with another reminder about Clinton's new CD.

Then, next up was a plug for the latest *People* magazine, with Princess Diana on the cover, featuring an interview with L.A. staff correspondent Tom Cunneff. She was in the news again since Prince Charles had just gone public with his confession about his mistress Camilla Parker Bowles. But in this case, even more important than Diana in the news, the new issue featured an article on George and Alana, including a description of how George jumped in their pool with his clothes on, after Alana's son offered him $50 to do so. To illustrate, George showed a couple of video replays of him jumping in. So the segment went full circle—from promoting *People* to showing how *People* was promoting the *George & Alana* show, although the feature was actually not entirely favorable, in that it noted that the show was "still afloat, albeit among the lowest-ranked of this season's new talk shows."[9] In any event, the article was promotion in a business where just about any publicity is good publicity, so by featuring *People* on the show, George and Alana made the most of it. Finally, to close out the show, director Martha Coolidge came on to talk about her new picture *Three Wishes*.

In short, these morning shows are like a celebration of pop and consumer culture. The focus is on TV, films, music, cooking, weight, and new fun or self-help products, with celebrity guests helping to pitch one thing or another. In turn, for those watching, the everyday more serious world is faraway.

late night and later

Unlike the morning shows, the late night comedy, variety, and interview shows do deal with the everyday world rather than trying to escape it. But they do so by making light of it, making fun of events and personalities in the news, and turning what is problematic or threatening into theater or comedy—a way of cutting everything, big names included, down to size. There is a certain amount of celebrity worship in the softball questions and chatty repartee with high-profile guests. By contrast, those subjected to barbs in the opening monologues, skits, top ten lists, and other segments, are fair game. And typically, these names in the news made fun of are not present at the show, making it easier to poke fun at them.

The typical format is to start with some comedy bits—introduced with some chatty opening remarks (a la Letterman) or a short monologue (about 5–10 minutes a la Leno). Then follows a mix of unpredictable bits, some of which have proved so popular that they have become standards. Some examples include Letterman's nightly Top Ten Lists and Leno's usual Monday night Headlines, featuring examples of human foibles in the news. Other frequently used bits include the tour of the studio or neighborhood with a camera following along; the man or woman on the street interview about a topic in the news, usually showing people who don't know anything about the subject or who make stupid comments; and guests who do odd things.

For example, there are Stupid Human Tricks on Letterman (like a guy who can blow up a balloon through his nose) and Personal Confessions on Leno (where a few audience members stand up and confess on national TV something they haven't told anyone, like the girl who tells her sister, "I once slept with your old boyfriend"). Then come the celebrities, usually promoting a new project or product. Typically, one of these will be an entertainer or group who will perform, as well as plug their current album or video. There are variations in personality or style from program to program, but this basic format has helped send Letterman and Leno to the top of the ratings. The other late-night or later-night shows use a similar format.

Interestingly, the comedy comments, monologues, and skits help to highlight what's important or troubling to us, like a bellwether of the day. For example, when I watched Letterman a few weeks after the O.J. verdict and while the U.N. was in town, [10] he began with a jibe at O.J., whose lawyer had recently petitioned Judge Ito to get some of his property back ("O.J. just got his passport returned by Judge Ito. Now he wants to know, 'When do I get my gloves back?' "). Then when Letterman picked up a big card on his desk to read the Top Ten List, it had the wrong copy on it: "You have the right to remain silent." "Let me correct this," said Letterman, and as he walked outside, camera behind him, he saw two cops, played by Jimmy Smits and Dennis Franz of *NYPD Blue*, holding a man against a car and about to read him his rights—at which point, Letterman appeared with the correct copy so they could use this instead. Then, after they handcuffed the man, Letterman plugged their premier on CBS the following night, after which he returned to the studio and read the Top Ten List. It was a clever way of giving them a plug as well as being a humorous comment on a serious problem raised by the O.J. trial and verdict—the lack of trust in the police by everyday citizens. But by adding a note of humor, turning the problem into something that looked ridiculous, Letterman helped viewers feel a little less tension about the problem. Through ridicule, tension was defused, since what was really a deep conflict in society was made to seem less so.

Similarly, Letterman's nightly Top Ten List helped to make

fun of, and thereby make less serious, problems related to Castro and the U.N. In the real world, there were debates about the U.N.'s continued relevance; the U.S. failure to pay its U.N. debt; and whether the U.S. should finally recognize Castro. But the Top Ten List made light of all of these concerns, as Letterman announced that tonight, from the home office, the Top Ten List featured Castro's top ten pick-up lines to women. (Among them: "You've started a revolution in my pants," "When I look at you I get a Cuban missile crisis," and "I can't spell Cuba without 'u'"). One more potential social/political conflict reduced to size.

Then came the celebrity guests to engage in typical celebrity chatter about their new project and how things were going for them (such as Matthew Perry to talk about *Friends*). And finally popular country performer Alan Jackson sang one of his hit songs and plugged his latest album.

As for Leno, that same week on the *Tonight Show*,[11] he was similarly providing his own humorous take on Castro at the U.N., O.J., and other events in the news. Again, his ridicule helped bring these serious matters down to size. For example, take the fear of killer bees back in the U.S. and the anger about how the Menendez brothers, now being retried, got a mistrial the first time with the abused child excuse. Leno's response was to note that the killer bees were back, but they were having trouble finding attorneys to represent them, because the attorneys weren't sure the parents "made them do it" excuse would work.

Similarly, Leno found a way to turn the problem of sexual harassment into a source of humor—using Boris Yeltsin's visit as the perfect foil. After pointing out that Yeltsin had come to the U.S. to learn about the American style of government, he showed a photo of Yeltsin pinching a secretary on the back as he walked by. "See, he's learning quickly," Leno observed, because he was learning to harass women.

Then after a dig at the smoking industry ("The Marlboro Man just died … It's proof he used the product … He's dead"), Leno had some reflections on the divisive O.J. trial and verdict ("Five jurors now have book deals.… We saw more of the trial than them … I say we should write books and sell them to the jury"). Finally after a few headlines showing human foibles and some sadly ironic actions (such as: "Anger Control Teacher Pinches Student into Coma" and "Arsonist Sets Blaze—Angry About Media Covering Him as an Arsonist"), it was time for the guests (Patrick Swayze, Rita Wilson, and the musical group Simply Red) to talk about what they were promoting.

Thus, between light banter with celebrities and making light of events and personalities in the news, Leno, like Letterman, helped viewers relax, put aside the cares of the day, and perhaps sleep more easily.

After their shows, the still later show hosts helped their guests do the same, using similar formats, though with slight variations in approach and the personality of the host. For example, Conan O'Brien on *Late Night*[12] is somewhat more laid-back, though he was doing send-ups of much the same subject matter when he introduced three "U.N. representatives" in costume in his studio audience and talked about the blocked streets around the U.N. screwing up New York traffic. Then, he had on some celebrity and musical guests—though less well known than on the earlier shows. As for Charles Grodin, he's more talky and cerebral, and starts off with some opinionated commentary, such as his discussion the night I watched about the difficulty of understanding the tax bill. Then he featured several celebrity interviews (Anthony Quinn was plugging his new book *One Man's Tango*) and a musical entertainer (Lainie Kazan plugging her album *Body and Soul*). As for the even later shows—I just went to bed!

the relationship and personal psychology shows: from entertainment to self-help

The relationship and personal psychology shows are the ones that have whipped up both big ratings and big controversy. The problem is that the very basis for their appeal—making relationships and personal conflicts entertaining and exciting—is the reason they are criticized. As critics point out, these shows are turning human tragedies and foibles into theater and battlegrounds, demeaning and humiliating people in the process. But that's what attracts the big audiences who come to boo and cheer. The atmosphere is a little like watching a football game or wrestling match, hissing the villains and egging on the heroes and heroines.

But is that seemly? Or is it a national embarrassment? There is a national war going on over these shows at this writing, led by former Education Secretary and Drug Czar William Bennett, a Republican, and Senator Joseph Lieberman, a Democrat from Connecticut. Much as in the campaign that led Time Warner to drop gangsta rap, Bennett and Lieberman held a press conference on October 26, 1995, to announce they were launching a campaign to pressure the producers and sponsors of trashy television talk shows to clean them up and for viewers to stop watching them. As Bennett explained at their press conference, he denounced daytime talk shows, such as *Ricki Lake*, *Jenny Jones*, and *Jerry Springer*, as "a case study of rot.... What is happening today is the pollution of the human environment."[13] Later in a talk with columnist Maureen Dowd, he went on to say: "Let's say this stinks and let's try to get this garbage off the air. We've forgotten that civilization depends on keeping some of this stuff under wraps."[14]

In turn, the talk show hosts and producers have started to fight back, defending these shows on First Amendment and freedom of choice grounds. For instance, Sally Jessy Raphael pointed to her own 4.5 million viewership and accused Bennett of taking a "real elitist view" in stating that he didn't think these people should be watching these shows. "These people have as much right to watch their show as he has to watch 'Nightline.'"[13]

Perhaps they do. But feeling the sting of the "bad taste" and "socially irresponsible" arguments against them, many talk show hosts and producers are reassessing their programs. For example, on the weekend after Bennett and Lieberman announced their campaign, two dozen talk show producers, executives, and hosts, along with some experts on social and health issues, held a "Talk Summit," to look at how their programs might "aim their influence in more socially responsible directions." Among the hosts were some who were especially singled out for exploitive programming, such as Rolanda Watts and Mark Walberg, as well as producers and executives from other shows, including *Sally Jessy Raphael*, *Geraldo*, *Jerry Springer*, and *Carnie*.[15]

Would this conference make any difference? Was it just a cosmetic reaction to the crackdown on these kinds of shows? Right now it's hard to tell how much the shows will change, since the battle is just beginning—and is certain to be argued out in the media—including on some of these talk shows—for some time. Still, there are some signs that the 1996 season will cut down on some of the excesses with more serious and sensitive talk shows. Some of the shows have already been canceled such as *Carnie* and *Gabrielle*. Others are being considered for possible cancellation if they continue to have poor ratings. Many of those remaining are cutting out some of the more guest humiliating excesses—or at least, saying they will. And several new gentler or message-oriented shows are being launched, such as shows by Rosie O'Donnell and Tammy Faye Messner (previously Bakker of Jim Bakker and Tammy Faye fame), who joined with Jim J. Bullock to create the Jim J. and Tammy Faye Show—now just the Jim J. show, since Tammy Faye left the show after about two months due to ill health. Even John Bradshaw, an author of self-help books, most notably *Homecoming: Reclaiming and Championing Your Inner Child*, will be getting a show called *The Bradshaw Difference* dealing with improving relationships and overcoming personal problems—as part of this new kinder, gentler talk show approach.[16] Will these changes continue? Time will tell.

human relationships as entertainment: bread, circuses, and the 1990s' coliseum

While the campaigners against trash talk may be lumping most or all of the relationship shows together, there's a big difference between the more entertainment-oriented, theatrical shows where this criticism is more justified and the others that strive for a higher goal of promoting a general understanding of the problem and helping the people on the show.

Unfortunately, some of these high-entertainment/theater shows are the most popular ones, most notably *Ricki*, number one in its 18- to 34-year-old age market as of this writing. But at one time, public executions and Roman circuses were considered top entertainment, too. So popularity isn't necessarily the most important criterion for judging the value of a program.

Certainly, when I watched these shows, I found them highly enjoyable, exciting, fast-moving. And I confess I was pulled along by their sense of drama, tension, conflict, unpredictability, emotion—all of the things that make good theater. But when one steps back and reflects on what's happening to the people on these programs, it's a different story. For these are real people exposing themselves to scorn and ridicule, and letting their emotions get rubbed raw. After their 10–20 minutes of fame, these people who have just revealed and demeaned themselves will have to go back to living their lives, often with the same people they just argued with or insulted on the show. And some of these people may have to weather breakups after these emotionally charged encounters. So while these shows may be enjoyable entertainment to the audience and viewers, they are often very destructive to their guests.

Perhaps, too, in a deeper sense, this transmutation of personal problems into entertainment for the masses is dangerous for us as a culture. That's because this process tends to undermine basic values about the worth of the individual, about what is good taste and manners, and the importance of personal privacy for individual identity. Instead, what is valued on these shows are celebrity, popularity, personal revelations, whatever appeals to and excites an audience.

Ironically, some media commentators have described these shows as mini-morality plays, in which those straying from important traditional values are portrayed as villains—like men who cheat on their wives, women who sleep with their sister's boyfriends, and people who lie repeatedly. So to an extent, these shows do affirm basic principles. However, at the same time, the excitement and titillation comes from seeing these villains break the rules, like the bad guy booed at a wrestling match. Then, too, these shows are glorifying all sorts of personal problems, family dysfunctions, and character disorders that may be better handled through private counseling with therapists or religious leaders. They certainly aren't handled very well in the few minutes on talk TV. It's like trying to get an instant analysis or solution in front of a national audience—instead of seriously dealing with an issue which can take time to fully understand and resolve, especially if it is a complex matter involving a long history of difficulty and/or involves many participants, as is true of many of these personal dramas.

notes

1. *Today*, October 25, 1995.
2. *This Morning*, October 25, 1995.
3. *Good Morning America*, October 25, 1995.
4. *Rivera Live*, October 23, 1995.
5. *Charlie Rose*, October 26, 1995.
6. *Equal Time*, October 26, 1995, featuring an August 1995 program.
7. *Rush Limbaugh*, October 26, 1995.
8. *Regis & Kathie Lee*, October 23, 1995.
9. Susan Schindehette, "Ex Marks the Spot," *People*, November 6, 1995, p. 79.
10. *Late Night*, October 24, 1995.
11. *Tonight Show*, October 23, 1995.
12. *Late Night*, October 26, 1995.
13. "Bennett Takes on TV Talk Shows," *San Francisco Chronicle*, October 27, 1995, p. A9.
14. Maureen Dowd, "New War on America's Talk Shows," *San Francisco Chronicle*, October 27, 1995.
15. "Talk-Show Summit Aims to Promote Responsible TV," *San Francisco Examiner*, October 29, 1995, p. A-7.
16. Bruce Handy, "Out with the Sleaze," *Time*, January 15, 1996.

chapter twelve

just how bad are the trash talk shows anyway?

ow that the battle against talk shows is raging, are these shows as bad as the critics say? Do the hosts and producers need to clean up their act? I sampled about 20 of these shows to find out. They ranged from the more entertainment-oriented "personal problems as theater" shows to the more serious "let's understand or resolve the problem" shows. Here's a sampling of what I found.

the problems into entertainment and theater approach

These shows use the same basic problems into entertainment approach, though they appeal to different audiences—from the shows with 20-something hosts appealing toward a teen and young adult market, like *Ricki*, *Mark Walberg*, *Carnie*, and *Danny!* (the last three since canceled), to the shows with hosts about 30 or older, directed toward a somewhat older group, like *Jenny Jones*, *Jerry Springer*, *Sally Jessy Raphael*, and *Richard Bey*.

Typically, after a glitzy opening, with up-tempo music, the name of the host in flashing lights, and a quick pan of the audience, a few teaser clips feature the encounters to come, such as a woman holding up the red panties she found as evidence of her mate's cheating in the beginning of one *Ricki* show. Then as the host enters with some fanfare, a short catchy title with the topic of the day flashes across the screen, such as: "You're a cheat and I have the proof" (*Ricki*), "Men with women who don't fulfill their fantasies" (*Richard Bey*), "Mom says I'm not old enough or good enough" (*Mark Walberg*), "Women who slept with their sister's boyfriends" (*Jenny Jones*), and "I'm still sleeping with my ex" (*Sally Jessy Raphael*).

The topics reflect conflicts over how people should behave; clashing personalities, life-styles, and values; and what happens when people overstep traditional moral boundaries to do the unacceptable like cheat on a mate or steal a friend's boyfriend. The excitement comes from breaking boundaries and flouting of traditional standards. But at the same time, the hosts and audiences express clear-cut values that people shouldn't do such things and should behave morally (such as don't cheat on your partner, don't sleep around, don't drink too much, don't put people down because they're unattractive or fat, and don't be a racist). As a result, as guests are introduced, they generally step quickly into clear-cut roles of villains and heroes. And in their few minutes on stage, there's little time to do much else—there's no time to understand the way in which the two or more parties involved in the clash may have each contributed to the problem. Instead, simplifying the problem and participants into victims or heroes to be cheered and villains to be condemned makes it easier for audience members and viewers to know who's right and who's wrong, who to root for and who to hiss.

Typically the amount of time per set of guests with a problem is about 10–20 minutes on the hour shows, with less time and more guests on the shows for the younger audiences, like *Ricki*, to create a faster pace, and with more time and fewer guests on shows appealing to an older crowd, like *Sally* and *Jerry*.

A typical playlet of problems and guests begins with one guest, usually the sympathetic victim, describing what has happened. Meanwhile, waiting backstage—and often a surprise to the first guest—is the person the victim is accusing. Typically, the hosts fills in the audience and viewers about what to expect before the first guest has a clue—like sharing a secret behind-the-scenes peek at what's to come.

Often, as the first guest proceeds, the sad or angry story he or she tells evokes gasps of horror or anger from the audience—a good sign the audience is engaged and moved. Then, the story line set, the host invites the next guest—usually the villain—to appear, commonly revving up the audience with words like, "Well, do we want to meet Henry who has been cheating on Mary?" Then, like a Greek chorus, the audience will cheer its agreement—yes, they want to meet Henry, only to begin booing and hissing as he strolls on stage. It is like a ritual in which they are ready to root for the first aggrieved party—and then in the second act, boo the villain, who now becomes like a defendant in a criminal case as the host and audience members pepper him with questions about why he or she acted like such a lout. Why did he cheat on his wife; why did she sleep with her sister's boyfriend; why did he gamble the family's money away; and so forth. But first, commonly, there's a commercial break that helps build tension.

Then, after a brief time for the "accused" or "villain" to explain, the accuser responds—an exchange that often leads to further revelations making what the accuser discovered even worse—for example, the husband didn't just cheat on his wife as suspected, but with her best friend, as he now admits.

Then, stirring up the problem even more, a third party to the conflict usually marches out at this point—frequently after the next commercial. For example, say the husband has been cheating on his wife, now it's time to meet the girlfriend. Or sometimes, the third party will be a supporter or critic, like the knowing mother-in-law or friend who has known about the situation, disapproves, but never said anything about it. So in "Act III," the victim or accused party now commonly has reason to feel even more upset.

Whatever the particular scenario, these confrontations typically build to a crescendo, as more information is revealed or more guests appear. Increasingly, the participants get more and more emotional and upset—particularly as they discover devastating information or are confronted with the host or audience members attacking them for their actions.

Then, like a moment in theater, they sometimes erupt strongly and unexpectedly. Great theater perhaps. But for the person involved, the emotions, the pain, are very real. For example, when he couldn't take it anymore, one man on *Jerry Springer* reacted by simply getting up and walking off the stage, because he couldn't deal with his feelings after seeing his gay twin brother who worked as a female impersonator, appear in drag in a tight black dress, long black wig, and long lashes. He was upset to begin with when his brother first appeared like this. Then when he was asked to watch his twin, now dressed in a long lace wedding dress and floppy white hat, go through a wedding ceremony to renew "her" vows with "her" longtime lover, that was too much. He hadn't attended the first wedding because he found it hard to accept his twin as gay; and now he found it even worse to go through this on national TV. So he stormed out—though after the commercial break he did return to briefly discuss what had happened with his twin who was now in tears because the plan for a joyous wedding renewal and "her" twin's acceptance were ruined. In other cases, these confrontations even lead to fistfights and kicking and screaming on air.

After the time allotted for a particular set of guests is over, it's time to go on to the next. Generally, all these battling guests have time to do is present their opposing positions and express their feelings. But there's hardly time to resolve anything. Instead, the show must go on, as the host concludes the segment with a statement to let audience members know what's coming next, such as: "And when we come back we'll meet a man who has four girlfriends at one time and they're all mad at him." As for the guests who just aired their problems, sometimes that's it and they're off the stage, though on some shows, they remain quietly on stage while the next set of guests go through the same sort of scenario.

Sometimes, though, there may be some sort of brief resolution, such as when a host brings out a psychologist to make suggestions. At times, this is after some guests are obviously distraught, such as when Richard Bey invited Dr. Judy Kuriansky, the author of *Generation Sex*, to say a few helpful words of advice after a program on which the men had explained what they thought was wrong with their wife or live-in lover. Other times, at the end, a psychologist will share some common observations, such as when Dr. Jean Cirillo noted on a program devoted to breakups that sometimes it's time to break up and that breaking up is never easy—it often hurts to break up. Another common way to end is for the host to point out how whatever occurred illustrates some moral principle, such as when Jenny Jones concluded a program devoted to one sister cheating on the other with this note of optimism: "Guys can come and go. But the family is more important. So if you are a sister, think twice before you get involved with your sister's boyfriend or mate."

And sometimes this wrap-up may be presented as entertainment, such as when Ricki Lake had a "judge" in robes weigh the "evidence" the guests had presented of their partner's cheating and decide on the appropriate penalty or result (such as "sentencing" one man to write 100 times: "I want to be like Kathie Lee," because the proof of his cheating was the panties his wife found in the car).

Unfortunately, such resolutions are generally too limited or banal to really help, and the efforts at humor often seem patronizing and demean the guests, given their serious problem. Indeed, it is such haphazard treatment of personal problems and difficult relationships that gives rise to the kind of tragedy triggered by *Jenny Jones*, when one guest later shot and killed a neighbor after the neighbor revealed he was the guest's gay secret admirer. Though often fun and enjoyable for audience members and viewers to watch, treating personal problems as "entertainment" is inherently demeaning and damaging to those participating.

Why do the guests do it? Among the reasons are the lure of celebrity, the chance to be briefly on national TV, the vision of some support from the audience or host, and the hope by some that some resolution may result. But whatever the reason, ultimately the personal cost to individual guests and the demeaning of American culture by turning serious problems into sport makes this entertainment with a too heavy price. The entertainment value isn't worth the personal and social cost.

entertainment or just bad taste?

When do these shows go over the line? When does entertainment turn into bad taste? Here are a few glaring examples I watched.

insulting women in bags on the richard bey show

Though I missed the *Richard Bey* show that *People* magazine singled out as among the *Worst of Tube*—when several heavy women sat down in melted chocolate, smeared their bottoms on a piece of paper, and Bey measured the results[1]—the show I saw was equally dubious.[2] Bey featured men who had fantasies of an ideal woman, but their own wife or girlfriend didn't measure up. The show opened with a line of four couples seated on the stage, and next to each man his partner was seated in a large body sack with a small opening so she could see and breathe. They looked like Arabian women at a bazaar.

The men began by stating their complaints, mainly that their women were too fat and had let themselves go and that's why the relationship was in trouble. For example, Lester complained he hadn't had sex with his wife for five months since he couldn't stand her anymore. Then, to explain why the women were covered with sheets, Bey commented: "We want to see how their men describe them before we see them."

Ironically, as the women were demeaned by being in these bags and being trashed, Bey described the theme of the show as "You deserve it Friday," pointing out that the most deserving of these women would get the big prize offered by the show—a make-over at a beauty salon in New York City followed by a gala vacation to the Bahamas. How would he determine the most deserving? As it turned out, the woman who was most humiliated during the program got the award.

To this end, to appreciative claps and cheers from the audience, the men continued to expand on their complaints and justify their objections. For example, Eric in griping about his live-in girlfriend Melissa whined: "I would like her to get a boob job and get in shape. The longer I'm with her, the more she's letting herself go. Pamela Anderson is my fantasy woman. And I'd like Melissa to have these nice melons to knock a person out. I want her to look good." Meanwhile, Melissa sat quietly in her bag.

But when the next man in line Lester began heaping on the insults—"She won't take a shower or clean the house. She just eats, drinks, and watches soap operas"—his partner Ginger finally couldn't take it anymore. She pulled off her body bag, revealing a very heavy, but attractive-looking brunette, a little like Roseanne, who shot back at him accusing him of lying and cheating on her. "But I do take showers … And you cheated on me four or five times … When he married me, I was already overweight … And I do cook … You don't work, you don't take care of our daughter…." Now what she really wanted from Lester, she told Bey in answer to his question: "I want love."

It was an incredibly painful and strained interchange, but the crowd seemed charged up enjoying the mounting tension. Meanwhile, Bey urged the other women still in their bags to "hold yourselves in there for a few more minutes." And his remarks in response to Ginger's plaintive plea to be loved seemed hardly reassuring: "We can't make him love you—but we can give you a chance for wonderful prizes to have a romantic experience to get in touch with others."

Then the other men further complained about their own women, until after a few minutes, the other women were finally invited to take off their sacks, revealing heavy, but basically pretty and personable women. After they had a chance to present their side, it seemed clear that these men were the biggest jerks. For example, after stating "I think I look fine," Angela described a trip to the restaurant with Carlos after she had gained about 20 pounds. "He started making pig snorts while I was eating, loud enough so the people around us could hear. He said he wanted to motivate me to lose weight."

Eventually, when it came time for comments and questions from the audience, most from female members, the general reaction was that these women deserved better treatment ("Can't you see this is a person, not just a body?"), and that they shouldn't put up with it anymore ("Why do you take this? Why don't you just walk out?").

At the end of the program, it looked like at least one—Ginger—would. But first, there was one last anger-provoking gimmick, the "Mismatch Fantasy Game," which the couples played together. Earlier the partners had each answered questions about what the man would say or do, writing their answers on large cards they now held in their laps. The questions were ones likely to provoke even more conflict, such as "Who would he most like to fulfill his bedroom fantasy with?" and "How many other women has your man been with since you have been together?" In turn, as the women guessed and the men revealed things like being attracted to his mate's sister and at having cheated even more than expected, emotions became even more heated. It was especially poignant for Ginger, for after she guessed there were 5 women, Lester held up a sign showing there were 10–15, and she screamed out: "I don't want to touch him now!" and turned away from him in a huff.

At the end of the program, psychologist Dr. Judy Kuriansky had a few banal platitudes about how "women who gain weight generally do so for love." But that certainly didn't do much to soften the very serious rift between Lester and Ginger made even worse by the show. As it closed, Ginger sat on the stage looking devastated and observed morosely that "I'll find somebody else who will love me … I feel so sad about what happened." Perhaps it was some consolation that Bey then announced that she was the winner who deserved the gala trip to the Bahamas, but it looked like she and Lester were finished. "I'll take it without Lester," she said, as the show ended and credits rolled.

Unfortunately, the whole episode seemed like awarding a glitzy and fleeting "Queen for a Day" award to a person who just saw their whole life go up in smoke. Meanwhile, further trivializing their personal pain, was the audience's cheers and boos during the process, like they were attending a prizefight or football game rather than the wreck of a sad personal relationship.

Thus, for me, the show seemed an especially dramatic illustration about what is really wrong with the basic premise of these shows in turning human heartache and misery into fun-filled sporting matches, game shows, and theatrical entertainment. For even when they "win," people's lives are being destroyed. The presence of a psychologist almost seems like an afterthought or cosmetic touch, because in reality, these people's problems are generally much deeper than can be dealt with in a few minutes on the show or in a brief discussion afterwards. And often, as in this case, their problems are made worse by what happens on the show. And the hosts, untrained as psychologists or counselors, are generally ill-equipped to deal with these problems either.

While Bey's show may be some kind of zenith, other shows come close. For example, following are a couple of more examples from the week I watched. And these are just from seeing these shows once during a single week. Just consider that these shows are airing five times a week for 13 weeks or more—and there are about a dozen of them in this category. That's a lot of personal dysfunctions played out on national TV.

setting back gay—straight relationships on the jerry springer show

For another bad taste award take *Jerry Springer*,[3] dealing with the problems of misunderstanding and hostility in gay–straight relationships, supposedly in the name of promoting gay self-acceptance and heterosexual understanding. But everything about the presentation of the subject, including the choice of guests, highlighted differences, showed hostility, and contributed to further antagonism toward gays.

The show's basic theme was family members who were unable to accept that a member of their family was gay. They wanted to tell that relative: "Please act straight!" Now the gay relative could explain why he or she couldn't and seek acceptance. Hence, the built-in conflict. And tipping the scale in favor of bad taste was the show's choice of the gay relative. While millions of gay people live everyday lives, dressing and pursuing a life-style much like everyone else, the selected guests included three gay men living like "flaming queens," including one as a female impersonator. They appeared on the show looking like they were going to a Halloween party in San Francisco's Castro District, a raucous gay Mardi Gras-like celebration. The choice of guests made for good theater, highlighting the confrontation between gay and straight. But it turned these relationships into something of a clown show, with rigidly disapproving "normal" family members opposing in-your-face and very fem gay men saying: "Accept me as I am or else." Fun to watch as theater, but heart-rending conflict and suffering, particularly when one gay men broke down in tears at the expected high point of the show.

For example, after Denise and April, a mother and daughter, were on first, complaining that their son and brother Chris was a flake, who liked to flaunt being gay, including wearing "fake fingernails" and once coming "out of the bathroom in a dress and full makeup," Chris appeared, looking like every conservative parent's gay nightmare. He was wearing bright red socks, high heels, long red nails, and lipstick—which looked even more out of place, because he was wearing an otherwise ordinary black casual suit. After he announced, "I'm gay and I'm proud," to a chorus of heavy audience boos, Denise and April described how Chris had embarrassed them at various times, and Springer confronted Chris by asking: "Do you enjoy flaunting it? Why?" And so the encounter went. The whole scenario seemed oddly out of phase with Springer's message at the end of the show that he hoped to promote tolerance and understanding. Rather, it seemed to pit polar opposite antagonists who came across more as stereotypes of squares and gays in a comedy film rather than real humans living everyday lives.

Similarly, after Carla and Gordon described their dismay with their 22-year-old son Philip, he flounced out with his long blonde hair worn Little Lord Fauntleroy style and explained how, since he came out at 16, he had always wanted to be a female, because he didn't like to do "guy things." Despite Springer's plea for toleration—"He's here for himself, not you"—his parents were clearly disgusted and showed little inclination to be swayed, even when Philip's sister Carla, whom he now lived with, spoke about what a wonderful person Philip was.

But perhaps worst of all was what happened to twin brothers Don and Ron. Don, who looked like a hunky African-American football player, appeared on stage first to describe the problem. They had grown up together and shared so much, from playing football to some of the same girlfriends. And then Don discovered that not only was Ron gay, but that he worked as a female impersonator and was living with a gay partner for 10 years.

When Ron came out, looking like Whitney Houston in long black hair, long lashes, and a slinky black dress, Don visibly flinched. Then, as Ron talked about finally feeling free when he "came out" and could express "who I am ... ," and described how he liked dressing like a woman and "I know I look fabulous," Don became even more upset. Springer then upped his discomfort even further, when he invited Ron's "husband" Bryan—a clerkish-looking white man with a trim goatee—to come on stage. He and Ron had been living together for 10 years, and had been married for 6, though Don had not attended the wedding, because he was uncomfortable with Ron's life-style choice. So now, because Ron had always regretted Don not being there, as he explained, Springer had arranged to give Ron the chance to renew his vows in another wedding ceremony for Don on national TV.

Unfortunately, though, Don couldn't handle this wedding anymore than the first one. As the next segment began with Ron coming out wearing a short white lace wedding dress and large floppy hat and veil, escorted by Bryan, Don at the brink of tears gasped: "I love you very much. But I can't be here. This breaks my heart." Then he walked off stage, as Ron broke down in tears as well. Though Springer tried to comfort him, "Do you want to go through with this?," as Bryan urged him to go forward so they could share their love, Ron was too upset. "I don't feel good," he said. Then he walked off stage, too.

It was an interchange full of real pathos—not an entertaining contrast of values and life-styles or an illustration of promoting toleration as seemingly intended. In the end, Springer managed to get both Don and Ron back on stage, giving each a chance to say he continued to love his brother, though Don was still hurt to see what Ron was doing, and Ron still wanted Don to accept that "This is me."

But now that the show was almost over, it was obvious this was a deep split between the brothers that couldn't be easily healed, and Springer's efforts to air their relationship only magnified their differences and sharpened the hurt. Though Springer concluded with a few final thoughts calling for understanding and toleration—"Good luck in your life choices. I hope you can find peace…. Today gays are coming out more than ever. Those flaunting it say this is who I am. But … many others don't understand"— his show had not contributed to much understanding. Rather, for the most part, it highlighted anger, confrontation, and misunderstanding—another example of how these shows in promoting entertainment values undermine the very relationships they claim to try to help and understand.

trivializing personal problems and pain on the ricki lake show

These personal problems as entertainment shows are also destructive in trivializing these problems, even turning them into comedy routines so they become something of a joke. The participants may appear to be laughing along with everyone else, but that can easily cover up the real hurt inside that gets ignored, so the feeling of fun can prevail.

An example is when Ricki Lake, whose fast-paced show is targeted for a younger audience, did a show entitled "You're Cheating—and I Have the Proof." After it began with some clips of a woman holding up some incriminating evidence that she found—a pair of bright red panties, Lake introduced a "mock judge" Bill Liebling, who would judge the quality of the evidence and case presented, and pass sentence.

Next came the usual opening description by the first complaining party, in this case Michelle, who explained that she had hired Veronica to help in the house and live with her and her husband, but had discovered Veronica's red underwear under her own bed—to which Lake responded: "Let's see the underwear." Whereupon Michelle held it up to loud claps and giggles from the audience, and Michelle's husband Patrick came out to loud boos and hisses to defend himself. But his responses seemed like they were scripted for a sitcom to provoke laughter, rather than sincere attempts to deal with the problem. For example, when Michelle stated, "He lies," Patrick responded, "Oh, no. It's not true I was with Veronica. It could have been the dog that brought the panties in."

The ensuing debate as to whether Patrick was really cheating with Veronica or not seemed more a game of did he or didn't he, than considering why he cheated if he did and what Michelle and Patrick could do about their relationship now, if anything. Turning their problems into comedy seemed hardly likely to help them continue living together successfully after the show. Nor did Lake's comments summarizing the situation toward the end: "Does he or doesn't he?… Hear the judge's verdict at the end."

Finally, after two more guest scenarios, when the judge did speak at the conclusion of the show, his remarks were like one-liners on Leno's *Tonight Show*, rather than serious suggestions to deal with the problem. But then, since their problems had been treated as comedy, his suggested solutions were right in keeping with this approach. For example, his suggestion to Patrick in the Michelle and Veronica triangle: "I suggest you spend a week watching the House of Representatives. They know how to screw things up more than the two of you."

While some serious nuggets of advice might be given now and then—and some of the interchange might have helped illuminate what was going on or clear the air for some participants—at what price? For when serious problems of communication, trust, and deception are turned into high comedy for the amusement of viewers and studio audience members, haven't we lost something, like understanding and compassion, in the process? I think we have.

other shows: other problems and put-downs

Given these approaches to handling personal problems and pain on these shows, it's no wonder the knives are out for them by former Education Secretary and Drug Czar William Bennett, Senator Joseph Lieberman, and others leading today's crackdown to promote more responsible TV. Not only do the shows showcase disharmony and dysfunction, but the emphasis on making these vignettes of pathos fast-paced, entertaining, and fun, further demeans the subjects. Furthermore, some of the techniques of building suspense, provoking confrontation, and setting up situations to reveal terrible discoveries of loss and betrayal can make things even worse. These dramatic techniques make the stories and encounters more emotionally charged and exciting—but they emphasize the personal tragedy and pain, and can trigger desperate acts, as when a straight man confronted by his gay secret admirer on *Jenny Jones* was led to murder.

Certainly, a wave of handwringing and claims of "We'll clean up our act" followed the *Jenny Jones* tragedy. But in the months since then, little seems to have changed. For example, when I watched,[4] Jones was doing exactly the same thing that had provoked the straight man to murder his gay neighbor—provoking unexpected revelations and encounters. On the program dealing with the theme "My Sister Stole My Man," Kim and Donna, now in their 40s, got a chance to confront each other and argue about how Donna seduced Kim's husband John resulting in an affair that went on for five years. Then in the next segment, Ruth Anne learned that not only were her roommate and best friend sleeping with her boyfriend, but her sister was sleeping with him, too.

Similarly, on the day that I watched *Sally Jessy Raphael*,[5] the show, dealing with the theme "I'm Still Sleeping with My Ex," featured a number of surprise discoveries. One occurred when Janet, who was 9 months pregnant and thought her boyfriend would stop sleeping with his ex and marry her, learned the bitter truth—he was afraid to tell her that he wanted to dump her to spare her feelings. But on the show he planned to tell her the way things really were. And Raphael herself engaged in a confrontation and revelation with one guest Johnny, who had been bouncing back and forth between his ex-wife Char and girlfriend Joannie. The blowup came when Raphael told him that the camera had caught his conversations with these two women during the commercial break and she had heard him tell both women, "I'm going to break your neck. I'm going to break your head." So now Johnny is shown to be not only the other things he is accused of being by his women and the audience, but Raphael tells him he is "stupid," too, at which point, he walked out in an angry huff.

In some cases the host or psychologist does try to offer some helpful observations on how one can learn from what just happened (such as Jones's observation after Kim's story that "sometimes it's hard to forgive. It's important to move on"). But this brief effort to offer help, which some have compared to drawing a message or moral in a modern morality play, is not much consolation. In fact, in many cases, these dramas end just as the tensions have risen to their highest point after an emotion-laden encounter (such as the moment when one guest has or is about to hit the other), not when the problems are resolved (which they hardly can be in the few minutes of air time devoted to them). Unfortunately, while these conclusions at emotional highs may be great for television theater, they often leave the guests in worse shape than ever.

To deal with this problem, some shows ask their guest psychologists or counselors to stay after the show to talk to the guests who are upset because of what just occurred or who want to talk about their problem generally. But with several dozen guests and several situations per program, this after-show counseling can hardly do more than provide a bandage for the more seriously hurt guests. And many shows don't, in fact, have psychologists to do this. Instead, after a few wrap-up comments on the show and a little conversation afterwards by the host, the guests are largely on their own.

In sum, I think these shows often not only offend good taste but are harmful to the guests they exploit. The guests have a brief taste of fame in return for airing their suffering on national TV. And then many suffer even more. I don't think the government should step in to control them, because these are matters of public taste and personal values best dealt with by personal choice. But I think the hosts and producers, as well as their viewers, should realize that these shows are not just fun entertainment; rather, they are having seriously negative effects on many people's lives, and therefore those in charge should reshape the approach of these shows accordingly.

combining entertainment and understanding in human relationships

In contrast to these fun with personal problems shows, many other shows do combine entertainment with a concern for understanding and self-help. In fact, there's a continuum between the more entertainment-oriented shows, with generally higher ratings, such as *Oprah*, *Gordon Elliott*, and *Maury Povich*, and those that more seriously promote understanding and assistance, such as *Leeza*, *Montel Williams*, and *Real Personal*. Then there are those that seem to be somewhere in the middle, like *Rolonda* and *Gabrielle* (since canceled).

What distinguishes these shows from the fun with problems shows is that even the ones with more show biz and production values showed a sense of social concern and responsibility and more respect for the dignity of their guests. The hosts did not go in for provoking confrontations and insults for the sake of drama and audience enthusiasm. They were not using bizarre stunts for theatrical effect at the expense of their guests like putting women in bags as on *Richard Bey*. In fact, I found that many of these shows that I watched did provide some good insight into real social and psychological problems that could help viewers and audience members, as well as the guests in two key areas. They provided for some added understanding of social issues and problems, and they also promoted psychological understanding and healing. Following are a couple of examples to illustrate.

looking at social issues and problems

The day I watched *Oprah*,[6] *Maury Povich*,[7] and *Gordon Elliott*,[8] they were each dealing with a serious social or personal problem in an interesting and relevant way. For example, on *Oprah*, the topic was what happens when a priest formerly accused of child abuse returns to the community. Should he be shunned or forgiven? The topic was inspired by a recent news event in which a popular Chicago priest, John W. Caldicott, was accepted back by his church after he was admonished and apologized for some questionable behavior. While he had the support of most parishioners, some members of the community and national groups criticized the decision, arguing that such a person should never be in a position to work with kids again. After presenting clips of Caldicott's news conference, the show featured comments from people on different sides of the issue, along with questions and comments from Oprah, audience members, and callers, resulting in a lively yet serious discussion, in which most felt such priests should be kept away from kids.

Similarly, Maury Povich, dealing with the controversial topic "If you kill someone, does that make you a bad parent?," treated his guests and callers with dignity and respect. For example, in one case, a man who had been falsely accused of shooting his wife in a robbery, had finally gotten his freedom with the continuing support of his son who believed in his innocence. In another case, two mothers debated whether it was an accident or murder when one mother's son shot the other's daughter and who should have custody of the kids, now living with their godparents. Also, Povich had one long-distance guest who was currently in prison for killing someone during a robbery but was nonetheless still trying to be a good father to his kids, and he felt that prisoners could be rehabilitated and still be good dads. In some cases, emotions raged, especially between the two mothers. But Povich managed to keep the dispute under control; as tempers flared, he got the parties to calm down—rather than trying to build their anger into creating good theater, as often occurs on the fun with problems shows.

Finally, Elliott's show helped to highlight the danger when faith in the American dream of success gets out of hand. To illustrate, he had on two sets of couples where the man was exhausting the family budget by engaging in questionable get-rich schemes that never paid off. Each man believed that eventually he would strike it rich and help his family pay the bills—though for now the expenses were leading to family fights, and in one case, the family might lose its home if they missed the next mortgage payment. While the two men—a younger dreamer who spent thousands on sweepstakes and an older man who constantly invested in new direct mail business offers—kept arguing why they should keep trying, Elliott, audience members, and a repre- sentative from a consumer's counseling group tried to persuade them to stop, explaining that instead of winning in no-win schemes, they were losing the love and respect of their families. Finally, by the end of the program, both men agreed to go to counseling sessions with the consumer counseling rep. So again, the focus in the show wasn't just on the conflict and problem, but how the people involved could resolve it—and how viewers could learn, too. It was a good example of a show that could both hold viewer interest and be socially responsible talk TV.

promoting psychological understanding and healing

TV talk shows can also credibly deal with relationships and psychological problems when they take more time with fewer guests to understand the problem and deal with it. This doesn't necessarily mean the problem will be resolved in 15–20 minutes; but at least, the issue can be presented more clearly, so the people involved can deal with it further or seek professional help. And some of these shows did have a psychologist who gave the problem some brief but reasoned analysis, provided further counseling after the program, or recommended sources of further help. Then, too, some of these shows presented a problem in a larger social context by including national statistics or a general discussion of the issue—another sign of socially responsible talk TV.

For example, the *Leeza* show I watched[9] dealt with the issue of teens wanting to get married too early, and she began by presenting some national statistics—that 70% of teen marriages end up in divorce—before introducing her guests: two sets of teenagers and their parents who didn't want them to marry so young. And in both cases, these appeared to be fairly ordinary, responsible teens and serious, articulate parents, who might be representative of other families who shared in the larger national problem of teens marrying too soon. These were not people with unusual problems living dysfunctional lives, as is so often the case on many of the "problems as entertainment" shows. Moreover, since Leeza had only two sets of guests, there was time to seriously consider the opposing positions of the teens and their parents and achieve some resolution or closure by the end of the program.

For example, first up was Carmen, an articulate 16-year-old raised with strong Christian values, and her older boyfriend, Jason. Both came from a middle-class African-American background, had agreed to no sex until marriage, and her parents very much liked Jason; they just felt Carmen was too young and wanted her to wait. In turn, Carmen made a credible argument for being responsible and knowing that Jason was the one. Then, at Leeza's invitation, audience members commented on both sides of the issue, with responses from both teens who had married successfully and those who regretted marrying too soon. The discussion went on in an eminently reasonable way. There was no yelling, no insults, no people locked into strong, unchanging positions; and at the end of the show, Leeza invited family counselor Linda Tatum to give her suggestions. When she did, she emphasized that there seemed to be a lot of love in the family, and she urged more discussion and compromise. In a similar way, Leeza guided the second set of couples—Jennifer and Jason, living together in a more punk life-style and not always practicing safe sex—into thinking about whether getting married now was a good idea or not.

Finally, though the show has been singled out by some critics in the talk TV crackdown as part of the "sleazy world of tabloid-TV trash," including in a critical *Newsweek* article,[10] at least the day I watched, I found the *Montel Williams* show another example of responsible talk TV in the sensitive way he handled what could have been a sensationalistic topic—about two fathers falsely accused of burning their son.[11] But instead of playing up the drama of the tragedy, Williams sought to show how the system had failed these two men by inadequately investigating what actually happened, and the show illustrated how both had suffered extensive financial losses and community sanction before they were finally cleared. For example, in the first case, the man, his wife, and child had been in a fire caused by a faulty iron, though a social service investigator leapt to the conclusion the boy had been burned by his father or mother and had the child taken away from them. Williams then focused on how the man struggled with homelessness, a nervous breakdown by his wife, and other problems to get his life back together and reclaim his son, with some help from a private investigator. Eventually, besides getting back together with his son, he gained a big insurance settlement when it was shown the cause of the fire was in fact the faulty iron.

Williams presented the second case—a Hispanic couple falsely accused of burning their 9-year-old son—in a similarly thoughtful way. After he introduced the situation, showing how the man had spent time in jail and lost his business, because a social worker thought the burns on the boy's leg were caused by a cigarette, rather than a skin condition, Williams had a guest social worker, family law attorney, and private investigator comment. When Williams or members of the audience asked questions or made comments, they seemed thoughtful, compassionate. So again, guests were treated with dignity and compassion in presenting their story, and Williams included both sides of the issue in his story. While it was obvious his sympathies and those of his audience lay with the falsely accused parents, at least he had on a social worker to defend the system. In short, it seemed an informative program presenting serious issues in a responsible way—not an example of trash talk TV.

summing up

In short, while some talk TV goes too far and can be justly criticized as being exploitive and in bad taste, some shows do try to be reasonable and responsible. And these aren't only the more academic, serious shows on cable or noncommercial networks. Shows can be entertaining as well as informative and still stay within the bounds of good taste—even within the limits of TV as a visual medium where most shows are a half hour or hour, broken up several times by commercial breaks. Though it is not possible to go into an issue in depth, it still is possible to present it fairly and treat the guests with dignity and respect. Confrontation, insults, heightened emotions, embarrassing revelations, and the like are not necessary. They may make great theater, but they contribute to personal pain and tragedy, and offend good taste.

Thus, while I agree that it's time to clean up the worst of trash talk TV, it's also important to recognize those programs that are in good taste, are socially responsible, and contribute to understanding and improving things for both viewers and guests. Then, such programs might be used as a model for future programming, while trying to clean up the rest.

notes

1. *People* magazine, December 18, 1995, p. 18.
2. *Richard Bey*, October 27, 1995.
3. *Jerry Springer*, October 24, 1995.
4. *Jenny Jones*, October 24, 1995.
5. *Sally Jessy Raphael*, October 26, 1995.
6. *Oprah*, October 26, 1995.

7. *Maury Povich*, October 23, 1995.

8. *Gordon Elliott*, October 24, 1995.

9. *Leeza*, October 23, 1995.

10. Jonathan Alter, "Next: 'The Revolt of the Revolted,'" *Newsweek*, November 6, 1995, pp. 46–47.

11. *Montel Williams*, October 23, 1995.

conclusion

where do we go from here?

Now talk shows—both on radio and TV—are at a crossroads. Not only is new technology changing them—from new satellite systems to the Internet, but we are going through a new cycle of reaction to the some of the excesses of the 1980s and 1990s.

On radio, the reaction has been the stepped-up level of angry political talk, arising out of frustration in a period of economic uncertainty and social and technological transformation, and in response, there have been efforts to crack down on this, resulting in freedom of speech arguments in response. Perhaps one big sign of the times was the controversy over the National Association of Radio Talk Show Hosts 1995 award to G. Gordon Liddy for his controversial remarks about individuals responding to FBI "attacks"—supporting his courage in making these remarks, not the particular remarks themselves. It's the essential free speech conundrum played out on much of issues-oriented talk radio today. How far can people go in saying what they want in the name of free speech? At what point does free speech turn into objectionable hate speech akin to yelling fire in a crowded theater? It's a controversy that has spilled over onto the Internet and Internet news groups, Web sites, and commercial on-line services, where similar arguments are being played out over what can be included, which is especially relevant for radio, since there are even some early efforts to put radio on-line, as technologies increasingly merge today.

In general, it seems likely that some kind of balance will be worked out between individual free speech and community standards controlling what's said on the other, but in the meantime the controversy rages on. Just what this balance will be and how radio will be regulated to achieve it is likely to be one of the continuing issues through the 1990s.

Meanwhile, on television, the reaction has been to the tawdriness of the tabloid and trash TV shows—both the daytime ones featuring dysfunctional and feuding people airing their personal and interpersonal problems and the sensation tabloid shows featuring the latest scandal of the day. Again, in response to government efforts to crack down, there has been the free speech reaction, though here too, there seems to be a shift toward finding a balance. And in this case, it would seem that much of this is related to market forces and the more conservative swing in community standards, so that many of the worst shows are just not doing well and are being canceled (like *Carnie, Danny!, Gabrielle, Charles Perez,* a *A Current Affair*), while others are experiencing slowed ratings (like *Ricki* and *Rivera*—down about 10 and 20%, respectively, since the fall of 1994),[1] so they are toning done the shows to be more responsible. Meanwhile, a number of new shows that are being introduced in 1996 reflect a more serious, sober, sensitive, thoughtful, or kinder, gentler approach—a reaction to the trash shows that just went too far. A recent *Time* feature on talk, published shortly before this writing, reflects this new tone. As author Bruce Handy writes:

> Daytime television ... is facing increasing pressure, both economic and political, to tone itself down.... There is evidence that there may actually be a limit to what audiences will watch.... Even the more established shows have seen their ratings fall.... Other shows in similar straits—including Mark Walberg's and Jerry Springer's—either have announced or are considering kinder, gentler makeovers.[1]

Meanwhile, new shows, like *The Bradshaw Difference*, hosted by John Bradshaw, the author of self-help books like *Reclaiming Your Inner Child*, and a talk variety show led by Rosie O'Donnell, noted for her quirky comedy heroines, are designed to show this greater softness and sensitivity.

Thus, it would appear that on both radio and TV, we may be in for a new period of readjustment and reconciliation to achieve a new balance. And to a great extent, this reflects both the voice of individuals calling for more responsibility and the market itself showing less of an interest in some of the more angry, violent, dysfunctional, and over-the-edge programming.

And this, I think, is a good thing. It shows a kind of maturing and search for balance in both radio and TV, a move away from some of the excesses that have led to what many have criticized as exploiting personal tragedy and subjecting guests to public humiliation, leading in some cases to disaster, like the murder following the *Jenny Jones* show. Many hosts themselves like Oprah Winfrey and Geraldo Rivera have gotten behind this call for increased reason and responsibility, in taking the higher road themselves, and it's part of a welcome trend. As a culture we have gone through a difficult period of high tech upheaval and recent social dislocations—and it's time for a national healing, a need to find a new balance and revived sense of personal responsibility and community. The recent trends in radio and TV seem to be both reflecting and leading these shifts—much as has happened in the past history of radio and TV, much as will be happening in the future.

It will definitely be an interesting development to watch over the next few years—and to see and hear talked about on both radio and TV, both reporting and making the news.

note

1. Bruce Handy, "Out with the Sleaze," *Time*, January 15, 1996, p. 64.

index